The Politics of Love

The Politics of Love

Sex Reformers and the Nonhuman

Carla Christina Hustak

UNIVERSITY OF CALIFORNIA PRESS

University of California Press
Oakland, California

Library of Congress Cataloging-in-Publication Data

Names: Hustak, Carla Christina, 1979– author.
Title: The politics of love : sex reformers and the nonhuman / Carla Christina Hustak.
Description: Oakland, California : University of California Press, [2024] | Includes bibliographical references and index.
Identifiers: LCCN 2023028625 (print) | LCCN 2023028626 (ebook) | ISBN 9780520395213 (cloth) | ISBN 9780520395220 (paperback) | ISBN 9780520395237 (ebook)
Subjects: LCSH: Love—Political aspects—20th century. | Sex—Political aspects—20th century. | Human-animal relationships—20th century. | Social movements—20th century.
Classification: LCC BF575.L8 H694 2024 (print) | LCC BF575.L8 (ebook) | DDC 152.4/1—dc23/eng/20230928
LC record available at https://lccn.loc.gov/2023028625
LC ebook record available at https://lccn.loc.gov/2023028626

Manufactured in the United States of America

33 32 31 30 29 28 27 26 25 24
10 9 8 7 6 5 4 3 2 1

For my niece,
who inspires me with her love and compassion
for all things big and small, human and nonhuman.

Contents

Figures

Acknowledgments

Through its many transformations over the span of fifteen years, this book owes its existence to a vast network of humans and nonhumans who have profoundly influenced its journey from doctoral dissertation to book. In its initial stages, this book was a dissertation focused on how sex reformers redefined practices of love in ways that radically challenged institutions of marriage, family, religion, education, and capitalist economies. Over the years, this book has evolved in its reorientation toward nonhuman actors who were crucial participants in sex reform. Moreover, this book has devoted heightened attention to the changing landscape of scientific knowledge, particularly in the rise of sexual science and the use of nonhuman bodies in shaping it.

This project began with multiple research trips. I am deeply grateful for the kind and generous assistance of archivists at the Beinecke Library at Yale University, the Smith College Archives in Northampton, Massachusetts, the Bertrand Russell Archives at McMaster University, the International Institute for Social History in Amsterdam, the British Library, and the Wellcome Library in London. In particular, I would like to thank Mieke Izermans at the International Institute for Social History for indulging me in many conversations about the Dora Russell Papers and for her kindness in opening her home to researchers. This research was partly funded by a University of Toronto travel grant and an Ontario Graduate Scholarship.

In its early incarnations as a dissertation, this book benefited from the academic community at the University of Toronto. I was fortunate to have an inspiring doctoral committee who saw the potential in my research and writing. My dissertation supervisor, Michelle Murphy, encouraged me to read broadly across disciplines, clarify my arguments, and sharpen my theoretical perspective. She helped me find my voice. Stephen Brooke and Elspeth Brown provided generous feedback on multiple drafts, holding me to a high standard of historical precision. In addition to my doctoral committee, I would like to thank Barbara Todd for her constant reminders to think about my audience. I am also grateful to have been a part of a supportive network of graduate students. Sarah Amato, Todd Craver, Brian Beaton, Nicholas Matte, Ariel Beaujot, Mike Pettit, Frances Timbers, and Julie Gilmour commented on specific chapters, providing suggestions on how to deepen my analysis. The friendship, support, and encouragement of Sarah Amato, Todd Craver, and Brian Beaton sustained me through roadblocks in the writing process.

In postgraduate life, my Mellon Fellowship at the University of Illinois, Urbana-Champaign, brought me into a new network of academics who offered much-needed guidance on what it meant for a work to transition from dissertation to book. David Roediger, Antoinette Burton, Dianne Harris, and Behrooz Ghamari-Tabrizi expressed an interest in my work and engaged in conversations on the nonhuman, socialist, and ecological aspects of the dissertation. Their thought-provoking questions encouraged me to continue to reflect on transforming the dissertation.

Although moving to Timmins, Ontario, in 2015 had seemingly put an end to ideas of publishing a book, it surprisingly became the ideal place to write. This is in no small measure due to the extraordinary people that I have met here. Rachelle Plouffe, Laura McCurdy, Angie Bernier, Jennie Lee, and Jason McLeod have provided me with the energy and emotional support to continue writing. I am deeply grateful for our entertaining conversations, walks around Gillies Lake, coffee breaks at Starbucks, trips to the cottage, art workshops, and ritual breakfast gatherings.

My family has witnessed the many stages of this book. They have shared my triumphs and struggles to write a better book. My father, Ron Hustak, and my uncle, John Hustak, have taught me that the most important things in life are often only possible with patience, perseverance, and a positive attitude. My sister has always encouraged me to challenge boundaries and imagine other possible ways of living. Sadly, my mother, Frances Hustak, and my grandmother, Mary Hustak, did not see this project reach completion, but I am grateful to them for teaching me the importance of paying attention to feelings. This book is dedicated to my niece who has so much to teach the world about unconditional love for humans and nonhumans.

My greatest debt is to the University of California Press, particularly my editor, Niels Hooper, for believing in my manuscript's potential to become a book. Niels passed on the manuscript to two insightful reviewers and patiently guided me through the revisions process. I wish to thank both reviewers for their careful reading of the manuscript and their astute comments on the art of writing. I am grateful to the anonymous reviewer who consistently pushed for a better book, urging me to write a more entertaining narrative by focusing on the "juicy bits" and suggesting better ways of communicating my ideas. The second reviewer, Alexandra Minna Stern, provided valuable insights on improving the historical narrative, clarifying my historical actors, and making the book more readable for a wider audience. Alexandra Minna Stern's work provided an inspiration for this book in its very early days as a dissertation. Lastly, I wish to thank Naja Pulliam Collins at the University of California Press for her guidance through the stages of the publication process.

Introduction

Love Stories for the Nonhuman

In January of 1920, Neith Boyce wrote to Mabel Dodge about her distinct feeling of "being an intimate part of something vast and harmonious—I've felt it most with 'nature'—trees and earth, with animals, and with those human beings who don't talk much." Boyce elaborated on this feeling as moving beyond the boundaries of the human, "a feeling of being part of it all, really the same thing as a tree or a horse or anything."[1] Boyce's letter is only one example of the profound role of nonhumans in the emergence of a new historically specific practice of love that informed the social and political activities of Greenwich Village bohemians. Neith Boyce and Mabel Dodge were part of a cohort of educated middle- and upper-class intellectuals who gravitated to Greenwich Village as a supportive community and experimental space for challenging conventional sexual morality in both their professional work and personal practices of marriage, sex, and parenting. These efforts to form a deep connective bond to both human as well as nonhuman others beyond the self galvanized new ideals and practices of love that were being pioneered by a group of radical intellectuals known as sex reformers in the early twentieth century. While the stories of sex reformers have long been told as stories of human rebels forming free-love relationships and mounting radical critiques of marriage and capitalism as sex slavery, these stories have primarily focused on sex rather than love and human actors rather than nonhuman ones.

By 1920, New York City's Greenwich Village had become a prominent bohemian community of political and social activists who were personally and professionally invested in reforming sexual morality. Sex reformers' critiques of sexual morality were driven by a specific meaning and practice of love that emerged out of a turn to the nonhuman. Within the Greenwich Village community, debutante and social activist, Mabel Dodge, and novelist Neith Boyce, were influential advocates of sex reform who identified with a larger transatlantic project of changing institutions by spreading love as a force for connecting *all* beings. Boyce's letter to Dodge exemplifies how sex reformers' efforts to cultivate love as an expansive force had implications for breaking not only institutional barriers but also ontological ones by making it possible to feel kinship with a tree or animal.

Although the World League for Sexual Reform was not established until 1928 in Copenhagen, its formation marked a crystallization of decades of efforts made by a socially and politically engaged professional elite that included artists, writers, physicians, nurses, psychologists, social workers, and scientists. Sex reformers were individuals who, in the late nineteenth century, turned critical attention to the problems of mid-Victorian sexual morality, particularly the gendered expectations for middle-class women to be sexually chaste and modest, deriving little enjoyment from sex. In contrast, Victorian sexual moral codes held middle-class men to standards of sexual self-control or self-mastery by refraining from masturbation and foregoing encounters with working-class prostitutes. To a number of late nineteenth-century intellectuals who were beginning to question the wisdom of these moral mandates, the current attitudes toward sex and the ensuing sexual practices needed to be reformed. Drawing on their scientific knowledge and professional influence, sex reformers publicized a range of sexual information including contraceptive knowledge, sex manuals on how to achieve orgasm, details on the varieties of sexual fetishes, discussions on the diversity of sexual orientations, and the multiple forms of sexual relationships from monogamy to polygamy to varietism. While sex reformers drew on breakthroughs in sex research, psychology, and biology, they were not only distinguished by their contributions to spreading insights into sexual knowledge in the hopes of also transforming prevailing social moral codes. They were a group also distinctly defined by their efforts to seek social and political changes via their visceral critiques of the state and oppressiveness of existing institutions. As they sought to overturn the culture of silence and enforced prohibitions around sex, sex reformers advocated for sexual freedom on a number of grounds such as the decriminalization of homosexuality, women's rights to sexual pleasure including access to birth control, and the legitimization of new forms of marital relations that would encourage a variety of sexual partners.

In casting an amplified lens on the diversity of sexual experience, sex reformers turned to sex as a practice that cut across species and pushed the boundary of what counted as "natural" sex to the variety of practices that could be observed in animals and plants. Moreover, as they extended "natural" sex beyond the parameters of the human, sex reformers also opened possibilities for drawing on nonhumans from plants to animals to manufactured devices to inform, shape, and enhance the human body's sexual experience. Mindful as to how this radical step might risk the ontological integrity and status of the human, sex reformers safeguarded the superiority of the human by differentiating sex in terms of sex with love from sex without love. As such, sex reformers reconfigured love in ways that fostered connection with others but also enacted a new form of violence in firmly excluding nonhumans and humans lower on the evolutionary ladder from an allegedly superior spiritual capacity for love.[2]

At the heart of this book is the question of how exactly sex reformers redefined and reinvented love, shifting the terms of social and political inequalities to an emotional register that made love a crucial criterion in measuring a body's status. As sex reformers turned attention to scientifically engineering sex as a practice of love, they defined love as a creative, generative, and positive force that would produce healthy new superior races who would take human civilization to its next evolutionary stage. As a force that contributed to growth, sex reformers articulated love as an experience of positive, mutually enhancing connections among evolutionary superior beings who felt this connection as mutual sexual pleasure, a higher spiritual elevation, and professional as well as domestic collaborations across gender roles. In the context of their ambition to create a more loving world on a global scale, sex reformers paradoxically construed love as a power to connect to human as well as nonhuman others but also an emotional capacity that legitimized social inequalities. In developing this new narrative of love, sex reformers presupposed several conditions of the historical legacy and privileges of white middle-class experience; namely, accessibility to a scientific education allowing for the knowledge of scientific practices of sex, a gendered and middle-class body that had internalized Victorian norms of sexual constraints, an experience of intellectual and professional work, and an identification with middle-class sensibilities of empathy, compassion, and acute sensitivity that dated from the eighteenth to the nineteenth century as a class status. These terms presupposed the background of the kinds of bodies capable of love in the new narrative of love forged by sex reformers.

Why sex reformers specifically seized on the scientific disciplining of sexual instincts as the practice of love must be situated in the trendiness and growing acceptance of evolutionary theory and sexology as scientific truths shaping new orientations toward nonhumans. Charles Darwin's attention to sexual instincts as crucial factors in evolutionary progress across humans and nonhumans established a kinship that bridged an ontological divide. Sexologists such as Magnus Hirschfeld, Havelock Ellis, and Richard von Krafft-Ebing writing in the late nineteenth century also drew attention to the significance of sexual instincts as crucial energies central not only to human happiness but to human productivity and the rise of civilization. As early as the 1880s, Sigmund Freud emphasized the costs to the health of upper- and middle-class patients who had repressed the animalistic sexual instincts at the core of the human psyche. In this context, young intellectuals well versed in fashionable theories taking hold in educated circles turned to reclaiming the cultivation and unrepentant indulgence of sexual instincts as the answer to reenergizing bodies crumbling under the pressures of modern life. As these intellectuals began to form and consolidate a movement to push for reforming sexual morality, they gradually identified themselves as sex reformers who advocated for a change in attitudes toward sex, the widespread dispersion of sexual knowledge, and the radical remaking of social and political institutions to embrace and nurture sexual instincts. Sex reformers positioned themselves at the forefront of an aggressive campaign to radically overturn existing social and political institutions to bring them into line with the emerging scientific truths about sex.

In the process of advocating for the reform of sex by subjecting it to the rules of science, sex reformers also reclaimed a moral ground for sex by insisting on love rather than lust as its outcome. However, as sex reformers construed love through the lens of popular scientific turns toward evolution and eugenics, they biologized and anthropologized love as an inherent potential in bodies that arose through the evolutionary progress of privileged "human" bodies. As sex reformers contextualized love as a scientifically disciplined practice of sex, they entangled love with eugenics, which involved careful mate selection and the strategic manipulation of reproduction to ensure the births of allegedly fitter, healthier, "wanted" children, which translated to nationally desirable populations of white, intelligent, middle-class babies. In the context of massive waves of immigration, rising labor radicalism, and a declining white birthrate, prominent sex reformers such as Havelock Ellis, Margaret Sanger, and Marie Stopes addressed birth control as a tool for population control over working-class, immigrant, and non-white populations and a tool for sexual pleasure and love among white middle-class couples. In other words, as sex reformers firmly grounded love as a scientific practice, they excluded the possibility for feeling love from not only nonhuman bodies but also from human ones believed to have failed to achieve the highest form of humanity along a modern measure of evolutionary progress with financial success, property, education, technological competency, and sexual self-control as its markers.

As sex reformers seized on reforming institutions along the lines of love, their version of love was deeply entrenched and forged out of a constellation of late nineteenth- and early twentieth-century developments that profoundly transformed human and nonhuman relations. Between the 1870s and 1890s, the seeds of the sex reform movement began to be sown as an emerging middle class of educated professionals began to identify the bodily effects of attempting to cope with the changing landscape of modern cities marked by rapid urbanization, an intensified pace of life due to new technologies, changing regimes of work, the rise of monopolistic companies with industrial magnates at their helm, and new societal goals of accumulating wealth and the conspicuous consumption of goods. It was no coincidence that amid these developments, American physician George Beard published a tract on neurasthenia in 1873, diagnosing the malady of nervousness gripping "brain workers" who found themselves unable to cope with modern pressures.[3] Identifying with the toll of "progress" on their bodies, sex reformers responded to widespread feelings of alienation, disconnectedness, and discontent by advocating love as a force that would productively channel sexual instincts to reconnect them to human and nonhuman others.[4]

Building on the intellectual, social, and political conditions of the late nineteenth century, the sex reform movement flourished in the Progressive Era as sex reformers positioned themselves as an alternative movement for social reform diametrically opposed to social purity, Comstockery, and the municipal housekeeping of progressives seeking to clean up corruption and sexual immorality, which included policing birth control clinics and criminalizing the spread of contraceptive knowledge. Instead, sex reformers hijacked progressives' narrative of social welfare and rebranded it as a mission to cultivate sexual instincts as a practice of love that would amount to healthier, happier, productive, and creative relations among humans as well as nonhumans. Sex reformers posed an alternative form of middle-class moral leadership that did not preclude sexual fulfillment but, instead, identified a new moral imperative of the scientific practice of sex as love. They, thus, positioned themselves as teachers and exemplars of modern love.

While sex reformers' politics of love highlights the fracturing and multiple positions of a rising professional middle class, it also sheds light on the complexities of socialist and feminist positions. Many prominent sex reformers such as Emma Goldman, Margaret Sanger, Hutchins Hapgood, Dora Russell, Bertrand Russell, Edward Carpenter, and Havelock Ellis have been considered influential advocates for feminism and socialism. However, sex reformers coupling their movement with a feminism that fought for women's rights to sexual pleasure conflicted and battled with other forms of feminism such as suffragism and the social purity that some feminists emphasized as the moral leadership of women based on their respectability as exemplars of virtue and chastity. Similarly, sex reformers simultaneously engaged with the working classes to encourage the control of their reproduction, curtail their alleged promiscuous unloving forms of sex, and learn from them about how to reconnect with primal instincts. Tracking how prominent sex reformers treated love in relation to socialism, this analysis of sex reformers sheds light on the multiple positions and complexities of socialism by foregrounding how prominent sex reformers who were known as advocates of social justice also shaped new definitions, practices, and ideals of love largely out of reach for anyone but white, educated, professional, heterosexual human couples. Although sex reformers invoked a shared evolutionary past of shared sexual instincts as the basis for connecting all human and nonhuman others, they continued to maintain their racial and class privileges by reinventing love as a new biological capacity that only emerged among those at the top of the evolutionary ladder.

Far from an isolated enclave of reformers, Greenwich Villagers connected with their bohemian British counterparts, who were equally critical of the emotional effects of capitalism and patriarchy. On both sides of the Atlantic, bohemian radicals shared a particular bond as the progeny of two nations that bore a historic relationship in building the success of global capitalist empires that had indoctrinated, trained, and sedimented a form of emotional citizenship. While shaped by the very trends of economic success and imperial advantage that they criticized, sex reformers bonded in their joint effort to proverbially bite the hand that fed them. Transatlantic sex reformers, who concentrated their activities in New York City and London, identified with shared inherited legacies of the rise of democratic institutions dating back to Jeremy Bentham and John Stuart Mill and the Founding Fathers of the US Constitution; free-market capitalism dating back to Adam Smith; and imperial legacies of the contest of colonial peoples in places such as Canada, Australia, Hawaii, Cuba, the Philippines, India, and China. For sex reformers, the critiques they shaped were critically linked to reflections on the costs of empire and capitalism for dominant rather than colonized subjects: namely, the burdens of empire on white, educated, middle- and upper-class subjects.[5] According to sex reformers who occupied the position of a critical bohemian vanguard within these hegemonic ranks, dominant imperial and capitalist subjects had emotionally and affectively suffered from upholding dominant institutions. Turning against the established institutions of Anglo-transatlantic human society, sex reformers turned to love as a force with the potential to overturn, reshape, and restructure the world by revamping all human and nonhuman relations.

Although the early twentieth-century sex reform movement was global in its scope, this book focuses on British and American sex reformers in how they formed their critiques of sexual morality from the privileged position of dominant historical actors at the pinnacle of imperial and capitalist power. Sex reformers' construction of love must be richly contextualized as a response to specific early twentieth-century concerns such as a declining white birth rate, fears of a "rising tide of color" amid massive waves of immigration, the malady of nervousness gripping white educated individuals, and fears of the future degeneration of "civilized" bodies unable to cope with modern evolutionary challenges.[6] This strand of sex reformers' critique of dominant institutions from within a modernized ruling class highlights the fractures, complexities, and multiple positions occupied by a white educated elite who were in a position to shape not only institutions but emotional experience. Focusing on British and American white middle- and upper-class sex reformers, this book casts an amplified lens on sex reformers' formation of a liberating incendiary critique of sexual morality while safeguarding their position of social and political dominance. To do so, sex reformers reinvented love as a scientific and civilized practice of sex associated with a white professional class differentiated from a promiscuous, animalistic, sordid, ethically bankrupt practice of sex associated with racialized and colonial subjects both within and outside of Britain and the United States. While sex reform was an international movement, sex reformers in other nations such as China, India, Germany, Austria, Russia, and Australia situated their advocacy for changing sexual morality within the context of their own particular histories, imperial formations, anti-colonial movements, and material conditions. To grasp the transformations of practices of sex and ideals of love in these nations is fascinating and beyond the scope of this monograph.

Because of its goal to elucidate a hegemonic narrative of love taking shape and creating new terms for inequalities, this book focuses on specific transatlantic sex reformers who had exceptional influence in shaping new practices of love, whether through their circulation of public works, political activism, bohemian social experiments, collaborations with transatlantic counterparts, or their presence at birth control and World League for Sex Reform conferences. Between 1890 and 1920, sex reformers emerged as an avant-garde intellectual elite within the broader white, educated, middle and upper classes as they enthusiastically embraced developments in sexual science to mount a powerful transatlantic socialist and feminist agenda to change sexual practices. For the most part, sex reformers emerged because of their exposure to British and American middle- and upper-class lifestyles including educational privileges and expectations of proper gendered sexual behavior. Through their exposure to a middle- or upper-class upbringing in two white imperial nations, sex reformers shaped their critique of dominant sexual morality and deployed the tools of their education to advance their cause. Sex reformers such as Emma Goldman, Margaret Sanger, and Dora Russell whose ideas reached a wide audience were particularly influential as architects of a new hegemonic narrative of love that profoundly affected how bodies sought to conform, transform, and compel themselves to feel differently from how they had been taught to feel under entrenched British and American institutions of social and political order. As for nonhuman and lower human bodies falling outside of the realm of privileged access to this new ideal of love, they were fetishized and exoticized as exemplars of a lost evolutionary past of human ancestors who were akin to animals in their indulgence of sexual instincts. In addition to harbingers of a lost Darwinian animal ancestry, nonhuman and lower human bodies became co-opted into sex reformers' agenda as exploitable resources and raw materials for fueling a privileged experience of love.

Throughout the following chapters, love is treated as a deeply historical artifact, grounded in the empirical details of sex reformers' engagement with political, social, environmental, spiritual, and scientific developments. Between the 1890s and 1920s, sex reformers were leading figures defining a new practice and ideal of love that was different from all of its past incarnations. At the center of this narrative of prominent and internationally influential British and American sex reformers is how their reconfiguration of love shifted the terms of social and political dominance to an axis of emotional citizenship. A close analysis of British and American sex reformers' politics of love elucidates how sex reformers transformed the burdens of upholding civilization into a narrative of the inherent rights of white "civilized" subjects to derive pleasure from dominance by indulging in sexual instincts while preserving their right to govern by insisting on their superior evolutionary capacity to experience love in its highest form. Through their formations of transatlantic bonds, British and American sex reformers jointly reconfigured love as a revolutionary force within the rising professional middle classes in response to their growing discontent in upholding global leadership in economics, Christian morals, technological innovation, urbanization, and democratic governance.

Although this book deploys many of the historian's tools to show how sex reformers reconfigured love out of a mosaic of late nineteenth- and early twentieth-century social movements, political conditions, scientific advancements, and environmental changes, it is also informed by the insights of affect theorists who have identified affects as spontaneous, disruptive, instantaneous atoms of feeling embedded in social and political structures. This merger of historical methodologies and affect theory offers a fruitful analytical framework for elucidating historically specific incarnations of affects while reframing historical narratives by telling a story through the lens of affect. Affect theorists have drawn attention to the importance of analytical precision in addressing feelings that range from the atomic particles of an immediate instantaneous feeling such as instincts and sensations to more organized structural molecular forms of feeling such as emotional states of love, sadness, or happiness that can involve a conglomeration of affective components. Moreover, affect theorists have demonstrated how affects are critical and ubiquitous components of social and political institutions that can be shaped by them as well as potentially disruptive or dissonant with them. The postmodern philosopher, Gilles Deleuze, has drawn attention to affect as a site for disrupting ontological distinctions between humans and nonhumans as their mutual apprehension of one another through a range of possible feeling highlights their fluidity, mutual transformation, and joint metamorphoses of their worlds.[7] The insights of affect scholars such as Gilles Deleuze, Brian Massumi, Nigel Thrift, Sara Ahmed, and Clare Hemmings are useful for grasping the social, political, and ontological implications of sex reformers' constructions of love as a very specific scientific bodily disciplining of affects such as sexual instincts, which unsettled and redrew the boundaries between humans and nonhumans.[8] Feminist science studies scholars such as Patricia Ticiento Clough and Rosi Braidotti have importantly forged a cross-pollination of affect studies and science studies to emphasize the specific implications of affect for challenging human and nonhuman boundaries.[9] Insofar as many affect studies scholars have cited prominent late nineteenth- and early twentieth-century intellectuals such as Henri Bergson, Sigmund Freud, and Charles Darwin, this book also urges affect studies to confront its own historical legacy as complexly intertwined in evolutionary paradigms of sexism, racism, and speciesism.[10] The historian's tools offer another level of precision to affect theory; namely, the insights that affects must be situated in a historical context of specific regimes, norms, and etiquettes of feeling that are shaped by political, social, and economic conditions, crises, and concerns at a specific moment in time.

Writing histories of sex reform through the lens of affect captures crucial insights on how feelings mattered as a contested site for shaping social and political power as sex reformers sought to reclaim the indoctrination of feelings by protesting the effects of existing institutions while also seeking to shape a new regime based on loving encounters. From this revisionist vantage point, histories of sex reform can tell hitherto underexplored stories of how bodies absorbed, felt, and metamorphosed in response to the new cultural imperative to cultivate sexual instincts. While other histories of sex reform have focused primarily on sex, my focus on affect shows how sex reform had a much more nuanced approach to the production, anticipation, and preparation of sexual encounters, which encompassed a network of human and nonhuman participants. Through the lens of affect, the depth and breadth of the sex reform movement's influence can be extended to everyday encounters with human and nonhuman bodies across numerous spaces, activities, and interactions. Given that bodily experience of desire, love, or sensations cannot be limited to one particular space, the history of sex reform through a lens of affect requires tracking all of the body's movements across space at a specific moment in time and shaped by specific cultural norms and institutions.

To grasp the historical specificity of affective experience shaped by the sex reform movement, readers will find a frequent reliance on a strategic selection and combination of sources, namely, private correspondence, academic publications, political tracts, speeches, conference proceedings, and autobiographies. Reading across these sources, it can be seen how sex reformers personally struggled to teach themselves a new ethic of love while also publicly espousing a transformation in bodily feelings in their published works, speeches, and conference papers. These sources show how sex reformers did not so much struggle with sex as they struggled to put sex on a scientific footing with the high expectations to achieve love at the expense of nonhumans and allegedly less evolved humans deemed to be objects rather than subjects of love.

This book is a contribution to the sex stories of the nonhuman, raising the question, what are the politics of including nonhumans as participants in reproductive science while remaining silent on matters of nonhuman love? Feminist science studies scholars have generated narratives of sex as a process involving the engagement of nonhuman actors. Building on the insights of these scholars, it is important to question the absence of love in contemporary analyses of sex and reproduction. Why, given the legacy of sex reformers, was the scientific relationship between love and sex severed and with what consequences for the nonhuman? In science studies, the scholarly focus on nonhuman sex has the advantage of fulfilling Latourian objectives in highlighting nonhuman agency.[11] While Bruno Latour's works presented an analytical opportunity for further exploring how nonhumans had real effects on human lives and worlds, feminist science studies scholars extrapolated these insights to reproductive bodies and genetic kinship across species. This focus on nonhuman agency, however, also reproduces a historical legacy of the exclusion of nonhumans from the practice of sex as love. Far from romanticizing acts of sex as love—the story of sex reformers' configuration of love as a science of sex—this narrative exposes the ontological politics at the heart of the making of reproductive science as a discipline.

What difference, if any, does love make to the existing narratives of reproductive science in science studies? If the scope of scholarly analysis of reproductive science is limited to the question of the joint participation of humans and nonhumans, then the picture is a deceptive equalization of all of the bodies involved. This approach would render Darwin's attention to plants, animals, and humans engaged in sex a seemingly democratic process of inclusiveness to the detriment of ignoring the varying hierarchical degrees of emotional agency. This seemingly ignored subtext of the emotional agency embedded in Darwinian narratives is one of the ghosts that an analysis of sex reformers' politics of love seeks to make visible.[12] In other words, bringing love into the analytical frame of science studies aims to highlight the bio-politics or institutional, cultural, and social management of reproductive bodies according to presumed capacities for love. Rather than simply considering the multiple human and nonhuman bodies involved in reproductive science, a focus on love addresses the specific nature of the relations between bodies in terms of desires, sensations, attraction, and emotional fulfillment.

The question of love in reproductive science broadens the purview of science studies to concerns about how reproductive science engages with the cultural politics of what counts as a family, which offspring (human and nonhuman) should be valued, and how institutions like fertility clinics operate according to a deeply politicized institutionalization of love. There is a substantial body of feminist science studies literature that draws attention to the diverse network of human and nonhuman actors that participate in the experience, materiality, and creation of reproductive bodies. Charis Thompson's seminal work, *Making Parents*, shows fertility clinics as collaborative networks of human and nonhuman actors that she calls "an ontological choreography" mobilized at the site of women's reproductive bodies. From a different vantage point on nonhuman entanglements in human reproduction, Sarah Franklin, Donna Haraway, and Myra Hird have shown the human and nonhuman crossings in shared genetic matter, thus making a case for biological kinship across ontological boundaries. Taking these arguments for biological kinship a step further, Luciana Parisi's *Abstract Sex* turns to sex itself as a shared creative process of mixing human and nonhuman bodies. From Donna Haraway's kinship with mice to Sarah Franklin's kinship with cloned sheep, like Dolly, and Myra Hird and Luciana Parisi's analyses of bacterial sex, feminist science studies has created a collection of nonhuman sex stories.[13] However, turning to love in feminist science studies begs the question of how Charis Thompson's ontological choreography might be reframed in light of questions of emotional agency or the question of how Dolly's capacity for love might alter or reshape Sarah Franklin's discussions of ontological mixtures or the issue of whether and by what forms bacteria can love might affect Hird and Parisi's discussions of sex.[14] Science studies scholars may find that considering how questions of love inform reproductive science furthers our analytical insights into the entanglements of science and culture and the possible limits of interdisciplinary boundaries.

Through an analysis of a historical episode of the encounter between love, sex, and science, this book engages with prominent themes that have shaped the trajectories of science studies. By taking love as an analytical lens for interrogating the making of science, scholars could offer new perspectives on critical themes of science studies such as the relationship between science and culture, the interdisciplinary crossings of arts and science, the production of knowledge, the objectivity of science, the historical contingencies of scientific knowledge, and the relationship between knowledge and power. To posit the place of love in science involves exploring how emotional affinities can shape the practices that produce knowledge and challenge any sharp divides between reason and emotion as well as science as a masculine domain and emotion as a feminine domain.

In the particular context of reproductive science, a scientist's assumption of the relationship between love and sex is crucial to understanding the design and context of the use of nonhuman bodies to further human reproductive knowledge. On the one hand, the use of nonhuman bodies in the context of reproductive experiments involves postulating the incapacities or irrelevance of nonhuman love while using the results of such experiments to inform human sexual practices. At the same time, how the results of reproductive experiments are unevenly distributed among human populations in terms of furthering the reproduction of some while curtailing the reproduction of others maps gender, racial, sexual, and economic inequalities onto cultural ideals of familial love and reproduction. The question of whose love is privileged or prioritized in the context of reproductive science shapes the selection of experimental subjects used to explore desires, hormones, contraception, and the maximization of fertility for the purposes of agricultural capitalism. As such, the domains of human and nonhuman reproduction are entangled at the intersections of reproductive science and agricultural science.

To what extent reproductive scientists are interested or not interested in questions of love is an issue that marks a critical juncture between science and culture. The story of sex reformers' politics of love as an engagement with sexual science problematizes the categorization of whom or what counts as a reproductive scientist insofar as sex reformers' lives transgressed boundaries of science and culture. These elusive lines between science and culture perhaps more importantly point to the mobility of nonhuman experimental subjects across these boundaries and thus open up the question of nonhuman participation in cultural ideals of love and how cultural ideals of love shape nonhuman lives engaged in reproductive experiments. Throughout the following chapters, nonhumans emerge as critical participants in grounding love in greater scientific certainty in the early twentieth century. The sex reform movement is therefore a pivotal chapter in the history of science insofar as scientific reasoning, methods, and techniques could be applied to love. This marked a critical turning point in expanding the domain of science to emotions. At the same time, nonhumans were engaged in transforming ideals of love to render love compatible with rationality, logic, and predictability and thus suggest the contributions of science to altering cultural practices of love. This role of nonhumans gradually unfolds beginning with chapter 1's attention to the role of animals in sex reform and then moves to plants, cosmic forces, and birth control technologies.

While the story of sex reformers' politics of love must be deeply contextualized in the historical conditions surrounding the scientization of sex, it is a narrative that furthers interdisciplinary conversations across the fields of arts, social sciences, and natural sciences. For example, sex reformers indiscriminately drew on cultural, artistic, and social scientific tools for understanding love with the scientific, biological tools for understanding bodies. This analysis of the early twentieth-century sex reform project as a mission to reconstruct love as a science of sex addresses how literature, art, biology, mathematics, ecology, psychology, and anthropology might be drawn into a collaborative relationship to address pressing cultural goals and uncertainties. In other words, the sex reform project suggests the dismantling of disciplinary barriers in efforts to draw on all possible useful tools to fulfill a cultural mission of overcoming the condition of neurasthenic bodies and the insecurities of love and marriage. Nonhumans also emerge at the crux of these interdisciplinary junctures: from the uses of sex manuals and contraceptive devices to produce middle-class love to the experiments on animals and plants that shaped marital sex advice and the creation of contraceptive devices.

Closely related to the theme of interdisciplinary crossings at the site of love, the story of sex reformers' mission to pin down love with greater scientific certainty also addresses scholarly inquiries into the production of knowledge. Each chapter approaches love as a form of knowledge to be excavated and mobilized through encounters between human and nonhuman actors. While in the first chapter sex reformers address love as emerging from a deep mental, physical, and spiritual knowledge aided by contraceptive devices, subsequent chapters highlight the ways other forms of knowledge that are seemingly focused on nonhumans such as physics, botany, ecology, and zoology are also reshaped and brought to bear on questions of the production of love. This book suggests that emotions like love can be productive analytical tools for excavating the production of multiple forms of knowledge. Love is, however, only one possible example for illustrating a larger point about how the analytical slipperiness of emotions actually invigorates analyses of knowledge production.[15] As readers will see, sex reformers turned to love as a problem site because of the uncertainty and difficulty of its capture, which thus invigorated significant transformations of various forms of knowledge including physics applied to sex, botany to birth control, and eugenics to human love.

With a particular focus on sex reformers' mission to ground love in science, this book engages with inquiries into the cultural traction of science's legitimacy, objectivity, and truthfulness.[16] Why was it so important to sex reformers to establish connections between love, sex, and science? As an example of the stakes of securing scientific legitimacy, the case of sex reformers turning to science as an authoritative discourse illustrates a crucial part of promoting birth control, sex education, and marital sex counselling as matters of fact, truth, and reality. Moreover, sex reformers' specific linkage of a scientific practice of sex with love gave science a moral function by differentiating promiscuous, presumably unscientific sex from a scientifically practiced sex as love. By exploring the specific historical episode of sex reformers' invocation of science to legitimize the cultivation of sexual pleasure, this book engages with the work of feminist science studies in demonstrating science as a narrative informed and shaped by cultural values. At the same time, this book's focus on the participation of nonhuman actors and changing human and nonhuman encounters also engages with the objectivity of science grounded in very real, concrete, and material conditions. As Sandra Harding and Donna Haraway have indicated, there is a "real," concrete, and objective aspect to science. This book, in particular, highlights the "real" material changes in the formation of a science of sex such as new experiences of sexual feeling aided by sex manuals and contraceptive devices, the practice of sex as a spiritual physics of tapping into atmospheric and planetary energies, the frequenting of farms and tinkering with plants, and the mixing of animal and human parts.

Through a focus on the early twentieth century as a formative period in the development of diverse sciences, this book takes a historical approach to elucidating a crucial theme of science studies, namely the contingencies of scientific knowledge. From the inception of science studies with Thomas Kuhn's crucial insights into paradigm shifts to Ian Hacking's discussions of the historicity of concepts, science studies as a field has been committed to demonstrating the changing nature of what counts as knowledge.[17] By exploring the relationship between sex reform and the rise of new sciences such as psychology, ecology, endocrinology, and sexology, this book illustrates the historical contingency of forms of scientific knowledge. Moreover, a focus on sex reformers highlights how these sciences developed as "truths" only in response to a specific cultural crisis of depleted sexual energies at a time when transnational communities of intellectuals began to equate sexual love with the creative evolutionary momentum of rising civilizations. Building on Theodore Porter's and Bernard Lightman's insights into cultural attitudes toward science, this book addresses how historical contingencies of scientific knowledge are shaped in relation to historical shifts in popular sentiments of trust and enthusiasm in science.[18] As shown through the case study of the sex reform movement, the forerunners of sex reform exhibited a profound faith and excitement in the possibilities for a science of sex to provide greater assurances of love.

While this book emphasizes early twentieth-century sex reformers' faith in a science of love to govern sexual relations, it also addresses Foucauldian concerns with relationships between knowledge and power with respect to the use of authoritative discourses to legitimize social inequalities.[19] In particular, this story shows how sex reformers' advocacy of a science of love was informed by eugenic assumptions of the higher spiritual and emotional capacities of white middle-class bodies and their entitlement to sexual pleasure. By applying science to sex as a path to love, sex reformers situated love as a privilege of a white, educated elite bonded by an appreciation of science and a willingness to govern their lives according to scientific practices. In doing so, this book highlights the production of love, involving multiple actors organized according to emotional, economic, political, and ontological hierarchies. This book gestures toward possible Marxist and Latourian collaborations in considering nonhuman laborers of love involved in a reproductive science invested in enabling human bodies to love. Although each chapter explores a different dimension of nonhuman participation in the transformations of human love, these love stories are unified by the theme of nonhuman emotional agency in doing the work of making human love possible. Whether it is contraceptive devices, cosmic forces, plants, or animals, nonhumans bear the scientific burden of shaping the context of love for human consumption and enjoyment without profiting from its experience.

Although this book focuses on a specific historical moment in a longer narrative of affective entanglements of humans and nonhumans, the unfolding of this story is informed by a Foucauldian genealogical method that stresses horizontal, nonlinear, connections across similar encounters and worlds. To elucidate how sex reformers' investment in love touched, transformed, and drew on multiple nonhuman worlds, this book is divided into chapters that look at these diverse landscapes of nonhumans from planetary realms to natural environments to scientific laboratories and bustling metropoles. As such, this is not a conventional linear history working from a definite beginning to a definite end. This is not a narrative that aims to show progress but, instead, to highlight a radical revision to not only our concept of love but also to our concepts of time and kinship.[20] Readers expecting a neat chronology moving from one clear definition or truth about love to the next will be disappointed. Although I focus on a specific time period, namely 1890 until 1930, I track love in what Michel Foucault considered the method of the genealogist. In doing so, I focus on connecting moments across time, highlighting the singularity of such moments while demonstrating how they build on and signal the recurrence of other moments.[21] It is perhaps fitting for a history of love to reflect the fluidity and interaction of past, present, and future in the same way that feeling, memory, and bodily experience does not abide by neat periodization. Love itself cannot be said to have a definite beginning or end. I would argue that love's temporalities are genealogical, connective, fluctuating, and recurring, rather than linear.[22]

The organization of the chapters emphasizes how sex reformers mobilized love as a connective force while holding it in tension with its divisiveness as a privilege for only some bodies. This structure of the book highlights the politics of love, which invokes connections with nonhumans as resources for love while denying these same nonhuman actors the agency of being able to love. In doing so, the book moves from a micro-politics of how sex reformers sought to engineer love by sexually experimenting with animal parts to a macro-politics of a metropolitan and global mapping of love that situated humans and nonhumans in an emotional evolutionary hierarchy defined by varying gradations of capacities to love.

In the first chapter, readers are introduced to how sex reformers took Darwinian evolutionary theory in radical new directions that inspired sexual experimentation with animal organs to fuel human sexual energies as the raw materials of love. Through these experiments, sex researchers introduced a new form of intimate animal exploitation in the production of love. Birth control clinics, sex research laboratories, eugenics conferences, and the offices of psychoanalysts were spaces that unsettled human/animal boundaries where sexual energies were concerned yet upheld love as a privileged human experience. Beginning with the literal space of new radical human/animal intimacies in the literal space of the laboratory, this chapter introduces a prominent theme of engineering love as scientific practice that will be extended in subsequent chapters that focus on other less conventionally defined scientific laboratories of love such as forests, farms, parks, gardens, churches, the cosmos, bedrooms, and city streets.

Chapters 2 and 3 elaborate on how sex reformers went beyond relationships with animals to encompass a vast network of "natural" nonhuman participants in their efforts to restructure the world and its populations according to a scientific practice of love. Chapter 2 devotes attention to the limits and possibilities of love among nonhuman environmental actors such as plants, rocks, mountains, sunshine, and other atmospheric agents. This chapter raises the question of how new sex reform injunctions to cultivate sex as love informed early twentieth-century back-to-nature movements, the discipline of ecology, and the fascination with plant-breeding. In doing so, this chapter shows how love is situated in idyllic landscapes, invoking romantic visions of pure nature reinterpreted through the discourse of eugenics. Chapter 3 pushes the map of love and its agents a little farther, going beyond the "natural" earthly places to other-worldly planetary realms. This chapter considers the role of supernatural nonhuman or occult forces in sex reformers' practice of love as the spiritual experience of sex. While exploring how the practice of love connected sex reformers to the cosmos, chapter 3 considers how access to the divine was contingent on which bodies were capable of love. Chapter 3 shows the spiritual dimension of sex as love as a crucial component in enchanting the body as well as the dangers of giving divine sanction to the emotional hierarchies of race, class, sex, and gender. At the intersection of spirituality, sex, and the body, sex reformers redefined love in relation to eugenic breeding as the necessary context for love.

Chapters 4 and 5 further expand on how sex reformers' efforts to incorporate nonhumans into a mission to scientifically engineer love did not stop at allegedly "natural" life forms but encompassed technological artifacts and metropolitan spaces. Chapter 4, for example, highlights how sex reformers' mission to elevate human bodily experience of love simultaneously compromised the boundaries of the "human" and nature through a reliance on intimate technologies to artificially augment human capacities to achieve love. This chapter highlights sex reformers' constructions of love as machinic intimate interventions into the "human" which ironically employed artificial nonhumans to exalt what sex reformers considered an evolutionary superior capacity of human bodies to experience love. In doing so, this chapter extends the scope of Darwinian evolutionary theory and its engagement with "nature" to nonhuman technologies as nonhuman actors. In the final chapter, we see how the idealized loving couple of chapter 4 is defined against yet depends on allegedly hypersexual energetic non-white, immigrant, lower-class, and colonized bodies. This chapter depicts an emotional hierarchy of bodies with those lower on the evolutionary ladder being deemed capable of sexual passion but not love. As such, chapter 5 broadens our perspective on love's actors to consider the human nonhuman or, what Dana Seitler calls animalized humans.[23]

Collectively, the chapters show that love is built out of human and nonhuman relations, informed by historically and culturally specific scientific truths about what those bodies can do or feel. As such, this book makes the point that love is construed and experienced in tandem with what culturally passes as knowledge about bodies. Throughout these chapters, sex reformers' entanglements of love and science offer a case study for considering love itself as a very particular kind of knowledge that is material, affective, and discursive. Each chapter explores a specific type of science or branch of knowledge that informed sex reformers' practices of love and, at the same time, defined the potential of bodies to love. The first chapter addresses the entanglement of love with endocrinology and zoology, showing how sex reformers engaged with animal sexual parts to sexually rejuvenate human bodies as a step toward achieving love. Chapter 2 elaborates on how sex reformers' mission to recreate love as a scientific practice involved a new environmental ethic that connected sexual science to ecology and botany in efforts to harness other kinds of "natural" nonhumans as material resources for love. Chapter 3 discusses sex reformers' turn to occult science, a mix of physics, mathematics, and spirituality, to redeem sex as a religious experience for bodies capable of turning sex into love. Chapter 4 addresses machinic interventions such as birth control technologies in the bodies of sex reformers as new scientific instruments for reconfiguring love as a science in engineering physical, mental, and spiritual connections between "human" highly evolved bodies. The final chapter explores how sex reformers' engagement with nonhumans as exploitable resources for engineering love also profoundly shaped new emotional hierarchies of racialized relations in metropolitan spaces insofar as love was situated in the context of Darwinian evolutionary biology that cast love as a privilege for the most evolved humans in contrast to humans deemed closer to the animal.

As this book offers a new perspective on love as the work of human and nonhuman intimacies, it is concerned with further developing a language for grasping the politics of love as both connection and division. Readers will encounter key phrases that cut across all of the chapters. One of the aims of this book is to encourage readers to consider how bodies are marked by assessments of their *affective potential* as a crucial axis of both exploitation and privileged experiences depending upon what a body is deemed capable of feeling. The phrase *affective potential* can be defined as the anticipation or future possibility of a body's capacity to feel, relate to, and transform with human and nonhuman others. As the chapters explore the political and cultural implications of assessing a body's affective potential, readers will repeatedly encounter the two other phrases: *the politics of love* and *radical intimacies*. What I refer to as the politics of love is an ontological politics that mobilizes love as a crucial mark of humanity thereby deeming those bodies capable of love as more human than others. Perhaps more importantly, deeming some bodies as more capable of love than others also invites the exploitation of less-than-human bodies as resources for love. While assessing a body's affective potential could be applied to any emotion, love has a particular relationship to defining the human, whereas anger, sadness, and fear are more readily ascribed to being shared among humans and nonhumans.[24] My use of the phrase *radical intimacies* highlights the risk taking in whom or what we become intimate with. For the human, the risk of intimacies with nonhumans challenges ideals of the purity of species and exceptionalism. For the nonhuman, the risk taking is one that opens them to other forms of intimate exploitation.

1

"Becoming-Animal"

Evolving Love in Animal Sex Experiments

In the early 1890s, William James, one of the prominent philosophers on the principles of human psychology, claimed that "The brains of mammals differ only in their proportions, and from the sheep's one can learn all that is essential in man's."[1] As a professor at Harvard University, James wrote this in the context of making the case to psychology students that the dissection of a sheep's brain could yield insights into the physiological structures and functions of the human brain. As a well-respected scientific authority and pioneer in the discipline of human psychology, James's claims of the intimate proximities between the brains of humans and sheep exemplifies an extraordinary shift in redrawing human/animal ontological boundaries. Insofar as James contended that it was possible to extrapolate from the brain of the sheep the fundamental principles in the human brain, he drew on a new scientific understanding of an evolutionary kinship between humans and animals and extended it to their potential affective commonalities.

By the time James had published his multivolume *Principles on Psychology*, which was soon followed by the abridged version *Psychology: A Briefer Course* in the 1890s, he had already embraced and applied Darwinian evolutionary theory to his understanding of the human mind, which encompassed a variety of affective components from reflexes to instincts to sensations to emotions. As an intellectually inquisitive young Victorian middle-class man, William James contemplated the profession of a naturalist in his passion for the scientific study of nature, accompanying Louis Agassiz on an expedition to Brazil up the Amazon River in 1865. In 1873, James taught his first course on natural history, focusing specifically on the comparative anatomy and physiology of vertebrates and, one year later, became the director of the Museum of Comparative Zoology at Harvard. James's career emerged out of an interest in examining the evolution of consciousness, driven by the question of what made consciousness so significant to survival that it became an object of natural selection.[2] Given James's insights into human psychology, his works provided a significant contribution to how sex reformers reconfigured love as a higher evolutionary phase of human emotional behavior. Sex reformers were not only familiar with James's works but one in particular, Hutchins Hapgood, benefited directly from James's teachings as a student at Harvard and reworked some of James's insights into the more specific direction of reforming sex with particular references to James's understanding of reservoirs of human energies as sexual energies.

As early twentieth-century sex reformers turned their attention to the importance of love, they inquired into the physiological mechanics of producing such love. Inquiring into the potential of organic materials from organs to tissues to bodily fluids for affective powers, they brought the animal and human into ever-closer proximities while ambivalently drawing evolutionary emotional distinctions between them. Through the emphasis on the possibilities of physiologically engineering love, sex reformers contributed to shaping arenas of sex research. However, this joint mission of sex researchers, physiologists, psychologists, and sex reformers found its inspiration in the anxieties around the loss of white, middle-class sexual energies and the declining white birthrate. As sex reformers drew attention to the pressures of capitalism and the effects of modernity, they turned to animals as potential affective resources to bolster white, middle-class sex lives. This historical moment was significant for reconsidering the boundaries of human sexual desire, love, and reproduction as the animal lingered in gynecologists' offices, birth control venues, physiological understandings of the human body, and psychologists' formulation of human minds. Ironically, white, middle-class professionals generally entertained eugenic concerns over purity of lineage while also disturbing the purity of human origins by drawing on lessons from animal inheritance. Yet sex reformers navigated this tenuous boundary of "becoming-animal" through an ontological politics of love that linked animal and human in sexual feeling but withheld love as a spiritual product of evolution.

Through attention to love, sex reformers forged new human/animal materialities between 1890 and 1930, which can be understood as a genealogical episode of Deleuze and Guattari's concept of becoming-animal. Deleuze and Guattari use the term *becoming-animal* to emphasize both the construction of the "human" and the possibilities for exceeding the "human." To this extent, Deleuze and Guattari's work de-territorializes the human by locating it within a flow of ontological fragments that can be detached, attached, and reattached to other bodies or worlds, thus, situating the "human" as part of an ontological process that edges it toward the "animal." In this sense, multiple human capacities can be understood as the range of feelings from emotions, instincts, sensations, and energies that flow across human and animal bodies. Moreover, sex reformers' focus on love as a particularly scientifically disciplined practice of sex involving the micromanagement of affects raises the question of the origins and limits of kinship. Sex reformers' interests in how reproductive research on animals could inform human practices can be understood through the lens of feminist science studies explorations into sex as a process across species involving messy mixtures and transgressions of human/animal boundaries.[3] Sarah Franklin's *Dolly Mixtures*, for example, addresses how sheep provided models for genetic cloning to be extrapolated to humans, which echoes late nineteenth-century turns to animal intimacies in sex research.[4]

From psychoanalysis to animal sex experiments, sex reformers embodied and materially inscribed Darwinian evolutionary narratives in the present through new scientific practices that drew on the animal in constructing the sexualized psyche as well as sexual physiology. As sex reformers closely bound mutual sexual satisfaction to love, they also drew upon the animal to achieve love while simultaneously denying the animal its own capacities and rights to love. Ironically, what sex reformers cast as the higher and exclusively human experience of sex as love depended upon the animal. Beyond the presence of the animal in navigating the metropolis as a Darwinian jungle, psychoanalysts, animal sex researchers, and sex reformers more broadly internalized and materialized Darwinian narratives in animal dreams, an animalized unconscious, the injection and transplantation of animal parts, and the revival of animal passions. The first section of this chapter explores how sex reformers in the 1890s initially turned to the developing sciences of psychology and zoology to ironically elucidate the mysteries of the human mind by exploring the purported animal within as the source of the driving force of love in sexual and psychic well-being. In the second section, this chapter turns to how

1920s sex research on reproduction intensified human/animal intimacies by yielding insights into the interchangeability of human and animal parts, which could be used to engineer love. These new and intensified human/animal intimacies emerged out of sex reformers' overarching project to create and disperse love, which they successfully popularized, enchanting the wider public with the possibilities for civilization in cultivating sexual happiness, and by extension, love.

ANIMAL PSYCHES: ANIMAL KINSHIP IN DREAMS, INSTINCTS, AND INTELLIGENCE

The late nineteenth-century invention of psychology as a science of human emotions ironically rendered the animal a crucial actor in the evolution of the human psyche as a product of the human longing for sexual love. Psychologists who were pioneering figures in the development of psychology configured the animal as a crucial actor in the modern love story of the human psyche, disturbing the sacred ground of the mind as a uniquely human artifact. Patricia Ticineto Clough has addressed Freud's construction of the psyche as a technological artifact, specifically emphasizing the psyche as a writing-pad that was inscribed by encounters with the outside world.[5] This openness of the psyche, however, stretches beyond a shaping of the psyche through material encounters to the very formation of the psyche out of a Darwinian animal inheritance that shaped the discipline of psychology at its very inception.

In the early stages of the sex reform movement, Darwin's turn to intimate genealogical ties with animals informed sex reformers' configuration of an animalized psyche. As late nineteenth-century white radical intellectuals turned to Darwin, they tracked down the traces of animal ancestors within a "civilized" body in the deep recesses of the mind, or what Sigmund Freud would eventually call the id, the mental repository of latent unruly animal passions. Wrestling with these animal impulses harbored within "civilized" bodies, sex reformers challenged the humanness of the mind itself by turning to basic animal instincts of sex and hunger as the foundations of the human psyche. The rise of the discipline of human psychology began with the animal, redeemed, exoticized, and made useful by sex reformers.

Freud, in fact, was part of a broader community of late nineteenth-century psychologists, which included Havelock Ellis, G. K. Stanley Hall, William James, and William McDougall, who cited a troubled civilized psyche at odds with animal instincts. It is not surprising that the first patients of practicing psychologists were predominantly white middle- or upper-class individuals who were considered to have attained the remotest distance from their evolutionary animal kin and, thus, bore the greatest burden in upholding human progress. For late nineteenth-century pioneers of psychology, evolution was as much about mental and emotional evolution as noticeable physical changes in the body.[6] Taking a broad global perspective on the evolutionary scope of human history, late nineteenth-century psychologists focused on the psyche as a racialized product of evolutionary development with a specific association between whiteness and the highest evolved form of the psyche. Across the works of Ellis, Hall, James, MacDougall, and Freud, there is an emphasis on reconnecting with repressed or submerged animal impulses that presupposed a vast continuum of bodies stretching from animals to allegedly savage, less evolved humans to higher "civilized" populations. At this critical moment of interrogating the mysteries of the human psyche, pioneering figures in psychology mapped Darwinian anthropological narratives onto global political and social inequalities of class and race that aligned white bodies with the most highly evolved human mind.

Although early pioneering psychologists were an embattled group persistently advocating psychology's claims to scientific legitimacy, the development of psychology began with their self-identification with the plight of their patients; namely, the psychic conflict between feeling purportedly primal animalistic sexual instincts while, at the same time, recognizing these instincts as a moral flaw and harbinger of the potential degeneration of civilized white races. Prominent American psychologist, Granville Stanley Hall's adolescence had been marked by the psychological conflict between overpowering masturbatory tendencies and a Protestant moral imperative of sexual self-control, which prompted his own bouts with mental suffering in the form of neurasthenia or nervous weakness.[7] In his monumental work on *Adolescence*, Hall would explain this very personal struggle in evolutionary terms, noting how "the child harks back to a remoter past; the adolescent is neo-atavistic, and in him the later acquisitions of the race slowly become prepotent."[8] Moreover, Hall acknowledged sex as a powerful persistent evolutionary force across organisms: "As these primitive sex elements differentiate one from the other, sex organs, secondary and ancillary to their needs in all their vast variety and beauty of form and exact adaptation to each other, throughout the plant and animal kingdom, are developed."[9] According to Hall, this psychological struggle was specific to modern civilized subjects who did not have outlets for channeling animal sexual impulses with the following dire consequences: "Sex asserts its mastery in field after field, and works its havoc in the form of secret vice, debauch, disease, and enfeebled heredity, cadences the soul to both its normal and abnormal rhythms, and sends many thousand youth a year to quacks, because neither parents, teachers, preachers, or physicians know how to deal with its problems."[10]

Like Hall, William James also suffered from neurasthenia in addition to bouts of depression and physical difficulties with his eyes, digestion, and insomnia. He therefore also had a vested interest in drawing attention to the particular plight of civilized bodies in conflict with their evolutionary impulses and kinship with animals. At the outset of James's *Principles of Psychology* in 1890, he addressed the tension between natural sexual impulses akin to those of animals and the moral imperative of "civilization" to stifle these tendencies. James contrasted the world of birds, frogs, and dogs with humans: "No one need be told how dependent all human social elevation is on the prevalence of chastity. Hardly any other factor measures more than this the difference between civilization and barbarism."[11] While interrogating the mysteries of the human mind, James elided the human with the animal at the site of affects such as interest, attention, and sexual instincts, indicating that "Our interest in things means the attention and emotion which the thought of them will excite, and the actions which their presence will evoke. Thus every species is particularly interested in its own prey or food, its own enemies, its own sexual mates, and its own young."[12] Havelock Ellis, another pioneering figure in psychology, wrote in his early journals at the age of seventeen about his desire to "throw off my reserve and physical nervousness which are now so hateful to me because I am so conscious of them."[13] At this same time, Ellis had embarked on his early teaching career in Australia and confessed his struggle to come to terms with his attraction to his student, Minnie, questioning, "Does that sensuousness render my love less pure?"[14] As the discipline of psychology developed as a way to navigate and mitigate this conflict, psychologists shaped a crucial scientific discourse that would prove to be foundational to the sex reform movement. Sex reformers would rely on psychology to make their case that the civilized expression of love need not be divorced from the cultivation of sexual energies.

As late nineteenth- and early twentieth-century psychologists began to develop a coherent science of the human mind, they were compelled to grapple with the question of animal kinship and evolutionary theory.

Early students of psychology therefore began to address the question of mental evolution, which had initially been raised by Alfred Russel Wallace, Darwin's cofounder of the theory of natural selection.[15] Like James, Freud too was influenced by evolutionary theories. In charting the phylogenetic memory of the psyche, Freud drew on his early readings of anthropology, which included Jean-Baptiste Lamarck's theory of acquired characteristics, Charles Darwin's theory of evolution, August Weismann's neo-Darwinism, and Ernst Haeckel's recapitulation theory of the reenactment of animal to human evolution in the stages from childhood to adulthood.[16] From Freud's days as a biology student to the end of his career, evolutionary theory shaped his construction of the psyche as a profoundly gendered and racialized site, associating hysteria, a feminized malady, with regression to the infantile stage of life and the primal stage of evolution.[17] As many historians have noted, Darwinism made a tremendous impact on mid-Victorian culture and this influence shaped the early lives and ideas of pioneering figures of psychology on both sides of the Atlantic.[18]

Psychology's debts to Darwin were explicitly mentioned in British psychologist William McDougall's 1908 publication, *An Introduction to Social Psychology*, which addressed the entanglement of the human mind with animal inheritance. Citing the profound influence of Darwin, McDougall advocated "only a comparative and evolutionary psychology." McDougall claimed that psychology "could not be created before the work of Darwin had convinced men of the continuity of human with animal evolution as regards all bodily characters." Once these affinities between animals and humans had been established, it remained for psychologists like McDougall to seize on the possibilities opened for "the quickly following recognition of the similar continuity of man's mental evolution with that of the animal world." In his work, McDougall drew on evolutionary narratives to explain the development of "the mental forces which we may trace in the evolutionary scale far back into the animal kingdom."[19] As such, McDougall's work exemplified the recurrence and rearticulation of Darwinism in the development of human psychology in response to the psychic crisis in white, middle- and upper-class bodies who were responsible for furthering modern evolutionary progress.

Psychologists who began to construct theories of the human mind in the late nineteenth century reinvented and reformulated Darwinian evolutionary theory in response to the pressing question of how emotions were situated in the dynamic drama of evolutionary progress. Situating the psyche in the context of evolution, psychologists critically positioned the animal as foundational to shaping the human psyche and bodily apprehension of the world. In 1890, William James's magnum opus, *The Principles of Psychology*, considered the animal as an animating central force in human mental life. James noted shared human/animal feelings emanating from "the whole history of civilization," whereby man exhibited "strong tendencies to rivalry, jealousy, and acquisitiveness." He referred to the hunting instinct as having a "remote origin in the evolution of the race." On the subject of rage, James retraced such human emotion to animal origins where "our ferocity is blind, and can only be explained from below." James, however, ambivalently experienced feeling with the animal. He brought the animal into both psychic proximity and distance with the human, explaining that "however uncertain man's reactions upon his environment may sometimes seem in comparison with those of the lower creatures, the uncertainty is probably not due to their possession of any principles of action which he lacks. *On the contrary, man possesses all the impulses that they have, and a great many more besides*" (emphasis in original).[20]

In fact, when James considered the subject of love, he specifically limited animal capacities to the level of sexual instincts. He invoked Darwin's discussion of wooing rituals among higher animal types. Under the category of love, James argued that "of all propensities, the sexual impulses bear on their face the most obvious signs of being instinctive, in the sense of blind, automatic, and untaught." James therefore posited evolutionary affinities and limits in the connections of animal and human emotional lives where their commonalities stopped at the level of sexual instincts as early un-evolved traces of love.[21] In James's formulation of the affective similarities of animal and human bodies, these similarities were limited to shared sexual impulses but stopped at the experience of love, which differentiated the higher evolved human from the animal.

Around the same time that William James reformulated Darwinism in framing the fundamental elements of human psychology, Havelock Ellis, on the other side of the Atlantic, also addressed the modern reverberations of evolutionary history in human affective experience. In 1894, Ellis's rather deceptively titled text, *Man and Woman: A Study of Secondary Characters*, if anything, showed man and woman as emerging bodies still caught in the web of their animal origins. Ellis suggested that the very differentiations of man and woman grew with evolutionary ascent, which, he presumed, intensified sexual attraction and furthered reproduction. Ellis's *Man and Woman* retold their origins as an emergence out of more ambiguously gendered ancestors that over time developed the "womanly qualities of the woman which are attractive to the man, the manly qualities of the man which are attractive to the woman."[22] Ellis told an evolutionary tale of the pelvis, describing how "the pelvis has developed during the course of human evolution; while in some of the dark races it is ape-like in its narrowness and small capacity, in the highest European races it becomes a sexual distinction."[23] Ellis also indicated that the higher development of the pelvis implied an evolution in emotion whereby "the persons best adapted to propagate the race are those with large pelvises, and as the pelvis is the seat of the great centres of sexual emotion the development of the pelvis and its nervous and vascular supply the greater heightening of sexual emotions."[24] Consequently, the white "civilized" woman's experience of her pelvis and, by extension, her greater experience of the intensity of sexual emotions ambivalently signified both her evolutionary superiority and intimate apprehension of the animal within.

Much like James and Ellis's works, William McDougall's works also formed part of the developing scientific "truth" that emotions were also subject to evolutionary progress with some emotions uniquely associated with the emergence of allegedly superior, white, civilized human bodies. McDougall's *An Introduction to Social Psychology* noted insects as purely instinctive, whereas higher organisms as they evolved became capable of more complex emotional experience. McDougall suggested that "instinctive activity" could be used to associate higher and lower animals. He claimed that "if no such instinctive activity occurs among the higher animals, we must suspect the affective state in question of being either a complex composite emotion or no true emotion."[25] As an avid supporter of the uses of psychology for eugenics, McDougall extended the emotional index of evolutionary status to racial difference among humans.[26] While discussing prehuman ancestors, McDougall blurred the animal/human boundary with "the minds of primitive human stock." In terms of affective capacities, McDougall drew distinctions between higher and lower animals as well as higher and lower humans. Far from a homogenous category, human beings, for McDougall, varied widely as a species in that "primary innate tendencies have different relative strengths in the native constitutions of the individuals of different races, and they are favoured or checked in very different degrees by the very different social circumstances of men in different stages of culture; but they are probably common to the men of every race and every age."[27]

McDougall drew on a popular discourse that noted how "civilized" men and women had weaker instincts because of their distance from the struggle for survival. Using the broad category of "innate inherited tendencies of the human mind," McDougall simultaneously introduced possible affinities with animals while rigorously marking affective racial differences.[28] This carried the serious implications of prescribing certain evolutionary limits to the range and possibility of an organism's affective experience, making certain emotions like love potentially beyond the reach of nonhumans as well as "less civilized" humans.

As psychologists situated the human psyche within the Darwinian framework of evolution, they mapped degrees of emotional maturity onto existing racial, class, and gender hierarchies. Sigmund Freud was beginning to consider the human mind as a conflicted site of clashing "civilized" cultural expectations entangled with an animal inheritance of overwhelming "natural" impulses of sex and hunger instincts. Freud's focus on female hysterics already positioned him within Victorian discourses of the insane as animalized humans. Darwin, in fact, used images of the insane in his 1873 work on *The Expression of Emotions in Man and Animals* to highlight the ambiguous and moving line between the human and nonhuman.[29] Freud referred to Darwin's work on emotions in his first major publication *Studies in Hysteria*, which he coauthored with Josef Breuer. Describing the case of forty-year-old, Frau Emmy von N, Freud noted that: "She played restlessly with her fingers (1888) or rubbed her hands against one another (1889) so as to prevent herself from screaming. This reason reminds one forcibly of one of the principles laid down by Darwin to explain the expression of the emotions—the principle of the overflow of excitation."[30] As such, psychoanalysis reproduced and embedded colonial politics and racial theories in the construction of the mind and in the experience of bodily feeling as psychoanalysis became a resource and accepted truth for grappling with sexual impulses. Literary scholar Gwen Berger explains the whiteness and masculinization of the Freudian unconscious in terms of how "the 'primitive' exists in a timeless, unevolved state associated with infancy, femininity, homosexuality, and neurosis. With the primitive forever marking this starting point of human evolution, Freud can trace the psychosocial development of the white, European, male subject."[31]

Far from a merely theoretical backdrop to the practice of psychology, psychologists turned to animals as critical actors shaping the psychic lives of their patients in the present. For psychologists drawn to

Darwinian evolutionary frameworks, the animal persisted in haunting the psyche and rising to the surface of modern bodies. This animal presence in the shaping of psychology as a discipline was most salient and literal in early twentieth-century animal experimentation in the field of physiological psychology, which relied on animals to draw conclusions about connections between bodily responses and mental life.[32] As early as 1884, William James's "What Is an Emotion?" in the journal *Mind*, drew on the experience of human encounters with bears to convey to his readers how fear is initially apprehended by the body and only later mentally apprehended as an emotion. James explained that when confronted by a bear, one runs and then one apprehends fear as the mind apprehends the body's movement.[33] By resituating emotions along physiological lines, James opened new possibilities for bridging mental life to affinities with animals. What may be surprising is that psychology's formation of the essence of human mental life uneasily opened such mental life to an ambiguous relation with and dependence on animals. Moreover, James's turn to human-bear encounters to illustrate his point on the experience of fear indicates how philosophers then and now find animals useful to think with.[34]

Although physiological psychology and psychoanalysis emerged as two different and often rival approaches, they shared a common practice of interrogating the animal as a crucial underlying actor in comprehending the psychic life of modern "civilized" populations. In Freud's practice, animals routinely intervened as critical participants that animated his patients' dreams and functioned as keys to their stories of psychological trauma. Some of Freud's early cases in the 1880s included a young girl who suffered from a deep memory of being chased by a dog and Frau Emmy who had fearful dreams of snakes and vultures, traumatic memories of wild horses, and profound fears of white mice in what Freud described as "animal hallucinations."[35] In 1905, when Freud published *Psychopathology of Everyday Life*, he extended animal intimacies to the broader condition of the human. In this work, Freud described an encounter with a friend who "said to me at that time in Andrassy Street, '*Nothing human is foreign to me.*' To which I remarked, basing it on psycho-analytic experience, 'You should go further and acknowledge *that nothing animal is foreign to you.*'"[36] In one of Freud's most famous cases, the Rat Man, he invoked the animal as a prominent affectively charged figure as the fear of rats came to powerfully represent deeper psychic conflicts. Freud configured the psyche as a human/animal hybrid as much as a civilized/primitive one. For Freud, psychoanalysis entailed grappling not only with infantile and archaic memories but, most importantly, the affect attached to the memory. As Freud and Breuer indicated in their introduction to *Studies of Hysteria*, "the fading of a memory or the losing of its affect depends on various factors. The most important of these is *whether there has been an energetic reaction to the event that provokes an affect*" (emphasis in original).[37] Freud cited affects as the primary site where human/animal and civilized/primitive boundaries were exposed as mirages.

James, Ellis, Freud, McDougall, and G. K. Stanley Hall exemplify early transnational formations of psychology through a new focus on sexual instincts as a common ground of affective evolutionary kinship with the animal. Sexual sciences like sexology and psychology emerged as new authoritative discourses to galvanize new cultural practices to probe the capacity for human feeling by cultivating animal inheritance. Freud's work must be contextualized within broader late nineteenth-century critiques of Victorian sexual morality that introduced new orientations toward animality as part of revitalizing white sexual energies to uphold civilization. Freudianism gained a foothold in Britain and the United States in the 1910s and 1920s, partly due to its resonance with the broader cultural fascination with sexual instincts, which cut across both psychoanalysis and the physiological psychology of William James in the United States and Havelock Ellis and William McDougall's contributions to the psychology of sexual instincts in Britain.

Late nineteenth- and early twentieth-century psychologists were critical figures in sex reform networks, as their ideas reached the broader community of sex reformers via their university teaching careers, public lectures, and engagement in circles beyond the field of psychology. During his career as a Harvard professor, William James, contributed to Harvard's mandate to educate manly bodies as well as intellects by encouraging athletics and propagating his theory of untapped reservoirs of primal energies in civilized male bodies.[38] James was an inspiration to many of his students, including Theodore Roosevelt, who went on to become a US president known for his strenuous life philosophy, and sex reformer Hutchins Hapgood, who cited James's view of these reservoirs of energies.[39] Scottish psychologist William McDougall began teaching at Harvard in 1920 and remained there until 1928. He became known as a pioneer in the "new psychology"; that is, the new early twentieth-century theories of psychology's application to addressing social problems and everyday life.[40] Far from isolated within specialized circles of psychological knowledge, McDougall's ideas became influential for teaching, social work, religion, and statecraft.[41] Both James and McDougall were also actively engaged in circles of psychical research, which also attracted a number of sex reformers. As a founder of the American Society for Psychical Research in 1884, James intertwined the mysteries of untapped human reservoirs of energies to new forms of spirituality, which reflected his interests in Swedenborgianism, mind cure, and theosophy.[42] Like James, McDougall also became active in the Society for Psychical Research.[43] And like many sex reformers, James and McDougall entertained the possibility that latent energies in human bodies could conceivably make cosmic connections across evolutionary time, nonhuman bodies, planets, the living, and the dead.

For sex reformers, psychological theories and practices informed by Darwinism offered new resources for probing latent animality as a source of sexual energies to revitalize weary civilized bodies in need of the animal to power white love. Sex reformers turned psychological theories on sexual instincts into a cultural practice, approaching everyday encounters as opportunities to rediscover the animal while channeling animal energies into productive, "civilized" pursuits. Although some sex reformers like anarchist Emma Goldman were fascinated by Freudian ideas as early as 1895, it took until around 1909 before Freud gained significant influence in the American radical intellectual milieu. At this time, American psychologist Granville Stanley Hall arranged for Freud to lecture in the United States at Clark University in Worcester, Massachusetts.[44] By 1909, Hall's well-known work on *Adolescence* had been published, drawing important attention to puberty as a pivotal but difficult phase in human sexual development because of the surfacing of inherited unruly animal and primal impulses. In *Adolescence*, Hall invoked recapitulation theory, whereby an organism relived the stages of evolution, overlapping the lifecycle with anthropological trajectories from animal to civilized societies.[45]

In Greenwich Village, around 1910, psychoanalysts such as Freud's disciple A. A. Brill, Smith Ely Jelliffe, and Beatrice Hinkle became popular names among sex reformers, who moved within a cultural milieu in which visiting psychoanalysts became a trendy practice.[46] As historian Joel Pfister has contended, Greenwich Village radical intellectuals treated their experience with psychoanalysis as "psychological capital" in the remaking of a white bourgeois emotional status in the 1910s.[47] Greenwich Village intellectuals such as Floyd Dell, Mabel Dodge, and Max

Eastman visited psychoanalysts and invoked psychoanalytic vocabulary as fashionable practices. Artists and playwrights such as Susan Glaspell, George Cram Cook, and Eugene O'Neill wrote plays that drew on psychoanalysis and its associations with cultivating animality, helping to popularize psychoanalysis as a mark of affinity with the avant-garde intellectual elite. In London's Bloomsbury, sex reformers Dora and Bertrand Russell engaged with other elite Bloomsburies such as James and Alix Strachey who became psychoanalysts and English translators of Freudian works.[48] Other British sex reformers such as Janine Riviere, Barbara Low, and Eden Paul became psychoanalysts and contributed to the sex reform movement by mounting a case for a less restrictive sexual morality informed by Freudianism.

As eminent psychologists on both sides of the Atlantic began to build the human psyche out of animal bodies and evolutionary theory, the animal became much more than a purely symbolic or discursive figure. Gilles Deleuze's discussion of Sigmund Freud's patient, the Wolf Man, indicates this invasion of the psyche by the real animal that disturbs and unhinges human ontological difference. Deleuze charts an alternative narrative to the implication of animals for psychology, showing the psyche as an arena for becoming-animal. Deleuze begins this renarration with "That day, the Wolf-Man rose from the couch particularly tired. He knew that Freud had a genius for brushing up against the truth and passing it by, then filling the void with associations." Instead of colonizing the animal within the domain of psychology, Deleuze redefines how the animal points to what exceeds the human. Deleuze argues that "he [the Wolf-Man] knew that Freud knew nothing about wolves, or anuses for that matter." While Deleuze is no historian, his point of how the animal was not to be taken as a purely symbolic construction within an entirely human mind captures the ambiguous ground of animal experimentation and evolutionary theory's relationship to early twentieth-century formations of psychology. However, Deleuze underestimates Freud's capacity for understanding real wolves and hybridized sex organs given Freud's own turn to evolutionary theory. Psychologists drew on animals theoretically and practically to construct the human psyche. For example, William James used pigeons in his physiology classes and William McDougall experimented with rats. For sex reformers, some of whom were psychologists and others who went to or conversed with psychologists, the psychological discourse on sexual instincts and evolution brought the animal into the experience of sexual feeling yet the animal continued to fall short of love.[49]

"BESTIAL FUSION OF HUMAN AND APE STOCK": BECOMING-ANIMAL IN LABORATORIES

At a birth control meeting on October 17, 1925, physician M. Deddow Bayly drew attention to the disconcerting experiments of Dr. Serge Voronoff, whose work raised the nightmarish vision of a prospective half-human, half-beast creation. Addressing Marie Stopes's eugenic organization, the Society for Constructive Birth Control and Racial Progress, Bayly discussed the horrific prospects of the practice of sexual rejuvenation, involving transplantations of animal sex organs into human bodies. In his talk, entitled "Voronoff and His Rejuvenation Experiments," Bayly warned against Dr. Voronoff's work on using monkey organs to revitalize human bodies.[50] To an audience deeply concerned with the purity of racial stock, Bayly invoked the specter of "this preposterous and bestial fusion of human and ape stock on the future of the race." Bayly also spoke to an audience that presumed the benefits of sexual instincts to clearly lie in furthering a heterosexual agenda of love and racial reproduction. Noting that these animal sexual organs may cure homosexuals, Bayly nonetheless warned that such benefits were outweighed by the need to "ensure that the cure is not more dangerous than the disease in so far as the integrity of racial life is concerned." At this venue of a conference devoted to birth control for women's bodies, Bayly's concerns over the potential "bestial fusion" of human and animal bodies in a prospective future race exemplifies the extent to which sex reformers had contributed to transgressing human/animal ontological divides through their promotion of sexual science.

Bayly's attention to Voronoff's work at a birth control meeting in London is perhaps a testament to the global reach of birth control and sex reform networks as well as the significance of Voronoff's disturbing crossings of human/animal reproduction. Much of Voronoff's popularity can be attributed to the popular fascination with sexual energies as the source of youthfulness.[51] Animal sexual organs earned the status of a particularly intense supply of sexual energies to rejuvenate aged bodies and cure all kinds of ailments from memory to wrinkles to sexual vigor. Voronoff, a Russian physiologist, worked as the director of the Department of Experimental Surgery in France. Voronoff's work took specific Darwinian kinship with apes to new intensified levels of concrete bodily mixtures across ape/human sex lines, registering deep ambivalence about such kinship in both prospects for powering human bodies with vital animal energies while risking the human in the impregnation of female apes with human sperm or the impregnation of human females with monkey sperm. He taught his technique of grafting ape glands onto human bodies to surgeons all over the world.[52] For this express purpose, Voronoff established a monkey farm in Grimaldi to supply monkey body parts while appealing to Belgium, British, Spanish, and French colonial governments for legal protection of chimpanzees.[53] One of Voronoff's more famous cases involved the ape Norah being injected with human sperm.[54] He had also gained notoriety for numerous successful rejuvenation experiments in men over a nine-year period. Despite the general excitement surrounding the seeming discovery of a source of eternal youth in animal sexual organs, some sex researchers and birth controllers worried about the potential offspring of such hybridization experiments. Bayly, in particular, worried that these rejuvenation experiments would lead a woman to give full credit to monkeys for her husband's sexual prowess. He insisted that she would wonder whether "her husband's power for becoming a father of her children is due to his possessing ape's glands in addition to his own."[55] Voronoff exemplifies the literal material and physiological turns that Darwin's evolutionary theory took many years after Darwin first proposed human and ape family ties.[56]

As scholars have grappled with the implications of reproductive technologies such as in vitro fertilization, cloning, and stem cell research, they have increasingly eroded human/nonhuman boundaries by considering the array of actors making reproduction possible. Insofar as scholars of science and technology studies have reshaped our perspectives on reproduction, they have approached reproduction as a process of making bodies that opens itself to creative combinations of hybrid bodies across the human/nonhuman divide. What Donna Haraway initially addressed as a cyborgian body composed of multiple human and nonhuman fragments can be considered the offspring of a mixed genealogical heritage of these new reproductive technologies.[57] The cyborg, in other words, can be considered the embodiment of what Charis Thompson calls the ontological choreography of institutions and actors that collaborate in the reproductive process.[58] In light of contemporary forms of reproduction, the purity of the human is compromised in its reliance on a network of nonhuman actors such as petri dishes, microscopes, DNA analysis, and computer logarithms of genetic predictability. Scholars of science studies have mainly focused on the merging of human and nonhuman objects or artifacts, or the organic with the inorganic. This focus, however, has neglected the animal/human entanglements in the longer genealogy of reproductive technologies. As such, contemporary scholars have perhaps unknowingly taken up the Darwinian mantle of a sex reform project in addressing the mechanics of sex as a lens for eroding human/nonhuman boundaries.

To some extent, psychoanalysis's encounters with animals offered its own repressed experience by confining the animal to the symbolic experience of a familial, oedipal, "civilized" conflict rather than directly engaging with "real" animality. In 1896, at a time of the search for ways to grapple with animal kinship, H. G. Wells's *Island of Dr. Moreau* anticipated the potential convergence, or perhaps Darwinian reconvergence, of human/animal boundaries in new surgical and technological human/animal hybrid bodies. Wells told the story of Edward Prendick, shipwrecked and stranded on the island of Dr. Moreau, a physiologist expelled from England for his experiments. On the island, Prendick encounters frightening creatures known as Beast People who have been created by Moreau through surgical re-combinations of animal and human parts.[59] As a sex reformer trained in zoology by Darwin's bulldog, Thomas Huxley, Wells was situated amid new intersections of human and animal sexuality made possible by evolutionary theory and sexology.[60] By the 1920s, sex reformers' figurations of the animal within, whether in Wells's novel or the staging of the animal in the psyche, took material forms in the bodily recombinations of human and animal organs, fluids, and energies.

As sexology developed and intensified its influence from the 1890s to the 1920s, it contributed to a model of the human body open to new intimate relations with animals. By the 1920s, sex reformers' efforts to excavate a latent animal other took the form of materially engineering the feeling of this animal presence. Drawing on new technologies such as contraceptive devices, gonadal extracts, and surgical alterations, sex reformers tested the potential for human feeling via new material intimacies with animal bodies while, at the same time, disciplining this feeling by subordinating it to the achievement of love and eugenic reproduction. In the surprising places of birth control clinics, birth control periodicals, and birth control conferences, the animal entered into the most intimate aspects of human emotional experience. Sex reformers in the 1920s experimented with these material reconfigurations of human/animal boundaries, radically entangling Darwinian inheritance, psychology, and new sexual technologies that offered a new model of the body as a sexological ecosystem.

As sex reformers shaped birth control movements in Britain and the United States during the 1910s and 1920s, they extended psychological explorations of animal subjectivity into the material reinvention of the sexual body. Birth control leaders such as Margaret Sanger and Marie Stopes probed the limits of the human reproductive body while drawing on sexual knowledge from animals. Sanger and Stopes radically contested the reproductive limits of the human body by probing the possibilities of new technologies to redefine sex and allow for a safe but disciplined and appropriately channeled cultivation of animal sexual instincts. The birth control movement's history has largely been taken for granted as a human story but birth controllers' attention to the techniques of managing sex drew on a wider array of actors than just human ones. Women's reproductive bodies converged with animal ones across a number of intellectual arenas such as sexology, breeding experiments, zoology, evolutionary theories, eugenics, and endocrinology. The animal, then, had a key role in what made techniques of sexual intimacy possible and what politicized such techniques along an evolutionary continuum extending from animal passions to human love.

Although Marie Stopes is widely known for her advocacy of birth control as a tool of love to ensure wanted children and pleasurable human sex, what is less known is her turn to zoology and animal sexual practices to make the uses of birth control possible. Stopes's *Radiant Motherhood* and *Wise Parenthood*, which followed her eminent publication of *Married Love*, focused on contraceptive interventions into the life cycle and, in fact, built on sexual knowledge of the animal. On March 31, 1920, Stopes wrote to Professor Hill that she had been researching the time of gestation and uterus retraction in common animals.[61] She told Hill that she had an interest in tigers, lions, wolves, foxes, leopards, pumas, apes, chimpanzees, other monkeys, or any "nice truly wild and graceful animals." She confessed her amazement "to find gaps in the knowledge about fertilization and the earliest stages in the higher animals. Is it true or is it merely that I do not know where to look, that the first divisions of human embryos, apes, and so on, are really not known?" While Hill affirmed that these facts were largely unknown, he directed Stopes to F. H. Marshall's well-known text on gestation. Marshall's work was filled with examples of animal reproduction out of which human sexual physiology was constructed and interwoven with nonhuman intimacies.[62] Couples, then, who turned to Stopes's famous marital sex manuals had their experiences partially built on animal reproductive bodies; thus, relying upon the animal to make love possible.

While Stopes exemplifies how the birth control movement owed a debt to animal sexual practices, scientists who primarily inquired into animal sex practices were, nonetheless, also influenced by sex reformers' popularization and advocacy of scientifically disciplining human sexual practices as love. Marie Stopes's correspondence with the notorious vivisectionist William Bayliss shows how the work of scientists was shaped by the politics of controlling women's reproductive choices. Bayliss had received much negative publicity from anti-vivisectionists who condemned his experiment on a dog, and he was well known among activists and intellectuals engaged in vivisection debates.[63] Some sex reformers, in fact, were particularly interested in scientific research on animals. Stopes and H. G. Wells, for instance, belonged to the Research Defence Society, which organized its members in opposition to anti-vivisection campaigns.[64] These lines of mutual support between sex reformers, birth controllers, and animal experimenters have yet to be fully explored. Bayliss's letters to Stopes indicate that he considered his expertise in physiology to extend beyond the animal. He not only corresponded with Stopes but suggested members for her Society for Constructive Birth Control and Racial Progress.[65] While Bayliss's work approached animals as useful for understanding the physiology of sex, it was love as a spiritual factor in sex that dominated his reflections on human sex. A few days after Stopes requested Bayliss to read her Prenatal Influence chapter in *Radiant Motherhood*, he wrote to praise her accuracy on the physiological claims.[66] Strikingly, Bayliss who primarily worked with animals and Stopes who primarily worked with humans found common ground across the animal/human divide at the site of sex and reproduction. Moreover, both Stopes and Bayliss could agree on distinctions between animal sex and a higher evolutionary product of human sex as love. These interdisciplinary crossings between sciences of human physiology and those of animal physiology exemplify the extent of the erosion of the human/animal boundary at a time of a Darwinian resurgence in sex reform networks.

Although Bayliss and Stopes could agree on the extension of lessons from animal sex to human sex, they also similarly addressed love as the limit of the animal-to-human extrapolation, redrawing that boundary not at sex but at love as a higher evolutionary capacity. Far from reducing sex to physiology, Bayliss, who experimented on animals and spent his time investigating the physical body, also emphasized spirituality and love as primary factors of human sexual experience. Bayliss's letter to Stopes in August of 1922 indicates the extent of sex reformers' influence on shaping ideals of sex as love. Bayliss admitted that he was drawn to Stopes's books because she discussed the spiritual significance of sex. Bayliss listed four main aims of sex: procreation, the relief of accumulated secretion, pleasure "apart from any love of the woman," and the manifestation of love for one woman. Holding love as the most important aim, Bayliss insisted that the sexual act should be "mutual love + trust between husband and wife prolonged + intensified thereby."[67] Outlining these specific objectives, Bayliss addressed love as a sign of the highest form of sex; a feeling and experience couples strived to attain in this period. This marked a significant link between Bayliss as a physiologist and sex reformers who introduced love into sexual physiology as part of the aim and mechanics of sexual technique. However, Bayliss's praise of Stopes's works and his support of her Society also suggest that he quite likely would have equated love with healthy, vigorous, educated, white, "civilized" bodies. By attaining the support of physiologists and other scientists like Bayliss, sex reformers and birth controllers grounded their visions of love in sciences of the body. Through this fruitful collaboration, sex reformers shaped a physiology of love built out of human and animal material and affective linkages.

Stopes's turn to animals occurred at a time when animal sex research and birth control movements informed one another across the collaborative work and divergent areas of expertise among sex reformers in Britain, the United States, and Western Europe. Margaret Sanger's *Birth Control Review* (*BCR*) was transnational in its scope. Although focusing on sex, love, and motherhood in the United States, the *BCR* also reported on birth control news in other countries such as China, India, Japan, and, most often, associated American activities with British initiatives. Sanger's periodical reflected the transnational reach of Darwinian animal intimacies and sex reformers' fascination with cultivating sexual feeling by cultivating the animal while, at the same time, avoiding the impediments of pregnancy. *BCR*'s news centered on women's reproductive bodies, but it included reports on groundbreaking animal sex research as the arena for testing new possibilities for achieving the intensities of animal feeling. Far from advocating unrestrained animal sex, the *BCR* encouraged "civilizing" sex through new technologies such as X-rays, intrauterine devices, and chemicals to allegedly perfect nature. The *BCR* included articles written by prominent sex researchers that reinforced sex reformer Margaret Sanger's mission to legitimize birth control as a scientific practice in tune with current trends and developing sexual science.

Sex researchers' contributions to the *BCR* also highlighted how they situated their work in the context of sex reform's politics of love insofar as they positioned emotions within evolutionary hierarchies of an organism's increasing sophistication and complexity. Although Lynda Birke has suggested that scientific objectivity has long been identified with suppressing emotion, early twentieth-century animal sex researchers warily investigated feelings out of concerns in undermining human evolutionary exceptionalism.[68] In the February 1920 issue of the *BCR*, Gideon Diedrich's "Biological Reasons for Family Limitation" traced the very origins of human sexual attraction and pregnancy to the evolution of a "copulating association" among animals. Observing that such an association existed in higher marine and land animals, Diedrich located intense human emotions of sexual desire within animal evolution. Far from a distinctively human practice, passion and attraction emerged out of animal inheritance. Telling this story of human sexual passion's animal origins, Diedrich explained: "That a distinct copulating association between parent organisms has only been developed at such a late stage in the evolution of life also makes it clearly evident that its development must have been caused by some powerful attractive force with the selfish individual to draw the male and female parents together into such an association."[69]

Diedrich not only addressed the development of sexual desire on an evolutionary scale but also presumed that heterosexual desire between male and female parents would be the form of attraction among higher evolved organisms. In a subsequent January 1924 issue of the *BCR*, Leon J. Cole's article, "Animal Aristocracy and Human Democracy," contended that the insights gained from nonhuman breeding could be applied to breeding an improved human stock.[70] Cole was a recognized expert in the field of experimental breeding, holding positions as a professor of genetics at the University of Wisconsin and as chief of the Animal Husbandry Division for the American Department of Agriculture. Far from limiting his discussion to analogies of animal and human reproductive physiology, Cole also went on to address the affective dimensions of reproduction, insisting that quality breeding among humans and animals did not amount to robbing human sex of its spiritual element thus marking a firm dividing line between animal sexual desires and uniquely human love. Sex researchers like Diedrich and Cole situated feelings on an evolutionary continuum, which addressed gradations of affective experience from animal sexual desires to human love. Featuring the work of sex researchers, Sanger's *BCR* exemplified the mutually reinforcing relationship between sex researchers who could articulate the political significance of their work in a sex reform forum and sex reformers who could articulate the scientific legitimacy of their campaign.

Reproductive scientist Donald Hooker's contributions to Sanger's *BCR* exemplified the degrees of convergence between sex reformers and sex researchers as well as human and animal desires. Donald Hooker's work on rat fertility and X-rays appeared in the *BCR* as a summary of his involvement in the 1921 Birth Control Conference in New York City. Hooker's circles of professional encounters thus straddled animal and human boundaries and laboratory and birth control spaces. Hooker, a researcher at Johns Hopkins University, attended the Fifth International Birth Control Conference where he presented his work, "The Effect of X-ray on Reproduction in Rats,"[71] thus, signaling the animal presence in human reproductive strategies. Hooker's work turned to questions of the use of the X-ray as a birth control mechanism to be initially tried out on rats. Yet, Hooker's experiments with rats were not limited to solely mechanical reproductive practices but, in fact, addressed the place of sexual desires in rat sex and essentially situated their desires at a lower end of an evolutionary spectrum of emotions in comparison with human love. Assessing the relationship between sterilization and masculinity, Hooker turned to the behavior of male rats that, after "rendered sterile by exposure to x-rays continue to exhibit normal sexual activity; that is to say they copulate with females."[72] Commenting on the absence of interstitial tissue, Hooker noted that this absence "precludes normal sexual life in that it is requisite to normal sex desire." This treaded on the ambiguous nature/culture divide with respect to whether observations on rats proved the "natural" and biological foundations of how sexual desire worked or the manufacture of such desire through the cultural norms informing the experiment. What X-ray sterilization on rats could teach about human intimacy shaped Hooker's concerns that "any method applicable to Birth Control must not abrogate the natural expression of love in marriage."[73] By insisting on how birth control could facilitate the "natural expression of love," Hooker drew on the political climate of birth control activism and sex reform to communicate how his work on rats engaged with contemporary concerns and debates on human sex. Hooker therefore associated the significance of his research with central arguments of the sex reform platform; namely, the importance of separating the indulgence of sexual desires from the consequences of reproduction.

Margaret Sanger's *Birth Control Review* evoked not only the diversity of professionals from social workers to clergy to scientists engaged in questions of women's reproductive choices but also showed the entanglements of human and nonhuman bodies in exploring ways to disconnect sexual desires and expressions of human love from the consequence of pregnancy. In the *BCR*, the human and animal entered into literal physical intimacies at the site of evolved practices of sex and reproduction. Diedrich explained the mother's womb as an evolutionary development of pregnancy, as a parasitic relationship. The womb had its own evolutionary story, as it developed through the gradual attachment of cells in the "parasitic habit of mammal embryos."[74] Diedrich used this connection of the human womb to other organisms in parasitic relations as an argument for birth control as a right to women's voluntary motherhood. On the grounds of pregnancy's evolution as a form of parasitism, Diedrich argued that "no human society has any moral, ethical, or biological right to dictate to a mother when and how often she shall allow a parasitic embryo to feed in her womb."[75] To this extent, Diedrich framed pregnancy in ways that situated the embryo as both an organic, intimately entwined entity as well as a foreign body. Diedrich addressed an ambivalent relationship between growth and parasitism in terms of the uneven distribution of energies between donors and recipients of life force and bodily matter.[76] Far from discouraging motherhood, however, Diedrich used this notion of the parasitic embryo to exalt the importance of motherhood. He exalted the maternal body as the locus of "all the civilizing and humanizing influences [that] have been brought into the world."[77] Diedrich not only situated voluntary motherhood as civilized and more truly human but simultaneously joined human and nonhuman physiologies in a shared birthing process among mammals.

Hooker's experiments with X-ray technologies on inhibiting fertility in rats is another example of how sex research entangled rat and human maternities and paternities in ways that resonated and could be used to reinforce sex reformers' calls for reforming sex. Significantly, Hooker's research pointed to the prospects of an effective male birth control technology and thus male participation and engagement in concerns around fertility.[78] He specifically distinguished the effectiveness of X-rays in male rats in contrast to the higher dosages required for female rat sterility. Hooker's intrusive gaze and interference in rat reproductive bodies also extended to work affecting the pregnant rat body insofar as X-rays delayed yet did not prevent such pregnancies.[79] In the context of this historical moment of animal sex research, female rats also became crucial historical actors in birth control research involving the submission of their ovaries to radiation.[80] In particular, to reach conclusions about possible human applications of X-rays for birth control, Hooker noted differences in female rats when "to reach ovaries the radiation has to penetrate deeper than is the case with the testes."[81] Hooker also defended his use of domesticated rats on the basis that he could easily follow their oestrous cycle, noting that "no experimental attack on the problem of birth control would be complete without consideration of the control of the oestrous cycle."[82] Like many sex reformers, sex researchers experimenting with reproductive technologies on animal subjects brought human and animal bodies into more intimate proximities across common sites of mammal embryos, sexual instincts, and reproductive processes while insisting on birth control as the distinguishing mark of the human in the capacity to scientifically discipline sex.

Sex researchers' articles in the *Birth Control Review* exemplified how reproductive experiments on animals and their desires extended to both the gender politics of sexual freedom for women as well as the racial politics of ensuring the reproduction of a fitter race. As the birth control movement and the rise of eugenics converged, sex reformers and sex researchers found common ground in situating their projects within the popularization of eugenics as a new trendy science of breeding that shaped the scrutiny of women's pregnancies and animal pregnancies Hooker, in fact, observed his rat subjects through the lens of eugenic concerns with "procreative normality" and the question: "Is there danger that offspring or children will be abnormal?" In this phrasing of "offspring or children," Hooker included rat offspring alongside childbirths. He specifically reassured his readers that after a temporary period of X-ray sterility, "the litters have been normal in size and there have been no monstrosities."[83] Hooker noted the scope of these animal experiments by citing the work of other researchers and prominent eugenicists such as Raymond Pearl, who experimented on fruit flies, and Clarence Cook Little, who also conducted mammalian breeding experiments.[84] Hooker, in fact, appealed to the knowledge of "those who have worked on mammalian breeding" to sympathize with the slow process of attaining experimental results.[85] His mention of C. C. Little is particularly significant given that Little prominently moved between worlds of animal and human reproduction, serving as chief of the Scientific Committee of Sanger's American Birth Control League. However, Little was more renowned for his expertise in breeding pure lines of mice for research to discern the inheritability of cancer. Little also considered his research as applicable to the formation of human eugenic social policies.[86] While Pearl worked on fruit flies and Little on white mice, Hooker also noted the work of Stockard and Evans on the domesticated rat. Hooker's awareness of other work in the field of animal breeding experiments suggests the prominent strand of animals in narratives of human fertility control.

Insofar as prominent scientists of breeding and reproduction collaborated with birth control activists like Marie Stopes and Margaret Sanger, they co-opted animals into reinforcing racial hierarchies *within a species*. Around the same time that Charles Darwin's theory of evolution and natural selection became influential in Victorian intellectual circles, his cousin, Francis Galton, became widely known as the father of eugenics, the science of better breeding, which was applied across human, plant, and animal life. In the early twentieth century, these connections were manifested in the motley array of members in Marie Stopes's Society for Constructive Birth Control, the Eugenics Society, and the International Birth Control Conferences. Birth controllers and animal sex researchers identified common ground in techniques of sexual science for disciplining sex by controlling the selection of sexual partners to breed a better race whether that race be defined as a specific race within the animal, plant, or human kingdom. As will be shown in the following chapter, birth control activists and botanists alike influenced by eugenics identified an allegedly superior racial being as one reproduced by loving sexual practices. The crucial ontological difference, however, was that a plant was reproduced by the botanist's loving practice of plant-breeding, which matched members of a superior plant racial stock. In contrast, a superior human was reproduced by allegedly racially superior parents who adhered to the tenets of sexual science to experience love as a higher spiritual capacity.[87]

As the birth control movement grew in tandem with the proliferation of sex manuals in the 1920s, popular practices of reinvigorating marital sex lives also drew upon new chemical and surgical intimate encounters with the animal. By this time, sex reformers had successfully popularized and romanticized sexual energies as the source of human vitality and civilization, thus contributing to the emergence of the popular phenomenon of seeking rejuvenation through injections of animal hormonal extracts. By the 1920s, rejuvenation was more than merely a fad. Scientists, journalists, physiologists, clinicians, and novelists expressed enthusiasm for how glandular science revealed the magical properties and hidden potential of the body.[88] Historian Chandak Sengoopta refers to the popular fascination with animal hormonal extracts as the "secret quintessence of life" and a magical formula for youth, success, and beauty. This phenomenon of rejuvenation occurred in a transnational context of leading

European, British, and American work in the developing science of endocrinology, emerging in tandem with the growing popularity of sex reform's attention to cultivating sexual energies as the first step to marital love. In the 1920s, animal parts became new material sources alongside psychoanalysis and sex manuals for enriching marital intimacies.

British gynecologist and sex reformer Norman Haire's medical practice exemplifies the extent to which animal sex research, birth control, and sex reform converged in the early twentieth century. Like Stopes and Sanger, Haire managed one of the early birth control clinics, the Walworth Women's Welfare Centre in East London, as an effort to educate and provide the poor with contraceptive advice and materials. Haire also identified his professional and birth control activism with the broader objectives of the sex reform movement, partnering with Dora Russell to organize the World League for Sexual Reform's 1922 meeting in London. Haire's consultations with patients offer a unique example of how sex reform agendas mixed with interests in psychology, evolution, and eugenics to inform medical diagnoses, patient attitudes, and new human/animal embodiments of new sexual technologies. Haire's correspondence with his patient, Mr. Brough, offers some insight into how animal sex research entered into managing human sexual health.

In January and February of 1922, Haire received several visits from Mr. Brough, who expressed grave concerns over his impotency. Haire approached Brough's case through the lens of a transatlantic medical discourse on sexual rejuvenation.[89] Initially, Haire attempted to sexually rejuvenate Brough by injecting a serum of bull's testicles into him. According to Haire, Brough showed some improvement through this boost of sexual force. He began eating better, putting on weight, and sleeping well. Although Brough's sexual performance was only temporarily restored, these other physiological improvements pointed to how physicians understood the effects of sexual energies on overall bodily health. With the problem of impotency still uncured, Haire suggested that Brough undergo psychoanalysis, which Haire himself could perform in an "amateur way."[90] Haire, therefore, drew on both physical and psychological methods for diagnosing impotency as an affective dysfunction that interwove body and mind. Haire's consulting room can be seen as a laboratory of love where testing Brough's powers of sexual feeling marked a crucial preliminary step toward enabling sexual instincts to reach their full potential of the higher experience of love. At the level, then, of gauging and augmenting sexual feeling in the human, animal parts proved to be useful. By the time of Brough's visit in 1922, sex reformers including Norman Haire had helped turn popular attention toward the significance of sexual energies for white, middle-class marital love.

When Haire turned to animal bodies as resources for enhancing human feeling, he drew on trends in biology and psychology that increasingly rendered the human/animal boundary porous. Several prominent psychologists such as William James, Stanley Hall, and Sigmund Freud were influenced by Darwinian thought on the animal ancestry of humans. They specifically tied feelings such as instincts as well as emotions to animal kinship. Brough, however, refused to undergo psychoanalysis, expressing his fears that it might, ironically, bring on insanity.[91] Instead, Brough opted for physically altering the body's parts in the hopes of producing sexual feelings. As a last resort, Brough requested Haire to perform a vasectomy for two reasons: firstly, Brough believed that, given his former bout with insanity, it was irresponsible for him to risk the chance of procreation, and secondly, he hoped the vasectomy would sexually rejuvenate him. Brough's decision shows how eugenics shaped concerns over reproduction with very real material effects on the body through procedures like vasectomies. Moreover, Brough's decision related to what sex reform discourses articulated as the wondrous power of sexual instincts for upholding civilization along a range of axes from breeding better bodies and improving overall health to artistic and literary inspiration. Haire's encounter with Brough exemplifies the reworking of human/animal intimacies across both the small and larger stages of birth control, eugenics, gynecology, and other medical and social interests in reproduction. Individual encounters between physicians and patients, birth control offices and clients, sex researchers and animals circulated in wider public and professional discussions of concerns over inter-species sex across human/animal divides.

Although human affinities with monkeys largely dominated the racial and scientific imagination, particularly in depictions of African Americans as simians, Darwinian evolution addressed a broad array of animal kin that became exemplified in the intensification of early twentieth-century human/animal intimacies in animal sex research. In fact, Voronoff's initial work involved experimenting with sheep. By 1931, sex reformers such as Marie Stopes and the eugenicist and psychologist Carlos Paton Blacker were well aware of John Baker's sex research on a variety of animals as part of the Department of Zoology at Oxford University's Museum. Baker's 1926 work, *Sex in Man and Animals* reflected the ambiguous territory between humans and nonhumans that emerged from late nineteenth- and early twentieth-century sex research, sex reform, and animal experimentation. John Baker's sex research on animals provides one case of the historically specific form of becoming-animal in the 1920s. In Baker's work, this "becoming-animal" concept emerged in the dynamic between the use of animals to "naturalize" human sexual norms and the use of human sexual norms to structure, observe, and pass judgment on animal bodies. There was no clear separation between the natural and the cultural that were entangled in the experimental context.

Baker's work attracted the attention of various experts and reformers as part of a growing professional discourse on sex that pathologized perversions and consolidated heterosexuality.[92] By the 1920s, sex reformers and psychologists shaped the growing cultural awareness of perversions, which also equated heterosexuality with evolutionary superiority and sexual maturity. Early on in his work, Baker cited heterosexuality as a product of the evolutionary development of higher organisms. Charting this development, Baker claimed, "No doubt the power to develop without fertilization was the earliest condition. Then, sexual reproduction having evolved, the ability to develop without fertilization was taken away by natural selection, so that the advantages of sexual reproduction could not be escaped."[93] Baker drew on an array of nonhuman bodies to argue that secondary sexual characters that differentiated gender and underpinned heterosexual attraction were instrumental to natural selection.[94] In doing so, Baker privileged heterosexuality as the sexual practice leading to higher evolutionary development.

Through his animal experiments, Baker offered further support for contemporary cultural turns to sex glands as the source of gendered behavior. Early twentieth-century endocrinologists showed that both male and female elements existed in each individual with gender ultimately determined by hormonal balance. Moreover, rejuvenation techniques to boost manly virility or preserve femininity in postmenopausal women entailed the use of animal sex organs; a practice known as organotherapy. In the early twentieth century, scientists turned to animal experimentation for investigating castration, transplantation, fertility, the estrus cycle, and infertility. At the time, Baker placed endocrine research across animal and human planes, arguing that "the interest of these glands for us is that the testis and the ovary of the higher animals secrete hormones, whose functions is to call forth the development of the characters of the appropriate sex."[95] Upon discussing the effects of castration on a young boy, Baker drew this human body into the network of nonhuman sexual physiologies, observing that: "in just the same way castration in other mammals results in a reduction of the penis and various glands, in the accumulation of fat, in greater growth by certain of the long bones and in loss of the sexual instincts. The tendency to fight other males and to copulate with females in heat is never developed or is lost."[96] To illustrate this point, Baker used a number of examples such as castrated sheep that failed to develop horns; castrated frogs without the instinct to croak or clasp the female in copulation; and castrated cocks unwilling to fight other cocks, crow, or copulate with the hens.[97] This array of disparate nonhumans indicated the range of nonhumans bonded by sexual experiences to their human kin.

When Baker turned to the subject of the removal and grafting of ovaries and testes, he suggested that the effect of glands on the production of sexual energies transformed animal and human gendered physiologies in similar ways. Baker claimed that ovariotomies in women resembled those in mammals. Juxtaposing the effects of ovariotomies in birds and in "primitive" women, Baker discussed the woman's growth of hair at the corners of her mouth and the decrease in her sexual instinct alongside the bird's growth of plumage and loss of sexual instinct.[98] Using the example of grafting on rats, Baker also suggested that gender physiology depended on the glandular production of sexual energies. Baker contended that grafting an ovary onto a castrated male rat or guinea pig would "feminize" it. Visible bodily markers of this transformation included the castrated rat or guinea-pig's growth of large teats, lactation, a female mating and suckling instinct, and the stagnation of male organ growth. Conversely, when testes were implanted in ovariotomized female rats or guinea-pigs, male copulating organs and male sexual instincts developed, female sexual organs failed to develop, and the coat became coarse like the male coat. As Baker's lens narrowed on animal sexual behavior and grafting, the line between human and nonhuman receded as heterosexuality and gendered bodies emerged as sites of the functioning of ontologically interchangeable parts.[99]

Baker closely scrutinized perverse animal bodies from sex-intergrade pigs to castrated sheep only to reaffirm heterosexuality and distinctively gendered bodies as experimental goals. Baker emphasized that important lessons could be learned from sex-intergrade pigs and hermaphrodite "freemartin" calves, which showed "a tendency to sexual abnormality is certainly inherited in mankind." According to Baker, the human anatomy of an abnormal individual resembled that of intergrade pigs and goats so that "it is reasonable to conclude that they are of similar origin." However, rather than use examples of hermaphroditism and sexual perversion to interrogate heterosexual norms, Baker emphasized that "the important point is to prevent the birth of sexually abnormal individuals." He went on to advocate a eugenic policy whereby "married people who have produced an abnormal individual or who have abnormal relations should be strongly encouraged to practice contraception." Drawing on his inquiry into animal sexual desires, Baker extended and naturalized what were then seen as human sexual perversions into the animal world. Baker's study exemplified the ambivalent turn to animal kinship whereby such perversions shared a kinship with animals. Yet, Baker also pointed to the need to reaffirm the human through birth control and the anxious reinforcement of heterosexuality among the ambiguous world of uncontrolled manifestations of animal perversions. Animals, then, provided sex researchers with the material canvas for assessing naturally occurring biological phenomena even while their animal experiments intensified cultural interventions and constructions of such bodies.[100]

News of animal research circulated within sex reform networks because of the potential usefulness of animal bodies for improving human sexual experience; thus, exemplifying the porosity of both disciplinary and ontological boundaries across human and nonhuman bodies and minds in psychology, zoology, and sex reform. Carlos Paton Blacker, a British psychiatrist, eugenicist, and birth control advocate, wrote to Marie Stopes in 1931 of the promising research being undertaken by Dr. John R. Baker. Blacker informed Stopes that Baker tested the strength of a particular spermicide on guinea pigs.[101] Blacker gave Stopes the details of how guinea pig and human sperm were rapidly destroyed by exposure to five grains of quinine. However, if placed in cocoa-butter, this action on human sperm was small. Blacker concluded that "this holds of the double-strength of quinine pessaries no less than of the single-strength. This clearly shows that the cocoa-butter somehow interferes with the spermaticidal power of the quinine."[102] Blacker noted that the cocoa-butter had less interference with chinosol in Baker's study. Among sex reformers, quinine was known as a key herbal contraceptive. Blacker was aware that Stopes had been working with the chinosol and cocoa-butter combination in creating pessaries and reassured her of its effectiveness in light of Baker's research. Baker's guinea pigs then entered into the possibilities for human sexual experience by demonstrating the effectiveness of birth control.

Given her activities as an international birth control leader, Stopes's awareness of current animal sex research suggests the importance of animals to shaping human sexual experience. When Stopes delivered a lecture in 1930 on "Present Day Technique and Clinical Results of Contraception" in London, she referred to Baker's experiments with contraceptives. She had heard of Baker's work before Blacker wrote to her about the news of Baker's guinea pigs in 1931. At her lecture, she recalled hearing Baker's paper at a sex research congress in which he endorsed the use of soap as a contraceptive.[103] Stopes, in fact, tested these contraceptives on herself. When she tested the soap, she broke out in a rash.[104] She also addressed the issue of the use of quinine, noting that it had been used with cocoa-butter since the 1880s. She also rejected this combination on the basis that it had made her sleepy for two to three days and other couples reported injurious effects.[105] Consequently, she endorsed the chinosol and cocoa-butter. Stopes knew of the work being done on guinea pigs to improve human contraceptives but warned that in vitro experiments with guinea pigs were also different from how human spermatozoa acted in human affairs.[106] This caveat highlights how animal research informed human experience to such an extent that Stopes found it necessary to insist on such caution in applying the findings from guinea pigs.

While sex researchers made the encounter between animal reproductive bodies and birth control technologies a test site for measuring affective potential, this potential essentially limited animals to normative considerations of heterosexual desire. Even when Baker's research pointed to perversions in animals, he took this as evidence of the need for scientific interventions into nature to "prevent the birth of sexually abnormal individuals."[107] However, this work on animal sexuality highlights what Oliver Hochadel refers to as the always ambivalent relationship of bringing animal bodies into close kinship with humans while also differentiating them from human capacities.[108] On the one hand, animal sex researchers used animal bodies to tweak and test the effectiveness of birth control technologies and assess sexual desires, but on the other hand, they framed sexual desire rather than love as the limited affective scope for animal sex. This politics of love that made use of the animal for human sexual experience extended to the social hierarchies that cast unfit human bodies, including undesired immigrants, racialized populations, and unhealthy, "feebleminded" or diseased others, along the lines of the animal.

The triangular relationship of a birth control leader like Stopes, a psychiatrist like Blacker, and an animal sex researcher like Baker became possible through the intensification of human/animal intimacies in the 1920s at the site of reproduction, sex, desire, and love. This exemplified unique crossings of human/animal lines, interrogating the artificiality of those boundaries as sex reformers, psychologists, and animal and human physiologists probed the origins of love more deeply. By 1930, animals too were caught in Freudian oedipal dilemmas; thus, more explicitly unfolding the Darwinian dimensions of Freudian psychoanalysis. In August of 1930, a number of these experts gathered in London for the meeting of the Second International Congress for Sex Research. The delegates met at the headquarters of the British Medical Association House in Tavistock Square, where a series of papers were presented bringing animal bodies into pressing conversations about human sexuality. The topics of the scheduled presentations included hormones, birth control, venereal disease, testicles, sterility, children's sexual development, hermaphroditism, and evolution.[109] Several papers focused on the sexual behavior of animals such as turkeys, guinea-pigs, hens, and rabbits to inform understandings of human sexual physiology.

Just as scientists like Baker and Voronoff grafted what they treated as interchangeable sexual parts between animals and humans, this physical interchangeability carried implications for psychical activity in animals. Professor C. Ceni, a presenter at the 1930 sex research congress in London, proposed to discuss his paper, "Experimental Studies on the Transformation of the Sexual Instinct into the Maternal Instinct in the Female and in the Male." Ceni's paper essentially placed turkeys on the proverbial Freudian couch, arguing that there was a transformation of the repression of sexual instinct and stimulation of maternal instinct in the turkey.[110] This is evidence of a site of scientific experimentation that corresponded to a cultural phenomenon of the exaltation of both men and women's capacities for mother-love, which sex reformers exalted for its transformative possibilities for a new social order. While discussing psychical activity in the turkey, Ceni also grounded psychical activity in the physiological functioning of the turkey's endocrine glands, thus suggesting visible material evidence of psychical sexual energies.[111] Ceni's paper is one example of how the disassembling and reassembling of the human and nonhuman sexual parts in animal experimentation also scrambled their ontologies and brought psychoanalysis and endocrinology into the same frame of efforts to understand interrelations of bodies and minds at the site of affect. On the one hand, sex researchers observed the potentiality of animal parts to fuel human sexual energies while, on the other hand, human psychical activity could be attributed to animals that sexually and physiologically functioned in similar ways through endocrine glands. Animal sex researchers highlighted the physiological sources and limits of a body's affective potential, which could stop at sexual desire or extend, at least in human bodies, to love.

The central role of animal subjects in the London Sex Research Congress in 1930 occurred in the context of a climate of overlapping areas of birth control, psychology, and endocrinology informed by Darwinian evolutionary and deeply politicized narratives of the emotional products of "civilization." The changing and increasing intensification of human/animal material and psychic intimacies can be traced from 1890, when Freud's publication *Studies in Hysteria* subtly gestured toward its Darwinian subtext, to 1930 when Freud's publication *Civilization and Its Discontents* told an evolutionary tale of the psyche and the oedipal family, dating back to ape kin. In *Civilization and Its Discontents*, Freud situated human sexual drives in an earlier history when "in his ape-like prehistory, man had taken to forming the families, and members of the family were probably his first helpers."[112] Freud attributed the evolution of the family to "the need for genital satisfaction" when "the male acquired a motive for keeping the female or—to put it more generally—his sexual objects around him."[113] Psychologists, only just beginning to ground psychology as a discipline, did not simply address animals in metaphorical terms but grounded the very foundations of the human psyche in the evolutionary theory of human/nonhuman kinship.[114]

What M. Deddow Bayly had described as "the preposterous bestial fusion of man and ape stock" at the birth control meeting in 1925, could easily have been applied to trajectories in psychology that addressed a plethora of animal intimacies with special attention paid to wolves and werewolves. Freud's very famous case of the Wolf Man, published in 1918, drew attention to the entanglement of the animal imagery of white wolves in a tree with the sexual and physical life of the Russian aristocrat, Sergei Konstantinovitch Pankejeff. Approximately, thirteen years later, Freud's disciple in England, Ernest Jones, focused specifically on the werewolf, a mythical but liminal human/animal hybrid represented in nightmares as manifestations of psychic disturbances triggered by deep-seated animal passions. Jones's work, *On the Nightmare*, first appeared in 1931, at a time when firmer and more explicit connections between animals and humans were being drawn across bodies and minds in sex reform, psychology, and zoology networks.

Jones situated nightmares within mythical, imaginary, religious, social, and literal intimacies with animals, tracing the theme of metamorphosis to "sources in dream experiences, for here the actual transformation of the figure of a human being into that of an animal and the occurrence of composite beings, half animal, half human, so often takes place directly before the eyes of the dreamer."[115] Although Jones acknowledged that the educated and literary elite also experienced these animal intrusions in psychic life, it is in "the untutored mind, e.g./ children and savages, [where] the gulf we perceive between human beings and animals is much less apparent."[116] As Freud's disciple, Jones also cast the psyche within Darwinian evolutionary frameworks that turned the psyche itself into a site of colonial and racial power that juxtaposed children with the affective potential to mature alongside the fixity of the "savage" stuck in both a Darwinian past and at the stage of psychic immaturity.

Jones's discussion of the werewolf as a variation on the nightmare as an "anxiety dream" resonated with both Freud's Wolf Man case in the specific context of psychoanalysis and the broader social and cultural context of "civilized" masculinity wrestling with animal inheritance in modernity.[117] Although Deleuze suggests that Freud failed to deal with real wolves, the figuration of the werewolf and the attention to it in psychoanalysis suggests broader efforts to grapple with growing human/animal intimacies that were marked at the level of conflicted encounters in feeling with the animal. For Jones, the surfacing of the werewolf in modernity embodied at the psychic level the difficulty of coming to terms with irresistible impulses, as an incarnation of "the savage and uncanny features characteristic of the wolf have made him specially suited to represent the dangerous and immoral side of nature in general and of human nature in particular."[118] Just as Deleuze suggests a need for reconceptualizing the Wolf Man case in genealogical relation to our present, Jones situated modernity's werewolves in psychic life within a longer genealogical relationship to early modern werewolves of religious and superstitious beliefs. Moreover, Jones situated werewolves in the gendered roles of psychoanalysis, identifying werewolves with sexually maturing Oedipal masculinity. Jones claimed that "it is perhaps not a matter of chance that hatred of the father was a striking characteristic in the actual cases of Lycanthropy, i.e. where people really imagined that they wandered about at night in the guise of wolves."[119] As such, Jones did take into account real wolves but rearticulated efforts to grapple with the fragility of human/animal liminality at the level of powerful irresistible impulses or affects that persistently exposed such fragility, manifesting in some cases in the nightmare and the embodied figuration of the werewolf.

Jones's and Freud's wolves are another strand in a longer genealogy of the continued fascination with lycanthropy and human/animal metamorphoses in new contemporary turns to affect as sites of ontological challenges to human/animal boundaries. Werewolves, for example, abound in the recent edited collection *The Animal Catalyst: Towards Ahuman Theory*, in which several essays focus particularly on Deleuze's "becoming-animal" as an animating and intellectually invigorating lens for rethinking the contours of human/animal ontologies. Deleuze's becoming-animal, however, resonates with the early twentieth-century sex reform efforts to reorient negative affects such as nervousness, fatigue, and nightmares toward positive affirmations of animal energies in the new vital healthy sexuality of Nietzschean supermen and superwomen. This affective reorientation both then and now involves an orientation toward love, albeit in a much different political and intellectual climate. For example, Chrysanthi Nigianni's "The Taste of Living" in *The Animal Catalyst*, drawing upon Deleuze, indicates that "to fall in love is an ahuman act: falling into the black holes of desubjectification, dehumanization."[120] Sex reformers' ethical platform of cultivating love as new encounters with the animal had similar de-territorializing affects shaped by new Darwinian and Freudian animal intimacies. However, in the late nineteenth and early twentieth century context of eugenics, empire, and the romanticization of marriage, new embodied proximities to the animal, whether in gonadal animal implants, animal dreams, or everyday exertions to channel animal impulses, carried the ambivalent status of simultaneously celebrating the vitality of animal passions while safeguarding the human as the "civilized" expression of such passions as divine love.

CONCLUSION

From the 1890s to the 1920s, the sex reform movement took shape in the context of grappling with new Darwinian animal intimacies that ultimately put the status of the human at risk. As sex reformers turned to the subject of the evolution of human love, they engaged in a politics of love. On the one hand, sex reformers drew inspiration from animals to cultivate intense sexual energies, intimately drawing animal and human bodies together both materially and psychically. On the other hand, sex reformers sought to safeguard the evolutionary status of the human by excluding animal bodies from the possibilities for transforming such energies into love. As such, sex reformers relied on animals as useful actors and experimental subjects in their efforts to cultivate love and ground it in science. Across developments in psychology and endocrinology, animal sex researchers' findings informed the larger cultural context of sex reform. As such, animals became important actors in early twentieth-century configurations of human love, birth control, eugenics, and marriage. What Gilles Deleuze has described as *becoming-animal* therefore has an important genealogical relationship to a period when sex reformers ambivalently grappled with the usefulness of animal bodies as affective resources to regenerate "civilized" human bodies and the risks of human degeneration into the promiscuity of animal passions.

As scholars across disciplines have turned toward the question of ethical encounters with animals in our post-humanist moment, they have drawn on both Deleuze's "becoming-animal" as well as Jacques Derrida's "The Animal That Therefore I Am." On the one hand, Deleuze and Derrida can be situated in a longer history of privileging feeling rather than reason as the basis for animal welfare, exemplified by the frequent invocation of Jeremy Bentham's claim that our treatment of animals should be bound to the question of not whether they can reason but whether they can suffer. Sex reformers, animal sex researchers, and psychoanalysts in the early twentieth century were also part of debates over animal welfare. Both H. G. Wells and Marie Stopes were part of a Research Defence Society in defending the use of animals for science. While Dr. William Bayliss confronted angry protests over his use of dogs in investigating the treatment of spinal injuries. Psychologist, Charles Loomis Dana, introduced zoo-phil psychosis as a new mental illness that afflicted feminized and overly sentimental anti-vivisectionists.[121] However, for sex reformers, animal experimentation was entirely consistent with a larger social, political, and ethical project of cultivating love that recognized and engaged with animal intimacies.

As such, contemporary scholars, as well as animal activists, are engaged in a genealogical project with late nineteenth- and early twentieth-century sex reformers who privileged a care and loving orientation to the world while challenging the boundaries between the human and the animal. Yet, for sex reformers, the project of cultivating love ultimately entailed exploiting animal intimacies along the lines of using animal parts and animal energies to revitalize "civilized" bodies. At the same time, as sex reformers advocated a loving ethic, they reinvented a form of emotional paternalism as part of a new emotional ruling class fit to lead "civilization" to its next evolutionary stage by virtue of an evolutionary superior capacity of love.

2

Eco/ontologies

Love, Sex Reform, and Environmental Sciences

While sex reformers considered animals as valuable instructive resources for generating sexual energies and refining breeding techniques to achieve love, they also turned particular attention to plants as crucial actors in human sexual intimacies. Sex reformers' encounters with plants exemplify the literal making of love on the ground through concrete, tangible, earthly, and organic materials. Plants were models for the perfection of human sex without being deemed capable of love in and of themselves.[1] Similarly, insofar as human love extended to gardening and the evolution of plants, it could be reflected by breeding and nurturing a perfected plant body. In both cases, however, sex reformers did not construe plants as agents of love but involved plants as indispensable supporting actors in making human love possible. Plants set the stage, landscape, and background for love, as well as sometimes being the product of it. Sex reformers initiated new plant intimacies with human bodies in the search for cultivating resources for remaking love in the twentieth century.

This chapter devotes much needed and deserved attention to a love story for plants with important implications for analyses of nonhuman agency in science studies. In particular, Bruno Latour's Actor-Network-Theory (ANT) has been pivotal to highlighting the significance of the nonhuman and redefining the role nonhumans play in shaping human lives. Playing upon the term ANT, Latour encourages a shift in the perspective of sociologists by taking on the role of an ant performing the hard work of managing and forging connections with materials on the ground. He contrasts the ant with the role of an angel that flies above the ground, separating oneself from lower forms of life and conceptualizing what happens on the ground without appreciating the messy material relations with the earth and the nonhuman.[2]

While Latour's Actor-Network-Theory offered significant insights into redefining the role of nonhumans, it leaves open the question of the nonhuman's affective capacities such as the energies, emotions, or feelings involved in the nonhuman's engagement with others. Can the ant or the ANT encompass love? What does Actor-Network-Theory look like when love is the product of a network of relations across human and nonhuman bodies? Some feminist science studies scholars have drawn important attention to affect, sex, and reproduction as lenses for reconsidering messy ontological relations across human and nonhuman bodies.[3] However, even these feminist science studies scholars have devoted little attention to nonhuman love stories and the possibilities for nonhumans to participate in love.

By analyzing love as an experience emerging out of human and nonhuman relations on the ground, this chapter addresses love as an ecological story as much as an ontological one. Building on developments in environmental sciences such as botany, ecology, and entomology, sex reformers applied new insights into constructing nonhuman actors in the creation of an environment for love.[4] Moreover, sex reformers' efforts to biologically engineer these environments also allowed plants to serve as models for human eugenic reproduction. Nonhumans played vital roles in sex reformers' efforts to shape "natural" environments that provided the necessary ecological context for making love possible.

Sex reformers experienced love as a force for transformation, not simply self-transformation or even social transformation but an ecological transformation in reorienting oneself to the world at large. This marked a pivotal moment in the history of love with particular implications for renegotiating relations with the nonhuman. Moreover, as sex reformers redefined love in an environmental framework, they also situated lovers as eco/ontological actors. I define the term *eco/ontologies* as a new becoming that involved the transformations of the self and the world through their specific modes of encounter with one another. As such, sex reformers turned attention to love as the mode of encounter, fostering mutually beneficial relationships for humans and nonhumans.

The story of love in sex reform highlights an important chapter in the shaping of ecological consciousness, as sex reformers were at the forefront of early conservation and preservation movements marked by loving relationships with the earth. Beyond drawing attention to the interaction of humans and nonhumans, sex reformers highlighted love as a force of connection entangling humans and nonhumans in a complex eco/ontological web of mutual transformation. As a force of connection, sex reformers re-crafted love as a site that unsettled distinct lines of separation between the human and the nonhuman, as one needed and shaped the other. In doing so, early twentieth-century love offers a critical lens for considering the entanglements of environmental sciences and sexual science.

REPRODUCTIVE ENVIRONMENTALISM: CREATING FERTILE CONDITIONS FOR LOVE, 1860S–1890S

Darwinian evolutionary science in the mid-nineteenth century marked a crucial moment for redefining the vital, active, and transformative sexual roles of nonhumans in shaping human lives. Far from an inert, monolithic, passive mass, nature, according to Charles Darwin, was a messy, volatile, interactive entity that was constituted by reproductive relations among diverse nonhumans. Although famous for drawing attention to human and animal kinship in human evolution, Darwin also addressed plant evolution and emphasized reproduction as a crucial force in shaping species' survival across human, plant, and animal kingdoms.[5] Nature and its nonhuman constituents were in motion, engaged in changing the makeup of the ground through sexual encounters that determined the kinds of plants, animals, and other nonhumans that survived and continued to populate the earth. As such, Darwinian evolutionary science introduced the significance of sexual desire, attraction, and reproductive relations but not necessarily love in the story of nonhuman relations in making nature.[6] Yet Darwin highlighted intimate sexual intimacies across animals, plants, and humans by addressing sex as a significant force in shaping their joint evolutionary destinies.

Through Darwin's works, nature emerged as a network of nonhuman actors whose active sexual lives constituted and reconstituted the world and its inhabitants. Between the 1860s and the 1880s, Darwin's works made reproduction a matter of environmental relations and the environment a matter of the health of human and nonhuman reproduction. Darwin upheld an evolutionary kinship among the highest evolved organisms in terms of how their evolutionary position was secured by sexual practices emulative of heterosexual reproduction. In *On the Origin of Species*, Darwin referred to "the remarkable effect which confinement or cultivation has on the functions of the reproductive system; this system appearing to be far more susceptible than any other part of the organization, to the action of any change in the conditions of life." Although Darwin's *On the Origin of Species* is famous for its discussion of animals, Darwin also devoted detailed attention to plants. On the topic of selective breeding, Darwin identified the same process for generating the best plants as for breeding animals. According to Darwin, plants and animals were remarkably similar in that "whether or not two or more species or races have become blended together by crossing, may plainly be recognised in the increased size and beauty which we now see in the heartsease, rose, pelargonium, dahlia, and other plants, when compared with the older varieties or with their parent-stocks." Darwin considered the influence of environmental conditions on the reproduction of "Domestic Races" of animals and plants. He claimed that "the conditions of life, from their action on the reproductive system, are so far of the highest importance as causing variability." As such, Darwin introduced a politics of racial reproduction on the ground that radically entangled the natural environment with the natural body. Most importantly, Darwin's attention to plants addressed their active participation in sexual practices, which influenced evolutionary momentums that could not be limited to humans and animals.[7]

Darwin not only addressed plants in the *Origin of Species*, but many of his subsequent experiments and published works were devoted to plant worlds of feeling and sexuality. Darwin brought plants into the ambit of human sexual worlds and romantic evolution by attributing a superior status to those plants that most closely emulated distinctly gendered bodies and heterosexual reproduction or "cross-fertilisation." At the outset of *The Effects of Cross and Self Fertilisation in the Vegetable Kingdom*, Darwin explains that "cross-fertilisation is sometimes ensured by the sexes being separated, and in a large number of cases by the pollen and stigma of the same flower being matured at different times."[8] In *The Different Forms of Flowers*, Darwin reiterated the case for the superiority of cross-fertilization, explaining that "I formerly applied the term 'heteromorphic' to the legitimate unions, and 'homomorphic' to the illegitimate unions." Although Darwin acknowledged hermaphroditism in animals and in numerous plants, he insisted on their behavior as distinctly gendered individuals. For example, he insisted that many hermaphrodite animals and plants "absolutely require the presence of another hermaphrodite for sexual union."[9] While Darwin did not romanticize plants as possessing capacities for love, he alluded to cross-fertilized plants as much closer to the romantic sexual norms of Victorian love. Darwin's early contributions to botanical science were not only entanglements of human culture and science but a pivotal chapter in unravelling the love stories of plants.

As Darwin's work pushed botanical science to probe the potential for plants to feel and perform sexually, environmental reform movements turned attention to how the human body was intimately affected by plants and other nonhuman agents such as sunlight, mountains, rivers, wind, and fresh air. The mid- to late nineteenth-century rise of environmental reform movements marked a cultural turn toward considering the human body as an ecologically situated entity shaped by environmental nonhuman actors.[10] In the 1860s, when Darwin was probing plant sexuality through the lens of Victorian sexual norms, environmental reform movements drew attention to preserving national parks and beautifying cities with green space. These movements emphasized how human bodies were vitally and intimately related to plant life. Darwin's transatlantic popularity in Britain and the United States coalesced with an Anglo-transatlantic environmental consciousness in preservation, conservation, and City Beautiful movements that highlighted the interconnectedness of human and environmental health.[11] As such, these environmental movements began to pave the way for further probing the roles of plants as participants in shaping human love as well as human bodies.

In the late nineteenth century, early environmental advocates insisted on the importance of green space and the preservation of wilderness in response to concerns over the health effects of urbanization on human bodies. At this time, when urban reformers in London, England, were making plans to create green space, American landscape architect, Frederick Law Olmsted, drew on his observations of parks in England to draft plans for American parks.[12] Olmsted considered parks and their array of nonhuman actors as intimately affecting and transgressing the boundaries of the human body. In his plan for a Chicago waterfront park, Olmsted addressed the "Gentlemen" of the South Park Commission to promote the park as reducing "rheumatic and pulmonary complaints and the epidemics of children."[13] Olmsted advocated for the creation of parks to fulfill the human body's occupational needs for "soothing, out-of-door refreshment."[14] Like Olmsted, John Muir, a prominent figure in the nature preservation movement, highlighted the bodily effects of nonhuman actors as energetic, soothing, revitalizing forces for human health. In a letter to his sister Ann in 1869, Muir extolled the porosity of human bodies to nonhuman actors, noting: "Now we are fairly into the mountains, and they are into us. We are fairly living now. What bright seething white-fire enthusiasm is bred in us—without our help or knowledge. A perfect influx into every pore and cell of us, fusing, vaporizing by its heat until the boundary walls of our heavy flesh tabernacle seem taken down and we flow and diffuse into the very air and trees and streams and rocks, thrilling with them to the touch of the vital sunbeams."[15] While Olmsted sought to create green space within the city to rejuvenate the bodies of urban workers, Muir ran specific nature tours of the Sierra mountains for white, middle-class men and women who gravitated to nature retreats for reviving bodies wearied and worn from purportedly upholding civilization.[16] Muir and Olmsted's advocacy of nature highlights an early attention to environments as affective ecologies whereby intended emotional effects of space were invested in capitalist projects across different forms of affective needs to enhance worker productivity.[17]

Although early environmental advocates noted the beneficial revitalizing effects of plants, trees, mountains, and other nonhuman "natural" actors, they did so in the context of a heightened attention to the detrimental effects of artificial inorganic nonhuman actors on human bodies. As historian Martin Melosi notes, by the 1890s a new environmental consciousness arose in response to urban problems of smoke, noise, overcrowding, refuse management, and water contamination, which heightened popular perceptions of bodily risk, permeability, and exposure to the environment.[18] In making a case for parks in 1870, Olmsted noted "the much greater rapidity with which patients convalesce, and may be returned with safety to their ordinary occupations after severe illness, when they can be sent to the Park for a few hours a day."[19] Olmsted situated parks as the lungs of urban environments to offer an "escape at frequent interiors from the confined and vitiated air of the commercial quarter to supply the lungs with air screened and purified by trees."[20] In his advocacy for park space, Olmsted drew attention to how the body was porously interwoven and mutated in response to the specific construction, forces, and effects of its environments.

While Olmsted sought to create a healthful natural oasis amid the contaminating air of the city, Muir turned to "wilderness" preservation as a nourishing bodily retreat for spiritually communing with nature. After leaving Madison University, Muir led a nomadic existence of walking, botanizing, working temporary jobs in the Midwest and Canada, and eventually journeying to the Sierras of California. Captivated by Yosemite and the Sierras, Muir devoted his life to studying the mountains while also prospering as a fruit farmer in the 1880s and 1890s. In a letter to his friend, Emily Pelton, Muir highlighted how his body was intimately opened to and affected by nonhuman actors, indicating that "as for the rough vertical animals called men, who occur in and on these mountains like sticks of condensed filth, I am not in contact with them; I do not live with them. I live alone, or rather, with the rocks and flowers and snows and blessed storms; I live in blessed mountain light, and love nothing less pure."[21] Like Darwin, Muir was much more willing and ready to commit to a kinship with plants than with racialized others depicted as less than human, notably Native Americans, who were driven out of national parks and denied formerly held privileges of hunting and fishing.[22] This new environmental consciousness heightened attention to the human body's intimate connections to nonhumans both in terms of the negative effects of urban nonhuman actors and the positive effects of natural nonhumans. As such, environmental movements also drew attention to the kinds of nonhumans that would participate in human love; namely, nonhumans making up natural rather than urban environments.

What Darwin, Olmsted, Muir, and others addressed as the body's permeability to the environment in the 1860s and 1870s mutated into a reproductive crisis in the white, modern, civilized body's dissipated sexual energies. In the 1880s and 1890s, several developments tightly wound environmental crises around reproductive crises: American physician George M. Beard's attention to the growing malady of neurasthenia among "brain-workers," the growing nativism and panic in white nations with heightened immigration levels of non-white populations, the growth of eugenics movements in Britain and the United States, and the fomented and anticipated world racial crisis of a declining white birthrate. Across Britain and the United States, the involvement of prominent intellectuals in an enthusiastic embrace of rising eugenics organizations coincided with their concerns over the impact of urbanization, particularly the abandonment of the countryside and growing elimination of green space. Muir's Sierra Club and other early twentieth-century environmentalists were also avid supporters of eugenics, which intertwined commitments to "pure" space with commitments to "pure" bodies.[23] Coinciding with the late nineteenth-century environmentalism of Muir's spiritual journey through the Sierras and Olmsted's development of parks, Edward Carpenter and Havelock Ellis began to intertwine the cultivation of "natural" sexual instincts with the spiritual immersion in natural spaces such as gardens, parks, farms, and the countryside. Although England did not have spectacular vistas like the Sierras, Ellis and Carpenter similarly identified with the principles underpinning American environmentalism and a longer tradition of British romanticism in the turn to nature to revitalize worn, enervated bodies coping under the modern strains of a new pace of life and urbanized environments.

As early as the 1880s, an intellectual vanguard of bohemian reformers began to respond to urban environments as a sexual crisis; thus, highlighting intimate relationships between bodies, objects, technologies, and nature. For these bohemian reformers, the solution to this crisis was a return to nature by seeking refuge at farms, in the mountains, and in the forest, as well as cultivating a primal past that presumed the present state of an evolved civilized body. Prominent socialists, Edward Carpenter, Havelock Ellis, and Edith Ellis, who met through Fabian and Fellowship of New Life socialist organizations, began to seek refuge in rural spaces as zones of sexual freedom as well as sexual vitality through encounters with nature.[24] In 1882, Carpenter established the farm at Millthorpe, becoming an avid market gardener while constructing a space beyond the constraints of dominant Victorian heterosexual morality. At the very outset of establishing Millthorpe, Carpenter's desires were inextricably mixed with the rural and rustic environment that stimulated his attraction to rugged working men.[25] During the 1880s, Bertrand Russell turned to Romantic poets' exaltation of the spiritually nourishing relations with nature to alleviate his sense of isolation in the sexually and emotionally inhibited environment of his grandmother's home.[26] This late nineteenth-century vanguard of reformers deeply concerned about the effects of the environment on sexual energies drew attention to the role of nonhumans in shaping the capacities for sexual feeling in human bodies.

Prominent sex reform couple Havelock and Edith Ellis situated the health and sexuality of the human body in intimate and interdependent relations with natural nonhumans. In the 1890s, Havelock Ellis's works on sexology advocated the importance of cultivating sexual instincts manifested in his own marriage and his retreat with wife, Edith Ellis, to the countryside. At their farm, Edith Ellis identified the physical labor of farming and the country atmosphere with cultivating new registers of sexual feeling. In 1896, Edith described her body's engagement with environments as nonhumans shaped her lungs, blood, and nose. She experienced the farm as "the spring is in my blood. The gorse here too is glorious, the sea blue and the sky too and my lungs are healed at last and my spirits getting up again and my nose mending after my Jehru

FIGURE 1. Edward Carpenter at Millthorpe in 1905, embracing the ideal of the rustic simple life. Photographer is unknown. Image is in the public domain.

adventure." Edith Ellis, in fact, found that "the sex question is forever with me in my farm."[27] While Edith and Olmsted's lungs were revived through green space in contrast to urban congestion, Edith experienced her bodily connections with the farm in terms of the important rejuvenation of sexual energies as forces of "civilization." Edith, Ellis, and Carpenter's entanglement of sex and space were informed by the 1890s turn toward reevaluating sexual energies as the cornerstone of "civilization," particularly in the context of Freud's early European lectures and the rise of British and Continental sexology.[28] As such, the 1880s and 1890s witnessed the beginning of sex reformers' environmental politics of sex reform, which involved cultivating sexual energies through nature.

Between the 1860s and 1890s, the rise of Darwinian evolution, conservationism, and early environmental activist calls for preservation entangled the health of the natural environment and the sexual health of human bodies. By the time sex reformers became a powerful cultural influence in the early 1900s, their reinvention of love as a product of human as well as ecological connection emerged out of the rise of environmental sciences and environmental movements. This marked a pivotal period in laying the foundation for addressing the importance of the sexual lives of nonhumans in making human love possible.

AGRICULTURAL WIZARDS: PLANT/HUMAN ENTANGLEMENTS IN EUGENICS, 1890S–1910S

Luther Burbank, a plant breeder internationally renowned for his success in producing extraordinary varieties of plants, attributed his accomplishments to an intimate relationship with his plants. Referring to himself as a "plant lover," Burbank contended that "there is no friendlier compact than that between man and the fruit tree."[29] Burbank's experiments with reproducing new varieties of plants involved a reciprocal affective relationship marked by his devotion to his plants and their responsiveness to his care by conforming to breeding techniques as they grew into healthy, beautiful, unusual hybrids. This love story of Burbank and his plants also attests to a darker side of love inextricably linked to the reproduction of fitter healthy racially superior bodies, which included plant "races" that were measured along an evolutionary continuum. In Burbank's gardens, plants were engaged with and materially affected by the infectious spread of sex reform's racial politics of love.

Between the 1860s and 1890s, early influences on sex reformers, which included a variety of intellectuals from Darwinian enthusiasts to romantic poets to early environmental activists and advocates, developed a naturalist approach to love that increasingly shifted to an interventionist approach to love. This interventionist approach to love involved a growing interest on the part of sex reformers in the precision of a science of sex beyond Darwinian sexual selection.[30] In the late nineteenth century, an educated elite and professional scientists shifted from a focus on naturalist approaches to science toward laboratory science and a changing scientific gaze through the use of the microscope that increasingly turned its attention to common sexual processes across plants, animals, and humans. Sciences such as botany and zoology could point to internal processes as evidence of kinship with plants and animals; thus, intensifying human intimacies with the environment. Historian Sharon Kingsland, in fact, refers to ecology as the "sister discipline" of genetics.[31] Sex reformers addressed scientific techniques of perfecting sex as a guide for achieving love at a time when the rediscovery of Mendelian breeding techniques taught that similar techniques could be applied across plants, animals, and humans to control reproduction.[32] Sex reformers situated their own techniques of sex within this wider environmental and scientific context of bringing nonhumans into the fray of human sexuality and the evolution of love.

While plant lives in experimental gardens across the world were shaped by pressing scientific questions about changing human reproduction, changing forms of human sexual intimacy owed a great deal to botanical investigations into plant sex. While historians have typically treated Stopes's botanical and birth control activities as separate chapters in her life, Stopes situated plants in human sexual politics and situated the practice of human sex as love within pristine environments.[33] At the crossroads of the worlds of sex reform and botany, Stopes is a unique and important example of the mutual shaping of ecology, sexology, and biology between 1890 and 1930. Several years before Stopes became a birth control advocate, she examined plant sex to discern the formations of racial strains, the evolutionary advance of heterosexuality, and the shift in higher plants toward distinctly gendered bodies. Stopes's initial training and foundation for sex reform, in fact, came from her study of plants' sex lives. At the same time, the question of human sexual essence came under close scrutiny by sexologists then recasting sex as the "art of love" among higher human bodies.[34]

FIGURE 2. Marie Stopes in 1904 at Victoria University of Manchester, in her early career as a botanist. Author of the image is unknown. Image is in the public domain.

The growing attention to sex in the late nineteenth and early twentieth century, shaped largely by sex reformers, influenced environmental sciences. Botanists, for example, turned their microscopes to plant sexual processes. In defining new plant sex research agendas, botanists investigated topics such as the potency of pollen, plant chromosomes as sex-determinants, and cross-fertilization in comparison to self-fertilization. In the late nineteenth century, botany changed from a genteel pastime for ladies interested in natural history to a science for male experts on controlling reproduction, which increasingly excluded women from pronouncing authority on fecundity, potency, and the embryonic growth of plants.[35] Yet this male-dominated profession of botanists nonetheless privileged the importance of sex and reproduction in the making of botanical science. Coinciding with the rise of sex reform, the rise of plant-breeding through Mendelian and Darwinian techniques became a thriving science, a cultural fascination, and a politically valued activity in Britain and the United States that thickened human/plant intimacies.[36] Botanists and amateur gardeners increasingly argued for the value of plant breeding insofar as findings on plant subjects could inform human eugenics. At the same time, botanists and amateur gardeners saw the prospects for eugenics to scientifically build a utopia of perfected plant, human, and animal bodies.

Whether a plant was grown on American or British soil, in a laboratory or in a garden, it embodied Darwinian breeding techniques of sexual selection; that is, the deliberate choice of mates based on specific qualities to reproduce offspring with anticipated idealized traits. Plant bodies reproduced by California gardener, Luther Burbank, and British botanist, Marie Stopes, exemplify how Darwinian narratives of plant romance joined scientific communities of breeders and plants on both sides of the Atlantic. Both Burbank and Stopes are featured as prominent case studies in this chapter, highlighting the transatlantic circulation of plants in sex reform love stories. Burbank's fascination with Darwin's techniques of sexual selection for plant-breeding was combined with his aesthetic appreciation of plants. Burbank first encountered Darwin's ideas on evolution and science at the age of nineteen when he attended lectures at the Mechanics' Institute. Upon reading Darwin's *Variation of Animals and Plants under Domestication*, Burbank acquired the knowledge of plant-breeding that informed all of his techniques in creating new plants. In addition to Darwin's methods, Burbank later attributed his plant-breeding success to a gift for anticipating ideal mates for plants to produce the most desirable qualities of color, taste, hardiness, texture, and vigor.

Like Burbank, Stopes's encounters with plants were informed by Darwinian ideas of human/nonhuman intimacies in terms of what Paul White calls "evolutionary kinship."[37] Stopes, in fact, drew attention to plants as long-neglected actors in the dramas of evolution, escaping human notice when "so quietly and slowly do they live and move that we in our hasty motion often forget that they equally with ourselves belong to the living and evolving organisms."[38] As the daughter of Henry Stopes and Charlotte Carmichael both of whom belonged to the British Association for the Advancement of Science, Stopes met some of the most famous British scientists, such as the father of eugenics and Darwin's cousin, Francis Galton. Moving within transnational circuits of botanical studies, Stopes undertook graduate studies in botany in Munich. Taking advantage of Germany's reputation in cutting-edge botanical research, Stopes engaged in the disciplinary shift from vegetable morphology to plant sexual reproduction as the defining mark of a plant's essence and evolutionary status. Although Burbank and Stopes experimented with plants in very different places, they shared a common set of breeding tactics that were materialized in the bodies of their plants.

Both Burbank and Stopes acquired international acclaim as plant scientists because of the insights they offered on how disciplining plant sex could reproduce more desirable, fitter plant bodies that could better withstand evolutionary challenges to survival. Although Stopes attained recognition as the first woman in the British Empire to earn a botany degree and published several scientific works on plant breeding, Burbank struggled to gain the respect and admiration of the scientific community. Stopes, in fact, was critical of amateur gardeners, whom she denounced in her publication *Botany* because their "results, as a rule, have been obtained by more or less haphazard crossing."[39] While scientists regarded Burbank with some skepticism, especially in his lack of precise record keeping, his work garnered intense attention from prominent scientists, who increasingly turned to botanical sex experiments for insight into perfecting animal and human reproduction.[40] Burbank's success in creating novel plant bodies attracted scientists to his Santa Rosa and Sebastopol farms, where he received visits from renowned Dutch botanist Hugo DeVries in 1904 and 1906. Liberty Hyde Bailey, botanist and director of the Experiment Station at Cornell University, also visited Burbank and acknowledged Burbank's remarkable plant-breeding achievements.[41] By 1904, Burbank's scientific contributions earned him a prestigious Carnegie grant of $10,000 and an honorary lectureship. Botanical communities of botanists, gardeners, and plant bodies were shaped by developing sexual sciences for breeding better and allegedly loved bodies; thus, bringing plants into sex reform networks.

Although botanists and gardeners focused on the significance of reproductive choices among plants, they seldom, if ever, acknowledged a plant's affective potential to love. For most scientific plant breeders, plant sex was devoid of love yet instructive for observing how disciplining sex could yield better offspring. Burbank, however, was an anomaly in the early twentieth-century botanical community in his insistence on the affective component of his breeding techniques. While Burbank did not go so far as to consider plants to be capable of love, he explained how the birth of his exquisite novel plant creations embodied his loving techniques of plant breeding. Collaborating with Burbank on his biography, Harwood addressed multiple dimensions of Burbank's early affective experience with plants such as his grief over the death of a "pet plant."[42] According to Harwood, Burbank's initial creation of the Burbank potato involved watching "this seed-ball with unusual care."[43] In 1871, Burbank began his ventures in agriculture, which resulted in his first famous creation of the Russet Burbank potato. Remarking on

FIGURE 3. Luther Burbank's experiments with breeding multiple varieties of cherries on one tree. Burbank (1849–1926) took this photo in 1922. Courtesy of the Library of Congress. Image is in the public domain.

the health of the snowball in his yard, Burbank claimed it "responded to my care."[44] By the end of the 1890s, Burbank attracted the attention of botanists as a "wonder worker" and "wizard" for his ability to create new plants such as the Burbank rose, the Wickson plum, and the Iceberg white blackberry, which were followed by the Burbank cherry in 1903 and the Santa Rosa plum in 1906.[45] At this juncture, botanists' curiosity in Burbank's plant-breeding successes earned him a space in the scientific community to articulate how disciplined sex led to better and loved plant bodies.

What Burbank shared with his botanist colleagues was close attention to how subjecting sex to precise scientific mating techniques could populate a world with planned, desired, healthier, and allegedly superior organisms across both plant and human bodies. In 1907, two years after the publication of Harwood's Burbank biography, Burbank drew explicit connections between plants and children in his work on *The Training of the Human Plant*. At the beginning of the chapter on "The Mingling of Races," Burbank expressed his fascination with plant-breeding in relation to "the similarity between the organization and development of plant and human life."[46] Through the practice of gardening and breeding, Burbank intensified plant and human intimacies whereby both plants and humans should be raised in "the only place that is truly fit to bring up a boy or a plant—the country, the small town or the country, the nearer to nature the better."[47] As a British botanist and future international birth control leader, Marie Stopes considered sex as a mechanism of reproduction that shaped evolution across human and plant kingdoms. As Stopes highlighted the significance of reproduction, she emphasized the importance of the sex lives of gendered plant bodies for determining the evolutionary rank of a species. In 1910, Stopes explained in *Ancient Plants* that "in judging the place of any plant in the scale of evolution it is to the reproductive organs that we look for the principal criteria, for the reproductive organs tend to be influenced less by their physical surroundings than the vegetative organs and are therefore truer guides to natural relationships."[48] Long before Stopes sought to harness women's reproductive power, plant reproductive bodies caught her attention as key determinants in the course of evolution. Plants were not only part of the early twentieth-century story of genetics, but they were also central to reconfiguring techniques of human sexual intimacy in birth control advocacy.

Stopes's publication on *The Human Body* in 1926, following her birth control publications *Radiant Motherhood* and *Wise Parenthood*, can be seen as a cumulative work, joining Stopes's expertise in plant sex with her more recent status as an authority on marital love. *The Human Body*, despite its title, undercut human exceptionality at the very site of origins, sex, and births. This work thus exemplified not only the extent to which human/plant intimacies intensified by 1926 but how evolutionary thought, ecology, biology, and sex reform became entangled in efforts to perfect bodies and environments. In *The Human Body*, Stopes specifically focused on gender, sexual, and cellular behaviors that joined human and nonhuman physiologies, stating, "Not only in man and woman, but in cow and bull, buck and doe rabbit, in fact in all the higher forms of life and in nearly all the insects and lower forms of life; indeed also in nearly all higher plants, and ultimately in most of the lowly and microscopic plants, there are two such differentiated sets of cells—the egg cells and the sperm cells."[49] Stopes noted these intimacies by positing an interspecies companionship at the level of eugenic hierarchies and gendered anatomies of egg and sperm interaction. Although Stopes admitted that human reproduction had a higher consciousness, she maintained that reproductive function was nonetheless "comparable with one that is found in all primitive animals and plants."[50] In other words, as Stopes investigated plant sex to determine how fitter plant specimens survived in an evolutionary struggle over time, she construed this as possible ways for also understanding human evolution governed by the same "natural laws."[51] To this extent, through the lens of Stopes's microscope, which observed traces of plant male and female cells, she brought together humans and nonhumans at the site of sex as a process. By joining these kingdoms at the site of sexual feeling, Stopes gestured toward the crucial place of plants in sex reformers' early twentieth-century framing of love as a scientifically perfected practice of sex. To judge and identify such techniques of reproduction for human love, plants and animals participated in the experiments to create human love.

Burbank's and Stopes's work with plants compelled plants to engage and embody the early twentieth-century racial politics of the eugenic breeding of fitter, healthier bodies that were cast as evolutionary superior races. Invoking love as part of his careful attention to the racial reproduction of plants, Burbank observed, "That such intimate differences of constitution should obtain between species that show many outward points of resemblance must always be a matter for surprise to the plant lover whose attention is called to it for the first time."[52] For Burbank, his skill in plant breeding was an act of love inseparable from reinforcing racial hierarchies. At the second International Conference on Plant Breeding and Hybridization in 1902, Burbank's paper "Some of the Fundamental Principles of Plant Breeding" was read to an audience of leading scientists, extolling the virtues of plant breeding to secure bloodlines of strong heredity. In his paper, Burbank divulged how his loving orientation toward plant breeding was inextricably tied to eugenic concerns of building heredity and raising human goals to "nobler" concerns of channeling sex toward superior bodies, indicating that "these silent influences [of heredity] are unconsciously felt ever by those who do not appreciate them consciously and thus with better and still better fruits, nuts, grains, and flowers will the earth be transformed, man's thoughts turned from the base, destructive forces into the nobler productive ones which will lift him to higher planes of action."[53]

Burbank also considered his work with plant births as transferable to human ones, particularly in terms of redefining love as the scientific disciplining of sex as eugenic mating. This linkage between eugenics for plants and people is perhaps unsurprising given Burbank's friendship with David Starr Jordan, a widely renowned and respected eugenicist, zoologist, and Stanford University professor. Burbank, in fact, categorized diseased human, plant, and animal bodies as undesirable, reproductive failures, insisting that "above all else, the child must be a healthy animal. I do not work with diseased plants."[54] Burbank's garden intermingled plants and people in the values attributed to life. He situated the American character within a racialized geography of a world characterized by "the North, powerful, virile, aggressive, blended with the luxurious ease-loving, more impetuous South."[55] Burbank's valuation of the North identified an Anglo-Saxon kinship of nations that materialized their historical ties as the search for racial origins informed biology and botany.

Stopes similarly invested plant sex with similar racial stakes for sex among humans and animals. She insisted that "naturally, when a race (as all races do) depends for its very existence on the chain of individuals leading from generation to generation, the most important items in the plant structures must be those mechanisms concerned with reproduction."[56] By 1912, botanists were well aware of the new more precise Mendelian method of mate selection. Stopes emphasized the importance of control over unruly plant sex, noting how "in the course of Mendelian work, one experimenter has two races of Stocks, one with white flowers and one with cream flowers. These were crossed in the usual way, and all outside pollen carefully kept from them."[57] For Stopes and other plant-breeders, Mendelism held the promise in directing evolutionary futures by controlling reproductive sex. Stopes and Burbank's control over plant-world narratives, involved plant bodies as differentiated, categorized, and marked by racialized identities of fitter or unfit "stocks." As such, insofar as Stopes and Burbank's plants were subjected to controlled scientific breeding techniques, their bodies enacted and corporealized the racialized concepts of superior and inferior stocks.

With Stopes's emphasis on reproduction as the most important evolutionary force, plants and humans engaged in both gender as well as racial politics that cut across species. More specifically, Stopes's human and nonhuman gender politics were profoundly racialized. In spite of the range of plant sexualities and identities, including hermaphroditism, multispecies insect pollination, and self-fertilization, Stopes privileged what most closely emulated normative human heterosexual reproduction.[58] In doing so, Stopes's work on plants was situated in a wider context of entrenching heterosexuality as a progressive evolutionary force that consequently treated nonnormative sexualities as degenerative, de-evolutionary, atavistic, and barbaric.[59] Within the plant-breeding world, Stopes's emphasis on heterosexuality as the sexual practice associated with the highest racially superior forms of life also dovetailed with early twentieth-century concerns over the white birthrate. As Stopes noted the kinship of plants and humans at the site of the centrality of sex in evolution, she also highlighted how plants, like humans, could be differentiated in terms of evolutionary superiority or inferiority. For Stopes and other botanists who devoted new attention to plant sexuality, reproduction was powerful insofar as it could be tailored toward racial purity and advancement in plant and human worlds.

Burbank's work in his garden and Stopes's work in plant laboratories exemplify how the nonhuman became engaged in what science studies scholar Patricia Clough has called the "worldwide meshing of bio-politics with an affective economy."[60] Clough explains this contemporary global political condition as "a marking of populations—some as valuable life and others as without value."[61] This kinship took an institutional form in the proliferation of agricultural experiment stations in the United States and the British Empire. In the aftermath of the 1862 Morrill Act, which established land grant colleges for specializations in agricultural science, and the 1887 Hatch Act, providing government funding for experiment stations, the United States acquired the reputation for producing cutting-edge plant-breeding research and resources.[62] Moreover, American botanists and their British counterparts developed close relationships through mutual work on sugar cane experiments at British colonial sites such as the Barbados, British Guiana, Jamaica, and Trinidad.[63] In this period of budding plant sex research, plant reproductive bodies became a site for rearticulating historical ties between white nations. Through probing the plant sexual body, American and British scientists retraced and rematerialized white lineage through alliances with German botanists who were considered forerunners in late nineteenth-century plant physiology.[64] At this time, Burbank's garden and Stopes's botanical laboratories provided microcosms of what plants might be able to teach humans about promises of love as eugenic reproduction.

Although Burbank and Stopes worked with plants on opposite ends of the Atlantic, they shared a profound faith in the scientific management of sex to produce better plant bodies and thus exemplify how transnational sex reform touched the plant world. Indeed, Burbank's and Stopes's experiments with plants highlight the emergence of a nonhuman sexology in botanical science as they engaged in a community of botanists inquiring into the sex lives of plants.[65] Through botanical experiments in plant breeding, plants materially embodied and performed the ideals of love espoused by their experimenters in the form of the reproduction of a superior plant body. Yet, experimenters like

Stopes and Burbank maintained a crucial distinction between human and plant worlds insofar as plants were deemed the objects but not subjects of love. Stopes's and Burbank's works highlight the limitations of plant bodies in capacities for love in spite of the fact that the importance of sex united human and plant evolutionary tracts. Ironically, it was not sex but love that marked the gulf between human and nonhuman worlds even though plant bodies served as models for the sex techniques employed for engineering human love.

CULTIVATING SEXUAL INSTINCTS: SEX REFORM'S ENVIRONMENTAL POLITICS OF LOVE, 1910–1930

Although sex reformers did not credit plants with the power to love, plants nonetheless participated in early twentieth-century sex reformers' reconfigurations of sex as love. As noted in the previous section, plants were subject to the same new sexual techniques of reproduction that, when similarly applied to human bodies, were deemed love. However, plants also participated in sex reformers' new practices of sex as environmental actors that could make love happen. Plants engaged in furthering the new evolutionary potential of human love, which, ironically, became the crucial ontological distinction between the perfection of plant sex and the perfection of human sex. As such, environmental sciences and environmental movements formed in close collaboration with sexology.[66]

Sex reformers' environmental politics of love drew on nonhumans as sources of sexual energies while describing encounters with nonhumans as loving relations of sympathy, connection, and intimacy. These loving relations, however, were inseparable from racial, sexual, economic, and affective differences that defined a human or nonhuman body's evolutionary rank. In this section, I use the word *cultivate* to emphasize how sex reformers redefined the practice of love in terms of actively and materially mixing with environmental actors and extracting energies from them. The word *cultivation* can be defined as the practice of working with another material, actor, or oneself with a sense that it has potential to improve. *Cultivation*, however, not only suggests this material excavation of affective potential in earthly and atmospheric actors but includes its social definition of perfectibility, refinement, and cultured experience. What philosopher of science Isabelle Stengers refers to as "achievement" applies here to the work of love in the human/nonhuman relations that shape and, indeed, cultivate its production.[67] Stengers's view of *achievement* is an important conceptual tool for situating the human as one partner among other nonhuman ones in a democratic space of mutual work.

My use of *cultivation* straddles the agricultural, social, and historically specific way these two meanings converged in early twentieth century sex reformers' advocacy of cultivating love as the practice of higher forms of sexual reproduction. Historically, the word *cultivate* also has particular significance in early twentieth-century developments of tissue culture when scientists began to stress the environment, milieu, or medium of the cell.[68] In other words, ecology and biology merged in early twentieth-century investigations of the cell rooted in a particular climate for cultivating life. As a science, cytology began to develop in the late nineteenth century, overlapping with growing interest across scientists and sex reformers in intimacies between plants and humans, with cells becoming common units defying seemingly ontological boundaries. Moreover, sex reformers' practices of love were related to their fetishization of manual labor, farm work, ranching, outdoor strenuous sports, and rural life, which allegedly reconnected the body to a primal state of sexual vigor while channeling such vigor into civilized love. As such, *cultivation* also appropriately captures the dual efforts of sex reformers to cultivate a latent Darwinian sexual past while cultivating the earth.

In their development of practices designed to cultivate the lost sexual energies of a Darwinian past, sex reformers retroactively read the evolutionary story from present to past by identifying bodies at the top of modern social, political, and economic hierarchies as those most civilized and, therefore, most in need of reconnection to early primal ancestors. As such, sex reformers privileged the cultivation of sexual energies as the mission of a middle- to upper-class white body, which allegedly carried the greatest burden of upholding the evolutionary progress made thus far in late nineteenth- and early twentieth-century societies. Darwin's story of evolution informed bodily enactments of racial and class status in terms of a specific affective character as white, middle- and upper-class bodies self-identified with bearing the affective costs of nervousness, fatigue, and sexual exhaustion, which required cultivating former animal instincts. More importantly, sex reformers simultaneously sought to secure the evolutionary gains of the white middle and upper classes by insisting that cultivating sexual energies would not risk reducing these bodies to lower-class or non-white human others but, instead, would elevate them to the higher spiritual experience of love. By situating love as an experience arising out of a rational, scientifically disciplined practice of sex, sex reformers implicitly identified bodies capable of love as those possessing specific privileges and concerns of race and class, such as an education, a profession, financial burdens, and an exposure to middle- and upper-class conservative sexual morality. As such, sex reformers shaped a newly emerging form of white cultural capital in terms of access to love and the scientific practice of sex.

To cultivate sexual energies, sex reformers advocated an active intimate engagement with "natural" nonhuman environmental actors in the hopes of reviving a lost ancestral body that marked the evolutionary baggage of carrying the weight of moving humanity to its next stage of evolution. Whether cultivating gardens, retreating to farms, or bonding with a distant Mother Earth, sex reformers sought the help of nonhumans to revitalize their bodies with the necessary energies to produce love. Critical of the pace of modernity, Hutchins Hapgood not only urged husbands to cultivate the art of love but joined such cultivation to deeper relations with organic nonhumans. In his article, "Cultivate Your Garden," Hapgood advocated the radical transformation of everyday practices "to cultivate our gardens, so to speak, to live creative lives, in an intimate though modest way."[69] Instructing his readers on how to cultivate their gardens, he advised, "Do fine work, live well with your husbands, wives, children, friends, resist public opinion when it is wrong or fanatical, resist change when it lacks the deeper culture, extend our capacity to love."[70] As a Harvard-educated aspiring professional writer, Hapgood dug in his garden to awaken within his body the evolutionary memory of lost connections to allegedly more primal beings who regularly lived by manual labor or ruggedly pioneered early frontier settlements or early on depended on relations to the land to survive.

Although writing about sex and love on the other side of the Atlantic, Marie Stopes's popular sex manual grounded the body's cultivation of love in gardens and woods through intimacies with plants. Like other sex reformers in Britain and the United States, Stopes drew on a tradition of British Romanticism, exalting the rural idyll, the picturesque, the sublime, and reinvention of the Edenic garden as the setting for cultivating love.[71] In *Married Love*, a renowned sex manual, Stopes situated love within a setting worthy of the praises of British Romantic poets, William Wordsworth and Percy Bysshe Shelley. For Stopes, woods and gardens played crucial roles in making sexual love possible, where "the pulling of rosemary or lavender may be the sweet excuse for the slow and profound mutual rousing of passion."[72] Stopes along with other sex reformers reinvented Romanticism's literary reverence for nature in light of the specific concerns of modernity's effects on the health of the human body.[73] Directing *Married Love* toward people in "civilized countries," Stopes suggested these particular bodies needed sex advice to cope with their heightened sensitivity to urban life. Stopes closely immersed those bodies within the different rhythms of city and country life with gendered consequences for intimacy. According to Stopes, the metropolis hindered intimacy, whereby "the overstimulation of city life tends to 'speed up' the man's reactions, but to retard hers." Stopes explained the very differently gendered Victorian sexual roles of men's need for self-control and women's frigidity: "The effects of fatigue, city-life, bad feeding and indeed of most outward circumstances may be very marked, and may for years, or all her life, so reduce her vitality that a woman may never have experienced any spontaneous sex-impulse at all." Just as city life shaped the context of devitalized and sexually unsatisfying marriages, Stopes prescribed the country as the place for rejuvenation and the cultivation of marital love.[74] More than simply drawing analogies between plants and humans, Stopes highlighted the sexual merging of plant and human rhythms with plants acting as crucial resources for uplifting and intensifying sexual experience.

Whether focusing specifically on mountains, parks, trees, or plants, sex reformers broadly cultivated relationships with nonhuman natures and, in fact, developed an environmental ethic as integral to the sex reform movement. Moving within the same Greenwich Village circles as Hapgood, Emma Goldman's periodical *Mother Earth* appealed to the educated elite's experience of a body suffering from a lost connection to its origins. In fact, *Mother Earth* became a rallying point for Greenwich Village sex reformers, with many of them, including Hapgood and Dodge, gathering at the *Mother Earth* headquarters.[75] In the March 1906 issue of *Mother Earth*, Emma Goldman and Max Baginski expressed the alienating effects of dominant Christian morality and capitalism in a narrative about Mother Earth. The story began with man's birth from "the womb of Mother Earth," which, over time, he came to reject as "there arose the dreary doctrine that he was not related to the Earth, that she was but a temporary resting place for his scornful feet and that she held nothing for him but temptation to degrade himself."[76] Soon, he came to believe that only through ignorance and asceticism would he be able to reach Heaven, "the very antithesis of Earth which was the source of sin."[77] Based on these beliefs in Mother Earth's inherent sinfulness, her calls to her children were resisted by man, who equated them with the beckoning of a seductress.[78] Baginski and Goldman claimed that this belief in Mother Earth's sinfulness

FIGURE 4. Portrait of Emma Goldman created circa 1911. Photographer T. Kajiwara. Courtesy of the Library of Congress Prints and Photographs Division, Washington, D.C.

encouraged man's devastation of her.[79] At this stage of the narrative, Goldman and Baginski linked ignorance with religious condemnations of sex and the body in contrast with knowledge and sensory material connections with the world. Through this narrative of Mother Earth, Goldman highlighted the contemporary suffering of the body inhibited from fully expressing its sexual desires because of an unnatural morality imposed on "civilization." Goldman and Hapgood were prominent voices of the sex reform movement, advocating a new environmental ethic of love in the hopes of transforming social and political relations affecting both humans and nonhumans.

Sex reformers practiced and promoted the active seeking of intimacies with nonhumans by placing their bodies in closer proximities, which extended to retreats to farms, frontiers, mountains, and forests. As seen earlier with Havelock and Edith Ellis's retreat to the farm, Mabel Dodge who operated within sex reform circles of New York City ventured to Finney Farm to transform, heal, and regenerate her own body in light of new sexological truths. When Dodge moved to Finney Farm shortly after the First World War, she drew on contemporary medical, sexological, and psychoanalytic wisdom that suggested fresh air, outdoor exercise, sunshine, and rolling hills would cure nervousness, a condition associated with the repression of female sexual instincts.[80] At the time of her move to the countryside, Mabel was being treated by psychoanalyst Smith Ely Jelliffe to cope with feelings of jealousy and frustrated sexual expression. Jelliffe, who had gained a reputation as one of Greenwich Village's prominent psychoanalysts, also self-identified with the plight of his patients in succumbing to the enervating effects of the city and, like Hapgood, sought to restore manly vigor by reconnecting with primal origins through manual and farm labor. In August of 1920, Jelliffe proudly wrote to Dodge, "So, I shine like a cook, a farmer, as plumber, carpenter + swimmer,"[81] thereby highlighting efforts at new nonhuman intimacies with nature, embodied in roles of farmer and swimmer, as well as tools in his roles as carpenter and plumber. As an expert in psychoanalysis, Smith Ely Jelliffe's efforts to initiate deeper engagements with nonhumans demonstrates the centrality of nonhumans to scientific transformations in diagnosing female as well as male sexuality as both a medical and social concern.

Far from an eccentric practice, Dodge's ventures to immerse herself in closer relations with nonhuman nature appealed to a transatlantic network of intellectuals, professionals, and activists who gathered at her artist colony in Taos, New Mexico. Dodge was visited by prominent intellectuals such as her Greenwich Village friend, Neith Boyce, British novelist D. H. Lawrence, and British novelist and renowned sex reformer, Naomi Mitchison. More than simply a metaphor for stimulating sexual desires, Boyce and Dodge immersed their bodies in the frontier atmosphere and terrain. Upon visiting Dodge in Taos, Boyce expressed her disappointment that "this place is too stimulating nervously but not tonic as I'd hoped."[82] She drew a distinction between the countryside of Massachusetts and the frontier, indicating that it has "an exotic quality—the Mexicans are mostly very poor + diseased—the Indians seem better off, though even poorer."[83] Boyce, however, also drew attention to encounters with nonhumans such as horses, mountains, and rugged terrain that invigorated her children. Writing to Hapgood, Boyce reported the energizing effects of the frontier on her son, Charles, who rode up a mountain, and her daughter, Miriam, who rode seventeen miles uphill to a ranch.[84] More than simply an emerging social practice of reliving historical encounters with frontier nonhumans, sex reformers justified trips to the frontier in terms of the evolutionary science of the body, which blurred lines between the social sciences such as sociology and anthropology and the natural science of biology.[85] British sex reformer, Naomi Mitchison, described the possibilities for the bohemian colony of Taos as an ideal site for anthropologists. Writing to Mabel Dodge in 1935, Mitchison responded to Dodge's complaints of the challenges of building a vibrant intellectual community in Taos. Mitchison suggested that "a colony of serious working anthropologists could bring you more of the kind of people you *really* need than anything else."[86] Mitchison's references to a colony and anthropologists as experts in human evolutionary history are critical to understanding how sex reformers' situated their bodies and frontier intimacies with nonhumans in scientific frameworks of evolution.

Sex reformers situated their encounters with nonhumans in the context of the specific gendered response of a white, middle-class body defined by its position within the drama of evolutionary history. Although both male and female sex reformers identified with nervousness and the dissipation of sexual energies, male sex reformers engaged with nonhumans in the hopes of restoring a rugged manliness of primal origins that had, to some extent, been preserved in the bodies of lower-class men who continued to work in trades of manual physical labor in working-class cultures that did not strictly emphasize sexual self-control. In a letter to Mabel Dodge, Neith Boyce divulged how "he [Hapgood] has become a perfect countryman, + that the other day walking down Main Street in Winchester, in boots and flannel shirt, he was taken for a wood-chopper! He loves this place, works hard + seems perfectly well here."[87] Boots, flannel shirt, and chopping wood served as props for reorienting Hapgood's "modern" nerves toward an idealized frontier manhood of primal affective intimacy with land. While male sex reformers dug for the lost origins of manly vigor, female sex reformers emphasized redeeming Mother Earth from patriarchal Christian characterizations of her as sinful, inert, and irrelevant matter intended, like animals, to be dominated by men. In contrast to male sex reformers, female sex reformers engaged with nonhumans in the hopes of reconnecting their bodies with "natural" sexual forces and undoing the bodily effects of Victorian sexual morality's emphasis on inhibiting sexual impulses.

By ecologically situating themselves in closer proximities to plants, sex reformers positioned their bodies in ways that opened them to ontological and sexual transformations. Casting themselves as exemplars for other white, middle- and upper-class couples, sex reformers engaged their bodies in an eco/ontological relationship with plants. In one of the most widely known and disseminated sex manuals of the period, Marie Stopes situated the body within the ebb and flow of its connections to earthly nonhuman others. At the outset of *Married Love*, Stopes positioned the achievement of marital love in the context of the co-participation of minds, senses, sap, rocks, trees, and whirlpools, circulating in love's ecology. Quoting from nineteenth-century British novelist, George Meredith's *Diana of the Crossways*, Stopes situates the human body's intimate entanglement with plants as "a finer shoot of the tree stoutly planted in good gross earth; the senses running their live sap, and the minds companioned, and the spirits made one by the whole-natured conjunction." Meredith goes on to describe "the speeding of us, compact of what we are, between the ascetic rocks and the sensual whirlpools, to the creation of certain nobler races." By foregrounding Meredith's quote, Stopes undermines any ontological separation between the flow of human sexuality and the rhythms of nonhumans. This environmental context of sexual love also implicates both plants and humans in the racial politics of reproduction where "nobler races" are inextricably linked with healthy and finer shoots rather than diseased ones.[88] Stopes, in fact, specifically intended her instructions on love for "people in English speaking countries" who were "civilized," "normal," and "who are married or about to be married."[89] Stopes associated these bodies who had the potential to achieve love with particular kinds of landscapes; namely, pastoral vistas that sex reformers on both sides of the Atlantic felt invigorated sexual intimacies.

Stopes situated sexual experience within the broader context of going-back-to-nature movements among early twentieth-century intellectuals, which required formulating new positive mutually nurturing relations with nonhumans.[90] As Stopes dwelled on the sexual technique of the married couple, their sexual physiologies were dispersed into the atmosphere as nonhuman others entered into this intimate ecology. For the young couple, Stopes emphasized that sexual love depended on coordinating bodily feeling with environmental rhythms. Stopes drew attention to sex as a practice that extended and opened human bodies to transformation through contact with others, demonstrating how "nature has so created us that we are incomplete in ourselves."[91] Although Stopes focused on the need for another human being, this incompleteness extended to nonhumans; thus, intimately interweaving the nonhuman into the very ontology of the human.

Stopes privileged heterosexuality as the practice of love by emphasizing the gendered specificity of the interplay of manly and womanly bodies with environments.[92] The young husband, for example, required knowledge of how his wife's body worked in tandem with the "moon-month rhythm in woman." Instructing the couple on how to ecologically situate their intimacies, Stopes advised the husband to work in tandem with woman's "rhythmic sex-tide which if its seasons were obeyed would ensure not only her enjoyment, but would explode the myth of her capriciousness."[93] Addressing the husband, Stopes stressed a measured, controlled moderation of "vital energy." According to Stopes, it would be "the greatest mistake to imagine that the semen is something to be got rid of frequently—all the vital energy and the precious chemical substances which go into its composition can be better utilized by being transformed into other creative work on most days of the month."[94] Drawing on a transatlantic and culturally familiar narrative of neurasthenic professional husbands, Stopes extended the problem of the exorbitant spending and fast-pace of city life to the fast-paced over-expenditure of semen. Stopes's sex advice in *Married Love* not only suggested the ecological momentums of human sex in achieving love but, building on her work as an expert in plant sex, hinted that human sexual rhythms were intimately aligned with plant rhythms.

Sex reformers' own sexual relationships also provide specific examples of how their encounters with nature extended beyond a mere proximity to plants to a much more intimate bodily engagement with nonhumans. Goldman's relationship with her tour manager, Ben Reitman, exemplifies how nonhumans participated in her own body's erotic experience. Around 1909, Hapgood recounted his impression of Goldman to Boyce, remarking that "he [Reitman] is the 'call of the wild' for her. Has shocked and violated her civilization, her heart and her soul."[95] Goldman and Reitman's appeals to nature to galvanize their mutual sexual excitement, at times, elided the most intimate parts of their bodies with nonhumans. In many love letters, Goldman and Reitman invoked nature to elicit sexual thrills through references to Goldman's "mountains of joy" or to Reitman's "primitive untrammeled nature."[96] Goldman exemplifies an ethic among female sex reformers that highlighted the crucial roles of nonhumans in the early twentieth-century transformations of female sexuality, marked by newly conceived sexological truths of the capacity of female bodies for sexual pleasure. As they strived to remake white female sexuality, female sex reformers turned to closer encounters with nonhumans.

Insofar as sex reformers experienced erotic feelings in the context of reliving evolutionary dramas, they brought nonhuman actors into the racial politics of the present, which situated lower-class and nonwhite others as primal others stuck at a lower stage of evolution. In these evolutionary dramas, sex reformers' intimacies with plants extended to primal and highly sexualized bodies deemed to be closer to nature. In Taos, for example, female sex reformers drew on the frontier mythology of Native Americans as barbaric and primal others already in tune with nonhuman elements of the soil, weather, and vegetation of a rugged frontier.[97] Like Goldman, Mabel Dodge and Neith Boyce situated intimacies in a primal narrative of shaking a civilization underpinned by Victorian ideals of female chastity. In writing to Dodge, Boyce divulged her bodily reconnection with a primal other, noting how she "cried most of one night because I regretted the old fierceness and wildness—which something perverse in me wanted—perhaps the red Indian!"[98] Many years after Dodge first engaged in psychoanalytic therapy with Jelliffe, she wrote in her diary of how she had "lived *through* the experience of identification with the Indians and the valley that has been Indianized by the Taos Pueblo." By forging these connections with the nonhuman environment of Taos, Dodge experienced a critical transformation in her body's experience of sex and transcendence beyond "the elementary sex life." In this same diary entry, Dodge juxtaposed her discussion of identifying with the Indian and the valley with her connections to her Pueblo lover, Tony. She explained that "*My* only root is in him and in my relationship with him, a relationship that has by now transcended the elementary sex life, the outlets of talk or activities in common that we had in the first years together." Indeed, Dodge situated and firmly grounded Tony with the frontier, explaining that "I have no real roots like Tony has, so I am very disconnected." Dodge contrasted her distance from primal others in noting her very rootlessness within the frontier and further magnifying this contrast in her role as "a pioneer" not only engaging with primal nonhuman nature but, at the same time, having "made a success of miscegenation" through her marriage to Tony.[99] Dodge's analogy between evolutionary progress and a growing distance from roots evokes the intimate entanglement of trees, plants, human bodies, and racial politics insofar as indigenous bodies were deemed closer to nonhumans and their rootedness in the land. Boyce and Dodge exemplify how sex reformers embodied racialized dramas of evolution in the very context of escalated sexual feelings as they struggled to achieve love. While drawing on nonhuman nature and allegedly primal others, sex reformers relied on them as bodily resources for sexual energies, never attributing the capacity for love to these bodies lower on the evolutionary continuum.

For sex reformers, evolutionary narratives of love blurred the boundaries between social and natural science as prevailing justifications for intimate racial logics. Dodge, for example, grounded her racial logic of frontier intimacies in terms of psychology and anthropology as well as natural sciences such as physics, biology, and chemistry. In 1938, Dodge wrote "On Human Relations" but situated the human within a racial as well as scientific history of race that could become consciously experienced through psychoanalysis. Dodge firmly connected psychoanalysis to other sciences and did not differentiate between its legitimacy in relation to other sciences. In reflecting on Freud's concept of libido or the force of sexual energy, Dodge posed the rhetorical questions of "What relation has it to electricity and to the atomic structure? Are these but different measures of one element back to which the scientists attempt to trace all life?"[100] It is important to note that Dodge wrote "On Human Relations" at the time of her life with Tony in Taos. Perhaps considering her own personal experiences of the struggles with sexual intimacies, Dodge referred to fears of liberating a "hidden fire" that would unleash a flood of the "buried racial and chemical life."[101] Positioning these intimate struggles within a long evolutionary narrative, Dodge pointed to the emergence of human psychic life out of a relation to wild animals. She associated the fears of allowing sexual impulses to surface with "the instinct of the wild animals who resist domestication."[102] While attributing a kinship to animals in the case of libido, Dodge contended that sexual energies transformed into love for humans at the pinnacle of a civilized society. In considering how sexual energies were driving forces for civilization, Dodge claimed: "Even in cases where ambition and desire for power and influence, or the pursuit of scientific study or great art are mastering a man, these are either the substitutes for love, denied its natural satisfactions, or the incentive of love to great enterprises."[103] As such, Dodge's search for love on the frontier was inseparable from her understanding of sexual and evolutionary truths of the human body. While Nancy Stepans and Sander Gilman have shown how late nineteenth-century biology developed within a framework of racial logic, sex reformers' frontier intimacies highlight the racialization of sexual science.[104] By extension, sex reformers' reformulation of love as a scientific practice of sex indicates the racialization of love itself.

Through sex reformers' mission to cultivate sexual energies through nonhuman intimacies with the aim of producing love, plants and other vegetative bodies became intimately entangled in the early twentieth-century racial politics of reproduction. Stopes published and disseminated her works internationally to extoll the importance of disciplining human as well as plant sex. By the 1920s, Stopes had attained the reputation of an international birth control expert who made the transition from an authority on plant sex to one on human sex. Stopes, however, did not forsake the plants in her turn to human sex advice to aid in the process of achieving love. In Stopes's subsequent books such as *Wise Parenthood* and *Radiant Motherhood*, she invoked the language of fructification, seeds, trees, germs, and fertilization, which forged a common ground between plant and human reproduction. Inviting her readers to place their practice of sex in the longer duration of evolutionary time, Stopes drew attention to intimacies with plants as "our bodies bear the impress of many past material phases of our evolution; and because in the past myriads of young were needed by any race that should evolve, we still produce a far larger number of germs awaiting fertilisation than can ever be fructified and imbued with individual life."[105] In doing so, Stopes situated the development of different races in both plant and human worlds within the trajectories of evolutionary progress, thereby bringing racial politics to bear on the plant as much as the human world of sex. Similarly, in *Radiant Motherhood*, Stopes emphasized the importance of birth control for preventing unfit births by drawing on a comparison with a tree. Using the example of how a "fine tree" can be debased by a parasite, Stopes warned young potential parents that they could suffer the same fate as the tree through the "debasing power of the inferior, the depraved, and feeble-minded," who were "appallingly prolific."[106] Significantly, Stopes here noted how unhealthy, lower, less desirable bodies were equated with prolific, promiscuous, undisciplined sex. These references to fructification and trees were "more than metaphor," a phrase Donna Haraway has used to emphasize that metaphors are deeply entangled in scientific knowledge production.[107] Stopes's slips into botanical terminology within marital advice tracts were not accidental or poetical flourishes but marked a subtle trace of a scientific view of the connectedness of human and plant bodies. Plants entered into these intimate narratives of human sexual love at a time when literal connections were being drawn between plant and human sexual processes.

As sex reformers turned attention to engineering human love through improved sex techniques, they drew upon evolutionary narratives that rendered plants and other natural nonhumans as crucial actors in human love stories. At the same time, sex reformers intervened in nonhuman sex lives through controlled breeding experiments. As exemplified by Luther Burbank and Marie Stopes's work with plants, these experiments were shaped by efforts to make reproductive practices conform to ideals of eugenic sex as love. What may seem to be an enigmatic overlap of sex reformers' interest in human sex and their engagement with environmental movements can be explained by their consideration of nonhuman actors in human love stories. In seeking to grasp the environmental conditions required to create love, sex reformers turned to nonhuman actors as well as the arts for shaping love as a scientific practice of sex. For sex reformers, the mission to engineer love entailed drawing upon a diverse range of ontological as well as discursive resources, thus confounding and exposing the artificiality of boundaries between humans and nonhumans as well as arts and sciences. This particular chapter of early twentieth-century sex reform transformations in love draws attention to human love's debts to plants and other natural nonhumans.

3

Planetary Intimacies

Physics, Occultism, and Nonhumans in Love

Darwinism radically opened the human family to a vast array of nonhuman kin that encompassed animals, plants, rocks, mountains, and earthly atmospheric forces. Yet, this challenge to the ontological sacredness of the human spilled beyond anthropology and biology into the domains of physics and spirituality. The human could therefore no longer be put on a pedestal far above animals or, for that matter, rocks, plants, dirt, and cosmic forces. Sex reformers reconfigured religion as a Darwinian cosmology of planetary intimacies among all humans and nonhumans. Situating love on a cosmic scale, sex reformers redefined the body's evolutionary status far beyond national earthly boundaries. To sex reformers, the practice of sex as love involved coming to terms with relations with allegedly lower-evolved forms of life as well as inorganic cosmic forces. While these forces were not the agents or recipients of love, they were instrumental to its production. Sex reformers focused attention on the evolutionary superior human body's potential for grasping the nature of God and the universe through the practice of sex as love.

Sex reformers' turn to love at the intersection of sexual science and spirituality resonates with the recent turn in feminist science studies toward human/nonhuman affective encounters.[1] While academic turns to the nonhuman primarily address the agency of lower forms of life such as bacteria, rocks, minerals, and insects, the nonhuman also includes ultra, superhuman, or supernatural forces.[2] To sex reformers, achieving love involved cooperating and participating with nonhuman forces in the context of a Stengerian commons or a Latourian network.[3] Whether we choose to use the languages of mathematics and physics or the language of emotions to explain forces of connection is a choice framed by the gender politics of knowledge. As histories of feminist and queer activism have shown, the imperative to speak through reason rather than emotion is integrally linked to privileging the mind over the body, culture over nature, man over woman, and human over nonhuman. Feminist and queer challenges to this dichotomous view of the world primarily occur in the context of interrogating biology.[4] However, as Karen Barad argues, the devaluation of bodies, and matter more broadly, can be understood in the context of rethinking how physics might describe bodies as open-ended, malleable, and shaped through their encounters with the world.[5] Both Barad's work on physics and ecofeminists' work on goddess worship exemplify genealogical threads connecting and diverging from early twentieth-century sex reformers' entanglement of sex, physics, and occultism.[6] Sex reformers' formation of love as a sexual science as well as the spirituality of sex offers a productive avenue for reconsidering intersections of science and religion. Stefan Helmreich, for example, has considered how computer programmers perform their work as fathers and gods giving life to data.[7] Other science studies scholars, such as Luciana Parisi, have considered technologies of sex as a lens for reconceptualizing sex as a process involving mixtures of organic and inorganic matter such as strings of DNA codes and silicon chips.[8] Yet, for the most part, science studies scholars are silent on the subject of spirituality. Sex reformers, however, offer a unique lens for considering how the boundaries of science and religion could be renegotiated through a focus on the relationship between sex and love.

REORIENTING CHRISTIANITY: SITUATING SEX AND SCIENCE IN A "DIVINE ATMOSPHERE"

In the process of reforming sex, sex reformers challenged the divide between science and religion as they probed the limits between the human and the nonhuman. For sex reformers, sex offered a gateway between the spiritual and the material as a process that allowed the human to engage with life-making cosmic and divine forces. This spiritual dimension to sex formed a critical axis for sex reformers' claims that sex practiced in a scientific way could be elevated to the spiritual platform of love. By reconsidering the status of sex in the context of a religious practice, sex reformers redeemed sex from its position as an earthly, material, ungodly, and sinful temptation. By repositioning sex from the margins to the center of religion, sex reformers disturbed the spiritual distinctions that separated the human as a paragon of moral sexual self-control and the animal as the exemplar of the immoral and irrational pursuit of sexual desire. Thus, for sex reformers, the scientific management of sex to achieve love involved pioneering a new modern religion that exalted the cultivation of bodily sexual desires as virtues rather than sins. By redefining the relationship between sex, science, and religion, sex reformers challenged a critical bastion of human exceptionalism, namely access to the divine.

While science studies scholars have reconceptualized sex as a process of connection across different entities from bacteria to plants to animals to humans, the history of sex reform alerts us to a moment when such a definition of sex emerged as a new form of spirituality. Sex reformers confronted a moral struggle to reconcile sex with religion as they defended the scientific practice of sex as love as a new morality.[9] Prior to becoming towering figures in the sex reform movement, Havelock Ellis and Edward Carpenter struggled to reconcile their traditional Anglican religious beliefs with overpowering sexual impulses.[10] In the 1870s, Ellis began to reflect on the unsettling effects of his experience of disturbing bodily feelings of sexual desire in conflict with moral guilt. Ellis experienced this spiritual crisis around 1878 when he first read George Drysdale's *Elements of Social Science* and Friedrich Strauss's *Old Faith and New*. Reading these works, Ellis experienced traumatic bodily feelings of "moods of deep melancholy [which] passed over me and were blended with thoughts of sexual origin when I read in the Elements of Social Science of the dangerous devitalizing effects of nocturnal seminal emissions and feared I might be impotent."[11] Like Ellis, Edward Carpenter wrestled with the Anglican Church's taboos surrounding sex prior to his rise as a transnational prophet of sex reform. As a mathematician and a curate of the Church of England, Edward Carpenter exemplified the convergence of science and religion in this period through which his vision of sex reform emerged. In the 1870s, Edward Carpenter's struggle with the institutionalized sexual morality of the Church resulted in the abandonment of his position as a curate.[12] By the early 1880s, Carpenter had turned to Eastern mysticism, believing that it was instructive for the worship of sex but disappointing in its failure to address the idea of love.[13] Ellis and Carpenter's early experience of the tensions between dominant Christian teachings and their bodily experience of sexual feelings exemplify a prevailing problem of how Christian moral prohibitions of sex were deeply imprinted on the body, inhibiting the indulgence or cultivation of any pleasure in sex. Ellis and Carpenter identified a problem widely shared among white middle-class men who, in the late nineteenth century, endeavored to merge the chasm between institutionalized Christianity and the cultivation of healthy, vigorous, manly bodies. On both sides of the Atlantic, rising professional men turned to muscular Christianity, which entailed reorienting Christianity toward the cultivation of manliness that forged ties between British and American intellectuals.[14]

Ellis and Carpenter's stories of bodily trauma incurred by the moral indoctrination of the Anglican Church's sexual taboos and the experience of sexual desire resonated with sex reformers who were delivering similar messages in other white, Christian nations. In the United States, sex reformer Emma Goldman's 1914 publication, "Love and Marriage" divulged how women's bodies suffered under this tension between "natural" overpowering sexual impulses and indoctrinated Christian values entrenched by the Church and promoted by the state, noting that:

> If, however, woman is free and big enough to learn the mystery of sex without the sanction of State or Church, she will stand condemned as utterly unfit to be the wife of a "good" man, his goodness consisting of an empty head and plenty of money. Can there be anything more outrageous than the idea of a healthy full grown woman, full of life and passion, must deny nature's demand, must subdue her most intense craving, undermine her health and break her spirit, must stunt her vision, abstain from the depth and glory of sex experience until a "good" man comes along to take her unto himself as a wife?[15]

Goldman, however, highlighted this experience as specific to middle- and upper-class women seeking the financial support of a husband with "plenty of money." Goldman addressed a common narrative of middle- and upper-class women's experience of their bodies as deeply resistant to fulfilling sexual desires in conflict with dominant tenets of Christian morality. This was, in fact, an important starting point for sex reformers making their case for how sexual morality needed to be revamped. International birth control advocate, Margaret Sanger's 1914 article on "Marriage" in the *Woman Rebel*, identified this experience of a woman's suppression of sexual desire as a common problem. Sanger criticized the Church's involvement in establishing sexual morality based on marriage, indicating that "Marriage, which should be the personal agreement between a man and a woman, should be no concern of the

State or of the Church. Never have either of these institutions interested themselves in the happiness or health of the individual."[16] In other words, for Sanger and Goldman, a dominant sexual morality dictated in white nations that extolled Christian values was deeply felt and affectively imprinted on the body.

Instead of renouncing either sex or Christianity, sex reformers reoriented Christianity around the bodily experience of "natural" sexual feelings, which was also consistent with the teachings of sexual science and evolutionary history. By turning the body into the vehicle for religious experience, sex reformers also sought to reform Christianity to make it consistent with prevailing wisdom and knowledge of sexual science. In particular, sex reformers reformulated Christian love as the spiritual and sensuous fulfillment of the body through its engagement with the world. Ellis, for example, drew on a prominent nineteenth-century shift in the history of English Protestantism that emphasized a loving God rather than a punitive one.[17] This significant interpretive shift, however, had maintained moral taboos around sex as a necessary evil of procreation. Shortly after the onset of his spiritual crisis in the 1870s, Ellis probed conventional understandings of Christ's capacity for love, radically extending the boundaries of Christ's love to include the spiritual value of sex. On January 4, 1880, Ellis redefined Christianity as an embodied affective experience that repositioned his body rather than the rational adherence to a set of commandments. Ellis seized on his experience of love as the conduit for bodily connecting with Christianity, noting how "we should, above all, love Christ simply as Love."[18] In fact, Christ was not even reducible to a human form. Instead, Ellis positioned all bodies as affected and open to Christ, or Love, as a universal force, engulfing and permeating the world as "a divine atmosphere, suffering, and interpenetrating all things."[19] By drawing attention to Christ's love as a "divine atmosphere," Ellis shifted spirituality from a primarily internal experience to a deeply social experience of the body's relation to its environment. He situated the body in a divine milieu that connected human and earthly nonhumans through cosmic forces of love.

While Ellis reoriented a relationship to Christ to enable a body to experience sex as a spiritual connection to divine forces, other sex reformers reinvented Eden, prophets, and Heaven. In 1921, Edward Carpenter, who had once been an Anglican curate, now exalted Adam and Eve as the new models that humanity must strive to emulate and Eden as the new Paradise. In his essay on "Civilisation and Its Causes," Carpenter blamed Christianity's "disownment of the sacredness of sex" for the contemporary condition of "civilized" men and women who have been severed from these lost origins of a connection to Nature.[20] Instead of castigating Adam and Eve as the sinful origins of sex, Carpenter preached a new sexual morality that would put humanity on a course to finding "the way back to Eden, or rather forward to the new Eden."[21] In this new Eden, civilized men and women would, like Adam and Eve, indulge in the "primitive condition of ease and contentment."[22] Swedish sex reformer, Ellen Key, whose works were well known in British and American sex reform circles, regarded sex reform as a new religious mission with sex reformers becoming "neo-Lutheran prophets of love."[23] Like many other sex reformers at the time, Key cited the body's experience of love as a vehicle for spiritual connection, indicating that "love—as we have already shown—has become a great spiritual power."[24] To make her case for the urgency to reconstruct a New Morality, Key reiterated a familiar narrative of the suffering of civilized bodies under the demands of modern capitalist regimes of work insofar as "the value of love—like all other personal values—sinks under modern conditions of work, which drain the vital forces and make people forget even the meaning of living."[25] While Key situated love as the pivotal spiritual force through which a body connected to higher supernatural powers, love only emerged through key commandments on disciplining sexual practices through careful mate selection, the use of birth control, and an overarching commitment to the evolution of the race. Rather than prohibit all sex as sinful, Key advocated a New Morality by which the crucial sins would be "All parentage without love; All irresponsible parentage; All parentage of immature and degenerate persons; All voluntary sterility of married people fitted for the mission of the race; and finally All such manifestations of sexual life as involve violence or seduction and entail unwillingness or incapacity to fulfill the mission of the race."[26] In this period, what Key referred to as "the mission of the race" involved the elevation, perpetuation, and evolutionary progress of specific populations deemed to be leading modern civilization, namely white middle- and upper-class couples which, in the context of Key's work, also implied love as the privileged experience of these populations.

Nineteenth-century developments in religion and science set the stage for sex reformers' reorientation of Christianity around the body's indulgence of sexual desires as central to this new spirituality. Ellis's reflections on the body's encounter with Christ's love in a divine milieu, Carpenter's anticipation of the sacredness of sex in a New Eden, and

Key's view of sex reformers as "neo-Lutheran prophets of love" are only a few examples of how sex reformers reconfigured sex as a bodily gateway for connection with higher spiritual forces beyond the human. Sex reformers' reformulations of Christianity must be situated in the context of the rise of new religions that took note of the physical and emotional significance of the body's experience of spirituality. In the mid- to late nineteenth century, new religions such as Evangelicalism, Pentecostalism, transcendentalism, spiritualism, Christian Science, and theosophy drew attention to the body as a significant agent for apprehending the divine.[27] Significantly, these religions emerged in response to popular spiritual dissatisfaction with traditional Christianity. As historians have noted, this period witnessed a turn from understandings of a vengeful punitive God to a loving one. Moreover, this period witnessed religious movements that questioned the church as the primary place of worship.[28] During this period, new religious leaders turned to spaces such as fields, forests, mountains, living rooms, and doctors' offices for connecting with divine forces. Moving beyond the church and beyond the human mind as the traditional loci of religious experience, new religious movements expanded the possibilities for new spiritual relationships with nonhuman others who might participate in a divine community connected by cosmic forces.

In the late nineteenth century, the coalescence of new developing sciences and experiments with religion presented an opportunity for conflicted anxious middle-class intellectuals like Ellis and Carpenter to reorient Christianity around the body's experience of sexual impulses. As the boundaries of science and religion became increasingly tenuous, late Victorian scientists and occultists shaped new perspectives and practices of sex as an encounter between human bodies and nonhuman planetary forces.[29] This rendered the human body more porous and open to transformation through encounters with earthly as well as cosmic nonhumans, given that planetary forces irreverently and indiscriminately circulated through all bodies and atmospheres. As late nineteenth-century intellectuals simultaneously turned to science and religion as tools to better understand and experience the body, they provided a context for sex reformers to develop a prominent early twentieth-century shift to a focus on sex as love. Sex reformers' advocacy of love can be seen as emerging from situating the body at the intersection of science and religion, whereby love involved both the scientific and spiritual practice of sex. As such, sex reformers reconfigured sex as an intimate experience of not only the connection of two human bodies but the necessary participation of nonhuman forces in making that connection possible.

SEX REFORM'S RELIGION: LOVE, SCIENCE, AND DIVINE REPRODUCTION

Prior to the onset of the sex reform movement, the late Victorian intellectuals who would emerge as leading sex reformers pioneered new relationships between science and religion out of their search to carve a place for sex within and across these disciplines. In the early twentieth century, however, these intellectuals identified as sex reformers as they centralized the body and, particularly sex, as the lens for revolutionizing traditional approaches to science and religion. Sex reformers notably turned to love as a force for expressing the interconnectedness of sex, religion, and science. Through this focus on love as a force of attraction and transformation, sex reformers entertained a much more fluid and embodied relationship between human and nonhuman bodies. By probing the potential for the human body to reach divine heights, sex reformers extended the human body beyond itself to nonhuman forces and thus, rendered nonhumans essential, albeit supporting, actors in the experience of sex as love.

As sex reformers devoted attention to the mystical properties of sex, they rendered religion's boundaries more porous and open to science. At the same time, however, they pushed the boundaries of science to take into account spiritual influences where scientists grappled with uncertainty in the limitations of scientific explanations. From the 1850s until the early twentieth-century, prominent scientists considered the place of spirituality in their practices of science. From the 1850s until the 1920s, new religions that drew attention to mystical forces in the atmosphere attracted well-known scientists such as Alfred Russel Wallace, Darwin's cofounder of natural selection, physicist Oliver Lodge, chemist Sir William Crookes, mathematician Bertrand Russell, and psychologist William James. Alfred Russel Wallace attended séances and considered the possibility of spiritual forces as he extended evolutionary theory to the progress of mental evolution.[30] In the area of physics, Oliver Lodge, an avid practitioner of spiritualism, did not discount the possibility of the existence of spirits in his theory of the ether as an invisible fluid substance that connected all things in the universe.[31] In the field of mathematics, Bertrand Russell considered mysticism's relationship to numbers as the language or code of the mysterious logic of the universe.[32] Like

Wallace, William Crookes and William James took spiritual phenomena as potentially scientific phenomena when they attended séances to investigate the practices of spiritual mediums.[33] William James, in fact, was one of the founders of the American Society for Psychical Research in 1884, devoted to the scientific inquiry into spiritual phenomena. Across investigations of physical and mental phenomena, scientists opened their methods and theories to religious influences.

Edward Carpenter is a transitional figure, bridging the late nineteenth-century proliferation of new forms of spirituality with the early twentieth-century rise in the popularity of sex reform. At the same time that Carpenter had served as curate for the Church of England, he also held a degree in mathematics from Cambridge University that was granted to him in 1868.[34] Carpenter's religious and mathematical interests converged in his search to grasp the spirituality of sex as a powerful connective force between human and nonhuman nature. Sheila Rowbotham, Carpenter's biographer, claimed that Carpenter applied mathematics to mysticism, particularly in his interests in the fourth dimension.[35] Across areas of spiritual and mathematical inquiry, Carpenter turned to occultist figures such as Jacob Boehme, Emanuel Swedenborg, and William Blake, who highlighted the spiritual dimensions of mathematics.[36] In the 1900s, Carpenter lectured on sun-worship and deities, forging new relationships between mathematics, astronomy, and spirituality with particular attention to sexual forces. By 1913, a fellow mathematician and occultist, Peter Ouspensky, visited Carpenter's Millthorpe commune.[37] Carpenter's turn to both mathematics and religion as different ways of considering sex as a connective force in the universe exemplifies how sex opened human bodies to transformative encounters with both earthly and supernatural nonhumans.

While Carpenter's personal experience of dissatisfaction with Christianity's moral tales preceded his engagement with Eastern mysticism, he considered how the West could draw upon the East as a guide for repositioning sex and love at the center of religious experience. As Carpenter delineated the possible future merger of the West with the insights of the East, he speculated on the significance of modern science's fourth dimension as comparable to Eastern spirituality's insights into the oneness and harmony of the universe. He noted how the "fourth dimension" introduced a different perspective which "makes it conceivable that apparently separate objects, e.g., distinct people, are really physically united; that things apparently sundered by enormous distances of space are really quite close together."[38] Emphasizing this illusory nature of separate and distinct entities, Carpenter introduced a spiritual and scientific vision of all entities mutually affecting one another, positioning the human sexual body at the crossroads of cosmic and organic forces. Carpenter drew attention to the male body's experience of the flow of semen as on par with the surge of godly forces through the body. Attributing an other-worldly and celestial character to semen, Carpenter claimed that "the male semen contains the five elements and the composition of it is determined by the attitude of the nine planets in the sky!"[39] These divine powers of semen enabled the body to apprehend the world on a higher spiritual plane of cosmic consciousness that Carpenter defined as "a glimmering embodiment of the deep lying truth that the whole universe conspires in the sexual act, and that the orgasm itself is a flash of universal consciousness."[40] As a prophet of sex reform, Carpenter raised the stakes of achieving orgasm from an act of sexual pleasure to a spiritual act of bodies conspiring with divine as well as mathematical forces on a cosmic scale.

By the 1910s and 1920s, sex reformers had engaged in personal struggles with the failure of religion, science, and mathematics to grasp the powers of love for perfecting sex as a spiritual experience. At this time, sex reformers experienced an unsettling sense of uncertainty, highlighting the precarious and contingent foundations of science and religion, neither of which alone could adequately account for the experience of sexual energies and the practice of sex as love. In pursuit of both knowledge and the spiritual potential of the body, sex reformers reinvented religion and gestured toward the spirituality of science, developing eugenic sermons, training birth control missionaries, and establishing rituals of sex performed as love. Sex reformers turned spirituality inside out: reorienting spirituality from a quest of internal and rational connection with God to a search for cultivating sexual experience through encounters with human and nonhuman others.

As a transatlantic bohemia developed in the 1910s, radical intellectuals mounted a critique of how feeling, specifically sexual feeling, was an effect of entangled political and religious formations of docile, capitalist, and patriarchal subjectivities.[41] Historians have shown that Greenwich Village was a radical heady intellectual and political climate, seething with new theories for remaking personal life and social institutions, but the Village was also a site for radical new formations of spirituality.[42] This reformed spirituality eclectically combined fragments of new religions with fragments of new sciences of energies and emotions. At the very core of this new spirituality, sex reformers positioned the performance of sex as love. For sex reformers, the turn to mysticism marked the formation of a new spiritual subjectivity defined by the extension of specific knowledge of the body excavated through sciences of biology, physics, and sexology into cosmic realms of the hidden potential of the body in its affective capacities to connect and transform through intimate relations with other humans and nonhumans. Mabel Dodge exemplifies how sex reformers addressed scientific knowledge of the body as a spiritual orientation toward an unknown evolutionary future. For Dodge and other sex reformers, the scientific management of sex through the tools of birth control, sex manuals, and eugenics was crucial to love and ultimately the design of divine reproduction.[43]

Dodge identified with new ideals of the experience of sex as love traversing arenas of science, religion, and social reform. Across Britain and the United States, sex reformers embraced mysticism as the intermingling of science, spirituality, and sex. Significantly, sex reformers' focus on the experience of sex as love led to crossing the boundaries of science and religion as useful tools for excavating the human body's potential to connect with nonhumans. Inasmuch as sex reformers sought to modify the social and political conventions of intimacy with other humans, these efforts included nonhumans in the context of mysticism.

In Greenwich Village, Mabel Dodge, a wealthy salonnière, became a renowned mystic among her coterie of sex reformers. When Dodge first moved from Florence Italy to Greenwich Village's Washington Square in November of 1912, she gathered together a number of intellectuals, reformers, novelists, psychologists, and other professionals who were involved in radical social movements and committed to changing rigid conventions of Christian sexual morality. She arrived in Greenwich Village with her second husband, Edwin Sherrill Dodge, and her son from a previous marriage, John Evans. Shortly after establishing herself among the Greenwich Village intelligentsia, she divorced Edwin and embraced bohemian love ethics which inspired her encounters with psychoanalysts, occultists, and Christian Scientists. Dodge pursued affairs with the radical socialist journalist John Reed and the artist Maurice Sterne as experiments in marriage as much as in spiritual growth.[44] As early as 1913, only one year after moving to Greenwich Village, Dodge wrote to anarchist Alexander Berkman naming their mutual efforts to challenge sexual morality as "spiritual dynamiting."[45] Dodge equated this spiritual transformation with the feelings that accompanied "varietist" marriage experiments, confessing to Berkman that "I do not believe or disbelieve in marriage but I believe in love which may exist either within the institution or outside of it providing that it is free."[46] For Dodge and other sex reformers, radical sexual intimacies were as much about social upheaval as a reformed spiritual orientation to the world. To them, sex reform was a religion.

Dodge positioned her body's affective potential at the crossroads of science and religion, which she regarded as epistemological tools for channeling sexual energies toward love. In 1916, when Mabel Dodge and Maurice Sterne experienced emotional struggles in their mutual commitment to a "varietist" ethic of non-monogamous love, Dodge sought the help of psychoanalyst Smith Ely Jelliffe for treating her "jealousy-complex." In her correspondence with Jelliffe, Dodge recalled therapeutic sessions where she divulged her experience of sex as a spiritual connection to mysterious higher nonhuman forces that permeated and communicated with her body. To Jelliffe, Dodge described in some detail the conception of her son John, explaining how "one night to my real horror something took me—took place in me—in spite of my straining not to bring it about + in spite of my willful non-participation."[47] Recalling this "willful non-participation," Dodge evoked the power of feeling in exceeding conscious intent and a force both registered in her body's potential for feeling yet also external to it. To Jelliffe, Dodge conveyed an experience of sex as an encounter with something not human that exposed the limits of science.

Drawing upon the insights of sexologists in describing her physical experience of sex, Dodge extended sexual feelings to the potential for connection with nonhuman godly forces. Divulging the intimate details of her sexual experience to Jelliffe, Dodge addressed sex as a mode for elevating the human body to its divine potential. She remembered that: "It was not only that the orgasm took place in the vagina because that has occurred more or less since the analysis directed it there, but, while my own will on that night seemed to be torpid—slow—indifferent, some other will in me seemed to act seemed to open up the walls of the uterus to receive the flow. I was amazed at it—I was even at the moment certain that it meant a baby—my body and an unconscious will in me had operated together."[48] Dodge's reference to "some other will" suggested an affective connection forged through the sensory apprehension of a force both external to and yet part of her, communicating across internal and external boundaries at the site of sexual feeling. This particular incident occurred during Dodge's relationship with Sterne, fifteen years after her son John's conception. Dodge consistently approached this other will as both a deeper cosmic force in the universe external to her and the unconscious part of her psyche that connected to that force. For Dodge, the mysteries of unconscious desires and the body's potential to reach the divine were inseparable.

While Dodge drew upon the insights of psychoanalysis and sexual science more broadly, she insisted on the importance of spirituality to grasp the experience of sex as love. In 1916, the same year that Dodge began to consult Jelliffe, she also sought the spiritual advice of Christian Science practitioner, Emma Curtis Hopkins, who was a disciple of Mary Baker Eddy.[49] Dodge became Hopkins's pupil, learning the Twelve Lessons in mysticism, with each lesson lasting one hour and leaving her "saturated, and the effect lasted until the next time." Joining the concept of the ether in physics to spiritual practices, Dodge referred to her friend, Bobby, as "practically supported in the upper ether by Emma Curtis Hopkins for years." For Dodge, such sessions were geared toward rejuvenating both body and spirit through love, recalling how Hopkins "stimulated and renewed one—causing the love and faith that life congealed to flow again." Hopkins, as a rather unconventional priest or pastor, operated not through offering scriptural insights but through "the love she felt for us," which, Dodge considered, was geared toward "the hidden self."[50] Dodge cultivated a new form of spirituality through sessions with Hopkins that were intended to probe and elicit the body's affective and divine potential of love, which connected the material body to higher nonhuman forces.

To cope with what she experienced as her own personal crisis of navigating constraining sexual and moral norms surrounding female sexuality, Dodge's focus on the site of affective experience opened new negotiations across disciplinary boundaries of psychology and religion.[51] In the fall of 1916, while seeing Hopkins and consulting with Jelliffe, Dodge also began therapy with Dr. Abraham Arden Brill, who was acknowledged by Sigmund Freud as his official American representative in the dissemination of psychoanalysis.[52] While Dodge introduced Brill to many leading figures of the Greenwich Village intelligentsia and even elicited clients for him, it was through Brill that Lincoln Steffens, the muckraking reporter, and other radicals heard of Freud's ideas. Dodge most directly confronted rigid boundaries between science and religion when her psychoanalyst, Dr. Brill, denounced her mysticism as a Jehovah complex. Dodge, herself, resisted these efforts to marginalize the spiritual intuition she grasped through her body. In her autobiography, *Intimate Memories*, Dodge divulged this struggle with Brill when she kept her visits to Ellice Curtis Hopkins a secret. According to Dodge,

"Brill called my mysticism a fantasy and frowned upon it severely. He became arbitrary and dogmatic. Anything religious was anathema to him. He consistently tried to remove every vestige of my belief in an inner power." She identified a crucial similarity between psychoanalysis's pursuit of the unconscious and mysticism's pursuit of cosmic powers. She had decided that "I should have referred to God and Nature as 'the Unconscious' and then they would have gotten by."[53]

Like Carpenter and Ellis's search for a new religion to express the spiritual experience of sex in London, Dodge and Neith Boyce cultivated the mystical powers of sexual organs to enable bodies to experience love. In 1919, Dodge wrote to Boyce, describing how she conceptualized the power of love: "I believe that this potency we have for discovery, understanding, and by which we attain to *all* in the end—*is* the power of love functioning up thro- the bodily generative organs to greater + greater invisible organs of generation—+ to greater + greater creations by us."[54] It was love that acted as a connective force, mediating between the cosmic and the organic, the human and the nonhuman. At the time of writing this letter, Boyce approached Dodge about communicating with her recently deceased son, Boyce Hapgood. Dodge replied that her mystical insights came about through sexual love: "By passionate love—I meant the love on earth of man + woman—+ not so much the love of mother + child. I haven't analysed it yet but I think that the love that functions through the generative organs is susceptible of all degrees of other-direction *power*. I think that your love on earth for Boyce was this other-directed—+ is that now, raised to a higher degree + power."[55] Dodge situated sex as a primary act for participating in the divine, while the love of mother and child might be an extension of that love through reproduction.[56] Dodge and Boyce's correspondence highlights an important historical transformation in not only the advocacy of women's sexual pleasure but a shift in what counted as a religious experience for female sexuality. In a dramatic turn from traditional Christian and social morality's association of sexual organs with disgust, filth, and perversion, sex reformers like Boyce and Dodge presented new possibilities for conceiving sexual organs as magical, enchanted, and spiritual.[57]

As sex reformers probed the mysterious potential of sex for human physiological and psychological development, they endowed sexual forces with the cosmic significance of pushing the human body beyond itself. What sex reformers considered the mystical powers of sexual organs turned the human body into a vehicle for spiritual connection to divine powers linked to the deepest truths and secrets of the universe. Whether sex reformers gravitated toward occultism, theosophy, or Christian Science, their receptivity to new religions derived from a sense of the spiritual importance of sex. As such, sex reformers commingled sexual science with spirituality, Darwinian evolution with cosmic evolution, and the human with the divine.

SPIRITUAL TECHNOLOGIES: BIRTH CONTROL AS A DIVINE MECHANISM TO UPLIFT THE HUMAN

While the advent of new technologies such as the X-ray, electricity, the telephone, and the camera were deemed to have spiritual properties, sex reformers drew particular attention to birth control as a technology for the spiritual experience of sex as love.[58] Not only did sex reformers advocate birth control as a technology for enabling the human body to achieve a higher potential for sexual feeling, but they also considered nonhuman objects such as intrauterine devices, sponges, and chemical mixtures as critical to elevating the human body to a spiritual connection with nonhuman cosmic forces. Sex, therefore, involved much more than the reconfiguration of intimacy between two human bodies; it, in fact, involved a community of supporting nonhuman actors to make the experience of love possible. Sex reformers' advocacy of birth control was as much a story about religion as it was about the social, political, and scientific transformation of sex as love.

Although some late nineteenth-century advocates of Malthusianism, the control of fertility to limit population, suggested that limiting births could be reconciled with religion, early twentieth-century sex reformers turned the reform of religion into a crucial dimension of scientifically managing sex as love. George Drysdale, Alice Vickery Drysdale, and Charles Drysdale were nineteenth-century advocates of family limitation or the right of women to control their fertility in the interests of preventing a population growth that would exceed available food and other resources to support it.[59] While the Drysdales did not consider fertility control to be at odds with religion, they did not position sex as central to spirituality. Similarly, Annie Besant, another nineteenth-century pioneer of the birth control movement, maintained that her social and political activities were consistent with her spirituality. However, Besant drew a sharp distinction between providing women with the means to control their fertility in the Malthusian interests of family limitation and the use of birth control to give women the freedom to indulge their sexual

FIGURE 5. Margaret Sanger and Charles Drysdale at the Sixth International Neo-Malthusian and Birth Control Conference exemplify the transatlantic collaboration of American and British birth control activists. Courtesy of the Library of Congress Prints and Photographs Division, Washington, D.C. Photoprint by Underwood & Underwood. Image is in the public domain.

desires without fear of pregnancy.[60] Besant, in fact, condemned free love and insisted on the importance of sexual self-control. Contrary to the early promotion of birth control as population control, sex reformers turned birth control advocacy into an argument for sex as a religion.

With the early twentieth-century development and proliferation of birth control technologies, sex reformers redefined birth control in terms of magic, enchantment, and probing the body's divine properties. In particular, the shared mission of birth control movements in Britain and the United States highlighted Anglo-transatlantic intimacies, as birth control leaders such as Marie Stopes and Margaret Sanger paid close attention to the necessary transformation of Christianity in response to birth control technologies. As such, divine nonhuman spiritual forces and technological nonhuman artifacts were important agents of social and political change, inspiring sex reformers to reconfigure spiritual practices to incorporate the use of these tools for uplifting the body.

While Margaret Sanger's birth control activism has primarily been told as a secular and predominantly human story, Sanger addressed the spiritual effects of birth control on women's bodies. Like Mabel Dodge, Sanger dabbled in occultism as an alternative and radical expansion of the spiritual possibilities of Christianity. Sanger situated birth control on a spiritual plane of cosmically connecting sexual bodies to the universe. On February 6, 1922, Sanger turned to astrologist, Elizabeth Aldrich, situating both the movement and her own body as leader of the movement within wider planetary cosmic forces. Aldrich responded to Sanger's request for advice on the fate of the birth control movement, indicating that "the whole Birth Control movement is largely a Neptunian affair. As I have said, Neptune is much conceived with suffering humanity."[61] Aldrich also put Sanger's battles with the clergy into astrological perspective. She told Sanger: "I observe with considerable interest that the conjunction of Saturn and Jupiter which spread so much havoc in our world, and which occurred September tenth, nineteen twenty-one, fell on the spot of your Progressed Venus and near your Radical Sun. I cannot remember the time exactly that your legal fracas with the police and a few (for one) of the clergy started. As this conjunction is still going strong, I have no doubt it was the manifestation in your life of this conjunction."[62] This fracas was likely the arrest of Sanger and the police raid on her clinic, orchestrated by Cardinal Patrick Hayes in 1916.[63] Contemplating a trip to spread the birth control campaign internationally, Sanger worried that her absence might affect the movement in the United States and consulted Aldrich. Aldrich reassured her that "This aspect of Sun sextile Uranus of which I have spoken, will give you remarkable magnetic power."[64] This reference to magnetic power linked Sanger to earlier eighteenth- and nineteenth-century beliefs in magnetic fluids connecting all bodies in the universe.[65] While Sanger is known for her efforts to ground birth control in science, specifically through collaborations with doctors, she also remained open to occultist forces in shaping her movement.

FIGURE 6. Margaret Sanger in 1922, amid the rising popularity of the birth control movement. Photograph by Underwood & Underwood. Courtesy of the Library of Congress Prints and Photographs Division, Washington, D.C. Image is in the public domain.

Transatlantic intimacies between American and British birth control activists were fostered and cemented by the advocacy for birth control's spiritual importance. In 1915, just one year prior to Margaret Sanger's confrontation with the police and the Catholic Church, Stopes and Sanger corresponded on birth control as a cause for the improvement of humanity. In September of 1915, Stopes and other leading British birth control supporters, including Edward Carpenter and H. G. Wells, sent a letter to American president Woodrow Wilson protesting the criminal prosecution of Margaret Sanger for circulating a birth control pamphlet. This letter objected to Sanger's prosecution on the grounds of the importance of birth control to humanity.[66] Sanger and Stopes also framed birth control as a universal issue in emotional terms of love that joined human beings across spatial and cultural divides. Shortly after the death of her young child, Peggy, Sanger wrote to Stopes of the work that birth control was doing insofar as "women are getting happiness out of love."[67] As such, Sanger and Stopes cast birth control as a movement that bridged nations through the appeal to love which positioned birth control in the spiritual domain as part of the essence of being human.

As Sanger battled religious authorities to make a spiritual case for birth control in the United States, Stopes engaged with British religious authorities in debates over the morality of birth control. In 1919, at the National Birth Control Commission's meeting in London, Stopes discussed birth control as a Christian practice of cultivating sexual energies to allow the body to fulfill its divine potential for love. To an audience of physicians, clergymen, politicians, and reformers, Stopes defended birth control as a spiritual and sexual technology for achieving the "highest potentialities of marriage."[68] Like Sanger, Stopes did not jettison religion as antithetical to science and sex reform but, instead, showed the contested and interpretive ground of Christian truths, particularly around sex as a divine practice of universal love. According to Stopes, "The insistence so often made in the name of a false Christian morality that the act of physical union should take place only for the procreation of children not only ignores profound physiological truths, but degrades one of the greatest religious truths."[69] Stopes proposed to the Commission that religious authorities failed to grasp sex as one of the "highest potentialities" that enabled human bodies to connect with cosmic forces. She explained that for the truly married couple "each is no longer a simple unit, but the two are fused and merged into a pair, and this is partly based upon and is correlated with the physical exchange of chemical and ultra-chemical particles."[70] For Stopes, the capacities for human bodies to experience sex as love presented an ambiguous ground between the scientific and the spiritual.

As both Sanger and Stopes actively engaged with clergymen, they collaboratively defined the human potential for love as attainable by bodies at the pinnacle of Western civilization.[71] Stopes's correspondence with Reverend Duncan Cameron in Stirling, Scotland, indicates the place of Catholicism in modern articulations of reproductive racism which aimed to stem the tide of the so-called unfit in economic and colonial terms. Cameron had, in fact, written an article for Stopes's periodical, the *Birth Control News*, and delivered a lecture titled "The Race Problem in Scotland" for her Society for Constructive Birth Control and Racial Progress. Stopes continued to correspond with Cameron a few years after this lecture. In November of 1928, Stopes praised Cameron's work, claiming that "I have watched with great interest from time to time small indications in the Press that you are so actively and usefully continuing to deal with the serious racial problem in Scotland of the low-grade Irish immigrants and Roman Catholics."[72] As a site of high Catholic immigrant populations from Ireland and Southern Italy, American and British birth controllers recognized New York City as an important and contested zone for their activities.[73] In her autobiography, Sanger also recalled the emotional experience of witnessing her Irish mother's exhaustion with numerous pregnancies.[74] She traced the origins of her activism to her personal encounters in nursing poor immigrant women in childbirth. She noted working in the Lower East Side of New York City among Irish and Italian Catholic women as well as Jewish immigrant women. Sanger remarked on the valuable work at her clinic among Catholic women.[75] In other words, Stopes and Sanger targeted white, middle-class, Anglo-Protestant bodies hovering at the top of the early twentieth-century evolutionary ladder who allegedly possessed the potential for love to move civilization to its next phase.

On both sides of the Atlantic, British and American birth control movements configured fertility technologies as not only spiritual tools of love but also eugenic ones.[76] Both American and British sex reformers exalted the Dean of St. Paul's, William Ralph Inge, for his support of eugenics. Although birth controllers emphasized Dean Inge as a progressive clergyman, he vociferously advocated for eugenic policies while refusing to promote birth control. In January of 1918, Inge wrote to Stopes to express his gratitude upon receiving her book on *Married Love* but assured her she would not convince him to associate his name with it.[77] In the 1920s, however, Margaret Sanger's periodical, the *Birth Control Review*, featured prominent clergymen including Inge, which appeared to lend religious validation to scientifically managing reproduction which entailed preventing unwanted children while encouraging love and sexual pleasure amid responsible families. As part of the religious propaganda for birth control, Sanger's February 1920 issue included an article titled "An English Bishop in Birth Control," which noted the famous Bishop of Birmingham, Dr. Russell Wakefield, and Dean Inge of St. Paul's as supporters of the mental, moral, and physical advantages of birth control.[78] By appealing to renowned clergymen on both sides of the Atlantic, Stopes and Sanger highlighted birth control as a tool for eugenic reproduction as a new formation of Christian love.

While birth control advocates focused on love as the evolutionary promise of the human sexual body, they also drew attention to love as an experience contingent on an array of nonhuman actors across the spectrum of cosmic forces and technical objects. From distant cosmic entities such as Venus, the Sun, or ancient gods to more proximate objects such as sponges and intrauterine devices, sex reformers highlighted a community of human and nonhuman actors intimately engaged in making love possible. Moreover, sex reformers took into account the possibilities for human bodies to connect with nonhumans as another factor in differentiating humans from the lowest and closer to the nonhuman to the very highest evolved human. As such, sex reformers reserved the spiritual potential for love for the very elite of humans along the evolutionary chain. As such, nonhumans were critical to defining the very essence of the human while they facilitated the experience of love.

Sex reformers' planetary politics of love raises profound questions about contemporary investments in affect, connectivity, and nonhuman agency. There is an important legacy of how love and care have historically operated as lenses for rethinking physics and religion in terms of grasping the ways that all beings, human and nonhuman, are connected by cosmic forces whether we call them spiritual or environmental forces. Although the academic turn to reconfiguring relations with nonhumans on a cosmic scale often romanticizes these relations as care or love, we must be mindful of deployments of love in the service of the violence of paternalism, colonialism, and capitalism.[79] Tracking the emergence of a new ideal of love between 1890 and 1930 is one way of alerting us to how love is never innocent, depoliticized, or divorced from power even at the point of love's rebirth or reconfiguration at different moments in time.

4

Reinventing Love as Technologies of Sex and Marital Intimacies

For sex reformers, the attainment of love as a scientific practice of sex involved an array of nonhuman actors that included inorganic machinic interventions. In combination with these machinic interventions, sex reformers highlighted a very carefully choreographed process of sex that gauged senses, energies, instincts, and emotions. Relying on very specific tools to manipulate affective as much as the physical facts of reproduction, sex reformers addressed the importance of intimate cooperation and seamlessness between bodies and birth control technologies. Marie Stopes, like Margaret Sanger, formed close networks with physicians who were in a position to support sex reform by supplying birth control and advising their patients on its appropriate and safe use. Moreover, sex reformers formed a transatlantic traffic of news on the latest birth control technologies in terms of their successes and failures.

Writing to Dr. Jane Hawthorne in June of 1920, Stopes provided information on where she could obtain cervical caps while also alluding to a specific case of a woman seeking contraceptive guidance. Stopes informed Hawthorne that she had advised the woman to avoid possible margins for error in applying these technologies by ensuring that her husband wear a sheath and upon wearing the cap, she should also insert a quinine pessary. While these measures could establish sufficient physical obstacles to pregnancy, Stopes also acknowledged an affective context by noting, "I think she needs a certain amount of encouraging—naturally, she must be feeling rather anxious about it." Stopes also emphasized the importance of providing women with guidance on how to properly use these methods and a certain degree of technical competence in applying them. Stopes queried, "Do you know anything about the gold pin method used so much now in America? It appears to be extremely suitable for the lazy or rather unreliable class which is so apt to make mistakes with ordinary methods."[1] Through the dissemination of birth control technologies and manuals advising on specific choreographed practices of sex, sex reformers highlighted an unnatural scientifically managed practice of sex designed in some cases to facilitate love and in other cases to stem the tide of allegedly rising populations of immigrant, racialized, and lower-class others.

As sex reformers in Britain and the United States formed transatlantic bonds in their experiments with the untapped potential of sexual bodies, they reinvented sex as a practice of love that could be broadly applied to new ways of being in the world at large. In other words, sex reformers established sex as an ontological practice that redefined the boundaries of the self as radically open-ended, permeable, and shaped by encounters in the world. What sex reformers called the "art of love" drew attention to a series of specific scientific techniques for practicing sex that not only relied on naturally occurring nonhumans but also included artificial nonhuman technologies. Accompanying these techniques, sex reformers introduced the metals, springs, chemicals, and rubber of birth control technologies into facilitating the body's experience of love. By challenging the boundaries of the self through new techniques and technologies of sex, sex reformers highlighted sex as a way of relating to others that could be broadly applied to public spheres of politics, ethics, and social bonds. Preceding the advent of Freudianism and perhaps setting the stage for it, sex reformers engaged with the rise of sexology in the 1890s to popularize the science of sex as the cornerstone of civilization. By advocating sex as a transformational engagement between the body and the world at large, sex reformers treaded a fine line between the hopes of strengthening the body through human and nonhuman resources and the fears of opening the body to contamination and degeneration through undesirable alliances with human and nonhuman others.[2] This ambivalence lies at the heart of sex reformers' politics of love in terms of which bodies were deemed capable of mastering the technologies and techniques of sex to achieve love.

As sex reformers advocated sexual techniques for cultivating and reviving the body's memory of Darwinian animal ancestors while also encouraging the use of birth control technologies, both animals and objects were brought into the network of actors engaged in making human love possible.[3] Arguably, animals, objects, and the scientific method of sex techniques were critical tools without which love could not be achieved. This particular moment is a historical example of what feminist science studies scholar Luciana Parisi discusses as the changing regimes of feeling in relation to technologies in the present. While Parisi highlights DNA biochips, prosthetics, and bionic retinas as examples of how technologies have recalibrated the body's potential to feel, a historically specific recalibration of love as sexual feeling occurred in relation to the techniques and technologies invoked by sex reformers.[4]

THE FEAR OF SLOPPY COPULATION

Paying close attention to the practice of sex as an art of love, sex reformers quite literally changed sex in this period and raised the stakes on sexual performance. With the advent of sex manuals designed to elicit mutual orgasm and ultimately love, sex reformers developed precise tactics, bodily positioning, and affective choreographies that refined the practice of sex. Beyond the wide dissemination of sex reform literature, sex reformers also gave lectures and attended conferences to popularize these high expectations of sex across Britain and the United States. While on an American lecture tour in 1924, Bertrand Russell sought to teach an educated professional class of Americans about sex, love, and companionship. When he recounted his experience of the lecture, Russell highlighted the lack of sexual skills in the art of love among the husbands of American women. He wrote to his wife and fellow sex reformer, Dora Russell that "American ladies are quite dreadful. They all rush up to me after a lecture +I almost have to use fists to get away. Poor things, they get no companionship, + they want it. They have to put up with nothing but sloppy copulation."[5] Although Bertrand Russell played the new role of British imperialist instructing Americans in the refined art of love, the higher stakes of sex were also a very real struggle in the Russell marriage. Bertrand at one point confided to Dora that he would consult a doctor to improve his sexual performance because "there is of course no hope [of marital happiness] unless I can satisfy you sexually."[6] In light of the new expectations of sex generated by sex reformers, "sloppy copulation" became a blow to masculine pride in sexual performance, which came under greater scrutiny in this period.

From the 1890s to the 1920s, sex reformers began to shape a scientific method for practicing sex as they drew on the studies of sexual desires, diverse sexual practices, and sexual anatomy, bodies, and practices. While historians, queer theorists, and feminist scholars have focused on sexology as sexual science, sex reformers drew on sexology as a science of love as much as a science of sex.[7] In 1898, Ellis's *Studies in the Psychology of Sex* devoted an entire chapter to "the art of love," which aimed to overturn assumptions that there is "no art of love to be either learnt or taught; it comes by nature." Instead, Ellis argued that "even the elementary fact of coitus needs to be taught."[8] In their specific directions for cultivating sexual pleasure, sex reformers presumed a highly choreographed act among a heterosexual couple carefully attending to the gendered specificity of the difference between male and female sexual rhythms. In particular, sex reformers situated this gender dynamic in the act of sex in terms of heightening sexual excitement in slower female bodies while tempering an overzealous sexual drive in faster-paced male bodies. Thus, sex reformers reinvented sex as hybrid natural and cultural act engaging a community of human and nonhuman participants in the production of love.

On both sides of the Atlantic, prominent sex reformers wrote sex manuals for married couples that widely disseminated the "art of love" as a scientific technique for practicing sex among educated middle-class couples. American birth control leader, Margaret Sanger's "love etiquette" required bodies to adhere to precise rules governing how to approach one another during the act of sex.[9] In *Happiness in Marriage*, Sanger advised the husband to hone his skill as a lover and discipline his body by controlling "the tumultuous power of his impulses."[10] Sanger set down an affective regime for the young husband who needed to "concentrate upon the psychic condition and mood of his beloved" and "note her response to his caresses, the caresses of a true artist."[11] To be a "successful husband-lover," Sanger also advised the husband to be aware of the female sexual cycle and "take advantage of her exact condition in this moon-monthly rhythm instead of beginning his lovemaking in the wrong period."[12] Despite Sanger's references to the husband as the piano-player, the artist, the composer, or the "successful lover," she also insisted that women were active participants in sex insofar as they allowed themselves to enjoy it.[13] Offering a description of the woman's role, Sanger claimed "She must learn therefore to relax. She must seek to fall into the rhythm of the love flight, as the continuation of a dance, a dance of soul as well as body."[14] Sanger went on to suggest how these bodies connected as "beings are co-mingled in a new and higher unity."[15] Through all of these prescriptive actions, Sanger indicated that "physical demands are harnessed for the expression of love."[16] Sanger's work is one example of a new genre of early twentieth-century sex manuals that highlighted love as a far from "natural" or spontaneous experience but one requiring an extraordinary amount of sexual and intimate work.

Although Marie Stopes's birth control advocacy largely emerged from her experiences in Britain, her 1918 sex manual, *Married Love*, offered advice that was consistent with the sex techniques of Sanger's *Happiness in Marriage*. Like Sanger, Stopes mentioned "the untutored male."[17] She, in fact, compared the male who solely sought to gratify himself to wild animals "who are not so foolish as man; a wild animal does not unite with his female without the wooing characteristic of his race."[18] Like Sanger, Stopes denounced the male's approach to "using the woman as a passive instrument"[19] and stressed that "without the discipline of control there is no lasting delight in erotic feeling."[20] Stopes also explained that "woman has a rhythmic sex-tide."[21] Both Sanger and Stopes suggested the importance of mutual understanding between husbands and wives to cooperatively achieve sexual pleasure. In Sanger's and Stopes's advice, this connection also took on the special character variously described as "spiritual union," "sex-communion," or "subtle spiritual alchemy." While Stopes and Sanger would agree sex was instinctive across animals and humans, precise scientific techniques were necessary to refine sex as a practice of love.

In their formulation of a corpus of sex literature to widely disseminate theories on the scientific practice of sex as love, sex reformers actively tested and experimented with these techniques in the laboratories of their own bedrooms. As part of a young, educated Greenwich Village elite, Hutchins Hapgood and Neith Boyce drew inspiration for practicing new sexual morals from the growing fascination with sexual science in the 1890s and early 1900s. During their courtship and throughout their marriage, Hapgood and Boyce actively engaged with newly emerging ideals of sex as they endeavored to coordinate their bodies in the practice of sex as an art of love. In the summer of 1898 at the start of their courtship, Hapgood confided to Boyce that "all the sensitive side of me is more sensitive for you—my senses sharper, my perceptions more alert."[22] In his letters to Boyce, Hapgood also divulged the bodily and emotional struggles in transitioning to this New Morality. On one occasion, Hapgood expressed the challenges of coordinating mutual sexual desires in both partners, telling Boyce that "To-night I made you miserable because I made you think of what I wanted because I am not

FIGURE 7. A portrait of Neith Boyce, taken between 1890 and 1910. Photograph by Frances Benjamin Johnston (1864–1952). Johnston (Frances Benjamin) Collection. Courtesy of the Library of Congress, Prints and Photographs Division, Washington, D.C. Image is in the public domain.

able to see you without making love to you."[23] Hapgood attributed these difficulties to the persistent hold of traditional sexual morality on Boyce's body, explaining that "your practical instinct tells you I'm unworthy, your maidenly feeling tells you to avoid me and it is only your liking for occasional companionship and the sense of being loved, added to womanly pity."[24] In 1905, several years after they had married,

Hapgood and Boyce continued a bodily struggle of eliciting mutual desire with the right timing and right intensity. For Hapgood, attaining the proper response from Boyce proved to be challenging as he regretfully recalled that "We did indeed have a grand time—you and I—that year of our (no, of my) love-making. I don't think your pleasure was as great as mine."[25] Reminding Boyce of his efforts, he asked, "Have I not tried always to arouse you and make you love me warmly?"[26] This exchange between Hapgood and Boyce exemplifies how the popular sex advice being disseminated by sex reformers had also been tried, tested, and tweaked in sex reformers' own sexual practices.

DARWIN IN THE BEDROOM: THE POLITICS OF LOVE IN EVOLUTIONARY PERSPECTIVE

As a scientific practice, the techniques of the art of love were primarily intended for the "civilized" and the allegedly highest-evolved bodies of early twentieth-century humanity. Sex reformers introduced the criterion of a body's affective potential to experience love as a new category for not only separating humans from nonhumans but for also differentiating "civilized" from "primitive" humans along the lines of race and class. In their efforts to orchestrate and perform sex in accordance with prescribed scientific techniques, sex reformers also engaged in a performance of their evolutionary status in the modern incarnation of urban jungles defined by racial and class hierarchies. At this historical juncture, Darwinian evolutionary theory captivated the imaginations of an educated middle class in Britain and the United States to the extent that they experienced their bodies as carrying the legacies of evolution with latent animal and ancestral impulses lingering in the deep recesses of the memory of the modern, white, middle-class body. British sex reformers Dora and Bertrand Russell both alluded to love as a "civilized" form of sex in publications that became popular in Britain and the United States. In Dora Russell's *The Right to Be Happy*, she defined a "real sex-union" based on love: "The civilizing of sex, of everything else, lies in the thought and emotion which give varied and supple expression to primitive passion."[27] Echoing these claims, Bertrand Russell's 1929 publication *Marriage and Morals* indicated that "sex intercourse apart from love has little value, and is to be regarded primarily as experimentation with a view to love." In *Marriage and Morals*, Bertrand specified the "white man" as the primary focus of sex reformers' efforts to reform sex as love. He claimed that "polyandry is another custom which an unread white man would suppose contrary to human nature." Russell addressed love as the emotional evolutionary product of "civilized' bodies, noting that "civilized people cannot fully satisfy their sexual instinct without love."[28] Insofar as sex reformers tied the performance of an evolutionary status to mastering the "art of love," they heightened the stakes of getting sex right; namely, both the stakes of appropriate gendered roles as well as whiteness.[29]

Through the creation of the "art of love," sex reformers paradoxically reconciled the need to cultivate "natural" sexual instincts of primal ancestors while protecting their civilized status by subjecting these sexual instincts to learned scientific rules that would enable these bodies to achieve the higher spiritual affective potential to experience sex as love.

Insofar as sex reformers relied on the cultivation of sexual energies to make the "art of love" possible, they turned to their own civilized bodies as microcosms of intimate reenactments of Darwinian evolutionary dramas. Neith Boyce and Hutchins Hapgood mounted this intimate performance of evolutionary status on a literal stage when they performed their play *Enemies* to an audience in Provincetown, Massachusetts. As the lovers in the play try to negotiate new non-monogamous terms for marriage, the male protagonist notes how they "did not swear to love one another eternally—we took one another for better, not for worse." Situating her body in a psychoanalytic and evolutionary past, the female protagonist suggests: "Perhaps I was not satisfied at the mother's breast, and you were. I seem to you a ravening monster, because you do not permit me to be a little child—Is there anything more unreasonable than a baby who is hungry for milk and warmth? Have you no sympathy for this deep starvation of mine, going to the distant unconscious past, to the womb, and perhaps beyond it? Can you not give me this infinite release, this satisfied freedom of instinct?" In his response to her, the male protagonist suggests that love is in the process of being transformed beyond conventional practices of marriage. He notes that "I did not love you, as you understand love." Throughout the play, the protagonists wrestle with their feelings as a civilized and bourgeois couple seeking to cope with the primal past of their sexual instincts.[30] Boyce and Hapgood's performance situated the efforts to revive a latent animal or primal body within the historically specific discourses of sex reform, Darwinian thought, psychoanalysis, and free love.[31] *Enemies* staged the paradox at the heart of sex reformers' practices of love; namely, the fact that love as an evolutionary capacity of civilized bodies depended upon the use of the nonhuman and primal others as affective resources to make it possible.

In their staging of *Enemies*, Boyce and Hapgood blurred the lines between fiction and reality, as *Enemies* publicly displayed the bodily struggles occurring among couples seeking to scientifically practice sex as an "art of love." Throughout the play, Hapgood's and Boyce's performances of the gendered roles in the evolutionary drama of cultivating primal passions illustrates what queer theorist, Judith Butler has famously described as gender performativity. Butler's definition of gender as a series of active, ritualistic, and repetitive acts captures how early twentieth-century sex reformers performed the prescribed gendered roles elucidated in sex manuals within the context of reliving Darwinian evolutionary dramas in the modern world.[32] *Enemies* mirrored how Hapgood and Boyce situated their own sex lives in terms of efforts to cultivate a primal animalistic other buried within the evolutionary memory of their own bodies. Around the time of her performance in *Enemies*, Boyce wrote to Mabel Dodge saying, "I've had my moments of jealousy and doubt. And I cried most of one night because I regretted the old fierceness and wildness—which something perverse in me wanted—perhaps the red Indian."[33] She also wrote to Hapgood recounting "their emotional history" and revealing "I am 'primitive'—that is, very instinctive."[34] Hapgood, in fact, explicitly referred to how evolution informed his own commitments to practicing marriage beyond existing morals. In Hapgood's critique of conservative claims that "radicalism meant the destruction of civilization," he professed his "general adherence to the doctrine of evolution."[35] In allying himself with a transnational platform of sex reform objectives, Hapgood explained the New Morality in terms of evolution in the following way: "Morality is a means by which the welfare of the race is furthered, and the conditions under which the race exists at the time have to be taken into account when we evolve a morality which will add to the general welfare." He went on to cite love as pivotal to this change in morality: "Love for one another seems to me a positive morality which will always endure. I cannot conceive of morality without love."[36] When Hapgood further specified what a New Morality based on this doctrine of evolution would entail, he firmly entrenched love in the racial politics of furthering the progress of "civilized" couples.

The extent to which Darwin's monkeys haunted the practices of sex reform can be seen in Hapgood's article "The Criminal Monkey," which positioned sex reformers' bodies at the crossroads of a lingering monkey heritage and the future superhuman body on the current evolutionary path. Hapgood's article appeared in the periodical *The Social War*. In Hapgood's story, sex reformers were the criminal monkeys. His story of the condition of modern society collapsed the Darwinian past of the evolution of monkey society with what Hapgood considered a current moment of evolutionary transformation. Within the society of monkeys, placid monkeys abide by conventions, happily swing from the trees, and only engage in habits established by tradition and eating decent food as "a peaceful, contented race." Hapgood associates the criminal monkeys with radical reformers of his own time. Both the monkeys and these reformers are dubbed "sinful" because of their challenge to tradition and the break from "organized society." Moreover, like sex reformers, a coterie of prominent intellectuals and artists, these criminal monkeys are an intellectual vanguard who, finding themselves beyond the traditional society, are "forced to use their grey matter and develop their hands." It is, then, the criminal monkey that becomes significant in the closer turn to the human.[37] Hapgood's invocation of Darwinian monkeys exemplifies how racialized associations of lower classes and non-white others with monkeys as the earliest stage of evolution were mobilized in sex reformers' politics of love. Insofar as sex reformers drew on the popularity of Darwinism as science, their constructions of love as a scientific practice of sex exemplify how a politics of social and political power shaped the construction of sexual science.[38]

Sex reformers turned attention to the modern manifestation of monkey society, invoking human kinship with monkeys in sexual instincts but redefining human evolutionary progress in terms of a body capable of scientifically disciplining these sexual forces to turn them into the higher, civilized experience of love. Hapgood points out the significance of this moment for the criminalized monkey that rebels against conventional morals: "Driven on by a terrible insatiable appetite they were gradually reconstructed and became Men." Hapgood positions himself and other sex reformers within this same kind of monumental moment in evolutionary history. His story slots many reformers, particularly sex reformers, into the evolutionary moment of nonhuman to human transition. Toward the end of his article, Hapgood specifically connects his own coterie of reformers to "criminal monkeys," claiming that contemporary criminal monkeys are "restless, troublesome, deeply disreputable individuals who are driven by the Vitalist Impulse philosophy of Bergson,"[39] a philosophy grounding evolution in energies. Hapgood's millennial vision considers a series of radical reformers then deeply involved in his Greenwich Village circle as shaping the future course of evolution. He credited anarchists, IWWs [Industrial Workers of the World], idealists, "restless moral criminals," and artists as those who "will have helped somehow, chaotically to carry on Evolution a step, into a race that we may call 'Supermen.'" This race of Supermen would, according to Hapgood, be the next evolutionary step of the human, "leaving Human Beings undisturbed, placid, well-to-do, perfectly adjusted to their well-worn environment, swinging in their traditional trees."[40] Hapgood's reference to the Superman attests to the extent to which sex reformers on both sides of the Atlantic drew on the figure of the Nietzschean superman, a mythical blond beast that drew its strength from primal energies and channelled these energies into making a stronger civilization.[41] As sex reformers embraced the science of evolution, they focused on tailoring new sexual practices toward compelling their bodies to embrace this evolutionary past in terms of psychoanalytic therapies devoted to probing the animal past in the unconscious and new forms of spirituality devoted to a millennial vision of reproducing the bodies of superhumans.

Hapgood and Boyce's performance of an affective evolutionary status extended to encounters with immigrant and racialized others in the diverse ethnic enclaves of New York City. At a time of unprecedented waves of Irish, Italian, and Chinese immigration to the United States, sex reformers ascribed a particular affective character to these populations. While living in New York City, Hapgood and Boyce indulged in "primitivism" as they engaged with Italians, Irish, and African Americans—the primal others in the modern urban incarnation of the Darwinian jungle. In 1901, just two years after they married, Boyce conveyed to Hapgood, "Your news always interests me too—all of your Italian and Irish adventures."[42] Referring to the "colonial Italians of distinction," Hapgood defined a specific affective character of "something primitive, passionate, and natural" and "in their private lives jealousy and lack of cooperation are virulently noticeable." Hapgood concluded that the Italians were "emotional about ideas as such, warm about abstractions, a feeling relatively rare in Anglo-Saxons."[43] In the Bowery district of New York, Hapgood engaged with Irish immigrants, recounting his experiences in articles on saloons, dancing Irish girls, and corrupt municipal Irish politicians. He described the world of Irish immigrants as a "picturesque, overcivilized, and yet barbarian world."[44] Sex reformers redefined the practice of "slumming" as racially and erotically charged encounters to cultivate latent ancestral passions through human bodies deemed to be closer to their animal origins.[45] In sharing a similar sense of the evolutionary distance of white bodies from primal others, British sex reformers also engaged in this affectively charged practice of "slumming." During a visit to New York City, Bertrand Russell shuddered at "the jungle poison invading our souls" in a cabaret as African American women danced near his group of American friends, poet Genevieve Taggard, and novelists Theodore Dreiser and Sherwood Anderson.[46] As sex reformers sought opportunities for cultivating sexual energies in metropolitan enclaves, they enacted a politics of love by intimately engaging with lower-class and racialized others in the hopes of drawing on their primal energies to make love possible for "civilized" bodies.

SOCIAL AND POLITICAL EXPERIMENTS IN THE ART OF LOVE

In addition to emphasizing the art of love, sex reformers drew attention to the necessary social and political conditions that would allow love to flourish.[47] Strongly committed to ideals of sexual freedom, many sex reformers experimented with "varietism" in their marriage, which involved allowing for a variety of sexual partners and opening the marital relationship to extramarital lovers. For sex reformers, varietist marriage challenged the principle of fidelity as the basis of marriage and, instead, allowed for the sexual freedom of both husbands and wives. Sex reformers, in fact, situated varietist marriages within the political context of feminism and socialism by seeking to eliminate a husband's economic and sexual control of his wife as a possession. Moreover, sex reformers also drew attention to varietism's implications for women, who would no longer need to feel that their economic security was contingent on their sexual virtue as chaste women. While sex reformers' advocacy of varietism as a socialist practice drew on a long tradition of free love in utopian socialism, sex reformers like Dora Russell were part of a New Left facing considerable opposition within socialist circles.[48] Although many historians have generally depicted women as victims of varietist marriages, suffering from the sexual liberties of their husbands, many women indulged, supported, and benefited from varietism, while many husbands emotionally struggled with the affairs of their wives.[49] As sex reformers experimented with varietism, they struggled with feelings of jealousy that signified a body's continued allegiance to capitalist and patriarchal investments in the ownership of a partner and, thus, a betrayal of sex reform ethics. Sex reformers invested considerable importance in the practice of love as both reflecting wider social, economic, and political relations and, in itself, a way of relating to others that could remake the world.

Typically living in bohemian communities in large metropolises, sex reformers used these spaces to test and perform varietism as a radical social experiment, what they regarded as the new sexual ethics.[50] Some of the sex reform couples experimenting with varietism included William and Margaret Sanger, Hutchins Hapgood and Neith Boyce, Emma Goldman and Ben Reitman, Dora and Bertrand Russell, and Jane and H. G. Wells.[51] In their experimentation with varietism, sex reformers struggled to conform to a new ethic of sexual freedom and permissible infidelity that often prompted feelings of jealousy. To sex reformers, jealousy was diametrically opposed to love insofar as jealousy attested to a body's affective orientation toward exclusively possessing and enslaving a partner by inhibiting their free pursuit of sexual desires. In his 1939 autobiography, *A Victorian in the Modern World*, Hutchins Hapgood referred to Chicago and Greenwich Village communities that upheld "varietism as a moral law."[52] He explained that: "Marriage on principle was not to be tolerated, since it was an enslaving institution; but, whether married or living in what was called free union, the unnatural idealism of the group made it obligatory on the part of the male not only to tolerate but to encourage the occasional impulse of the wife or sweetheart toward some other man; or, on the part of the woman, a more tolerant willingness to have her man follow out a brief impulse with some other woman."[53] Acknowledging some of the struggles varietism posed to masculinity, Hapgood claimed that in varietist marriages, "The woman was in full possession of what the man used to regard as his 'rights,' and the men, even the most advanced of them, suffered from the woman's full assumption of his own privileges."[54] While Hapgood spoke primarily of American communities, varietism also held sway as moral ethic across the Atlantic in London's Bloomsbury. Bloomsbury radicals such as Vanessa Bell, Virginia Woolf, and John Maynard Keynes treated marriage as a mere outward conformity to convention but, in practice, they allowed for a new sexual ethics that dispensed with fidelity. Dora Russell, in fact, described the Bloomsbury group as living by a "code to regard this [marriage] as not very important in sexual ethics."[55] Within sex reform circles, varietism took hold as a radical experiment for overturning the conventional basis of the institution of marriage.

In their practices of varietism, sex reformers repeatedly struggled with jealousy as the very antithesis of an ethic of love that encouraged sexual freedom and openly welcomed extramarital lovers as extensions of family. In the early years of marriage, Boyce and Hapgood were committed to a varietist marriage as a practice of love based on sexual freedom. In January of 1899, Boyce praised Hapgood's lack of possessiveness, noting his proposal that "we might for a time proceed in separate orbits coincident at only remote intervals—I wonder if you meant it? If so—then you are certainly the least jealous of men. But you may try it if you like."[56] As Ellen Kay Trimberger has pointed out, the ideals of love in this period were difficult to maintain and, by 1916, Hapgood and Boyce were demoralized by their mutual jealousy over extramarital affairs.[57] In 1915, Hapgood confessed his failure to overcome jealousy over Boyce's relationship with a lover by the name of Fisk, feeling "ashamed of my conduct about him—I have not tried to cut you off from him, but I have shown too much feeling about it."[58] Boyce also lost much of the earlier enthusiastic idealism of free love relations. Referring to Hapgood's lover Lucy, Boyce explained that "I told her that no one could maintain two complete love-relations at the same time. She has lost [her husband] John's instinctive feeling for her—and hers for him—at least for the time. You and I lost ours for one another, to some extent—but I think it's clear that it isn't gone completely."[59] Bertrand and Dora also wrestled with feelings of jealousy. In December of 1927, Bertrand wrote to Dora, "As long as I know you need me I am happy. My vanity was hurt—that is the main thing in jealousy."[60] On a separate occasion, Bertrand lamented, "I wish we never landed ourselves with lovers, but now we have obligations to them + can't end things suddenly."[61] During the process of divorce negotiations in 1933, Dora reminded Bertrand of their agreement to live in a varietist marriage. Dora expressed her willingness to have welcomed Bertrand's lover Patricia Spence (known throughout her life as "Peter," as her parents had wanted a boy), and their expected child, Conrad. Dora told Bertrand that "you had the legal marriage, and the home with John and Kate [the Russells' children], and liberty for any other tie as well." The Russells and the Hapgoods exemplify how sex reformers radically reinvented the marital contract in ways that they regarded as a set of practices more consistent with love but often disturbed by feelings of jealousy.[62]

To sex reformers, jealousy was a mark of the vestiges and emotional residue of hundreds of years of conforming to patriarchal and capitalist structures of the family. Emma Goldman and Edward Carpenter situated the emergence of the nuclear family unit within the annals of evolution as an outcome of the extension of private property to the bodies of women and children. Sex reformers contended that the chasm between a male breadwinner and a female housewife created a marriage of dependency and possessiveness rather than freedom and love. For varietism to work, both husbands and wives needed to participate in both regimes of work and domesticity and thus free women from the conventional marital contract of bargaining sexual duties for economic security. For the most part, sex reformers emphasized a transformation in gender roles in terms of cultivating women's work in intellectual and professional capacities while cultivating men's involvement in domesticity and childcare. In the case of the Hapgood-Boyce and Russell marriages, Neith and Dora's professional work was important to fostering intellectual companionship as one of the conditions for love. On a night train bound for Chicago in 1904 to work for the *Evening Post*, Hapgood expressed his faith in Boyce's talents by reassuring her, "You are bound to do good work, work that will give you fame and respect, and some money."[63] As a shared activity that intellectually bonded them, Boyce expressed her love for Hapgood as an appreciation of his "instinct for work + experience—that energy in you is part of what I love!"[64] Similarly, Bertrand Russell encouraged Dora's professional work, proudly remarking that "You have already sold more copies of your book than I ever sold of any book before '*Education*.'"[65] Recognizing the importance of Dora's work, he offered to "be only too delighted to take on the domestic work now that you can earn so much money."[66] These marriage experiments in redefining gender roles to create an atmosphere more conducive to love presumed a traditional white, middle-class home in need of reform to nurture, white middle-class women's education and professional work.

While the Hapgood-Boyce and Russell marriage experiments sought to foster the intellectual and professional development of wives, they also sought the transformation of the traditional role of the husband by emphasizing male domesticity and fatherhood. Bertrand, for example, wrote to Dora in 1929 that "They [John and Kate] both felt your going, John quite as much as Kate."[67] In September of 1929 during one of Dora's absences, Bertrand reported that "the children are very flourishing" and "I took them to St. Ives + we went out in a motor boat."[68] In his reports to Dora on the children, Bertrand practiced the modern formulation of fatherhood as masculine domesticity and playmate to the children.[69] Hapgood felt an intense fatherly connection as an emotional transformation of white middle-class manhood whereby "a father loses his keenness for his male intellectual labors by being put in a position where he pays sympathetic attention to children, becomes feminized, as it were. I feel a little tendency that way myself!"[70] About ten years later, Hapgood also noted how his devotion to his children had affected his professional life. He agreed with his editor, Lincoln Steffens, that "I, for many years, had been a good mother and that that had been good for you + for the family but not for me or for my work."[71] By considering himself "a good mother," Hapgood identified the extent to which the new ethic of love in varietist marriages redrew the lines of gendered labor and thus, unsettled the ontological distinctions of the body.

Although varietism was far from a mainstream social practice, sex reformers regarded their varietist experiments as pioneering ventures leading to an alternative form of marriage among human societies in the next stage of evolution. As Stephen Brooke has shown, the Russells were part of a coterie of sex reformers who considered emotions like love to be transformative forces in building new worlds.[72] In *The Right to Be Happy*, Dora Russell indicated that "I know of nothing more likely to transform society than that men and women should love one another without stint or fear, and unashamedly yield to the physical tenderness they feel for each other and their children." As their experience of jealousy reveals, sex reformers experienced their bodies as caught in a transition phase of evolutionary development at the crossroads of an Old Morality and a New Morality. As noted previously, Hapgood embodied this transition as "A Victorian in the Modern World" or as a "Criminal Monkey" caught between Darwin's monkeys and the superhuman of the evolutionary future. Like Hapgood, Dora Russell also considered the efforts of reforming marriage as a transition period toward a future of Nietzschean supermen and women. In *The Right to Be Happy*, she commented on the imperfect trials of modern marriages in the grip of an evolutionary transition, claiming that "Our suppositious band of moderns therefore—they are not to be called super-men or women—must be ready to demonstrate by the effortless grace of their lives and the harmony between their activity and their thought that they possess a view of life adequate to conquering their environment."[73] By positioning their own varietist marriages within evolutionary time and place, sex reformers drew attention to how the lingering presence of the nonhuman in the past and the superhuman of the future spurred meaningful social and political transformations in the present. Varietist marriages highlighted sex reformers' ambivalent experience of their bodies as affectively trained in an Old Morality in tension with a New Morality that attempted to reorient that body toward love as a connection with nonhumans.

LOVE MACHINES: SEX MANUALS AND BIRTH CONTROL DEVICES IN THE 1920S

By the 1920s, sex reformers popularized new technologies for perfecting sex as an art of love. Sex reformers treated sex manuals and birth control devices as tools of love when used by middle- and upper-class married couples.[74] Whether sex reformers promoted birth control devices as tools of love or methods of population control to prevent the births of unwanted or unfit children depended on the race and class of their audience.[75] This occurred in the context of widespread late nineteenth-century fears of a global decline in the white birth rate and the degeneration of a white race.[76] To sex reformers, learning to embrace sexual energies as a source of vitality and creativity was the panacea to the looming failure of white civilization. Although sex reformers maintained that sexual instincts were natural impulses shared with animal and primal others, they developed technologies to guide, refine, and intervene in the sexual body to gauge its potential for new possibilities for sexual experience. These technologies participated in gauging human bodies for new types of feeling, moving, being, and connecting with one another to achieve love.

In addition to developing new techniques of sex, sex reformers also advocated new technologies for facilitating the practice of sex as love. Like sex manuals, sex reformers pointed out the role of birth control technologies in altering human bodies to make sex better. In the 1920s, Dora Russell defended the use of birth control technologies as the application of art and science, whereby, "Sex love is not an act of sinful indulgence only permissible to man and woman that a child may be born; it is the expression of the intimate love and comradeship of two human creatures, who will use it by mutual consent, when time and circumstances seem good to them, to create the children of their dreams."[77]

Unsurprisingly, Stopes and Sanger extended their expertise in teaching sex as marital love to encompass the best technological devices to transform and transcend sexual bodies into loving ones. A few years after Stopes published her famous marital sex manual, *Married Love*, she wrote to a number of physicians on the effectiveness of specific birth control technologies. Dr. Norman Haire, for example, corresponded with Stopes regarding the Mensinga and Matrisalus, two pessaries used in Holland.[78] They also exchanged letters concerning the gold pin method, which involved inserting a gold pin into the uterus, running the risk of inflammation and causing abortion.[79] Stopes, however, became a staunch advocate of the Pro-Race pessary, explaining to Dr. Helena Wright its practical advantages and easy use in fitting over the cervix and, if positioned properly, allowing female patients to reach it with their fingertips.[80] Dr. Janet Hawthorne, in fact, wrote to Stopes in May of 1920, drawing a specific connection between the use of the pessary

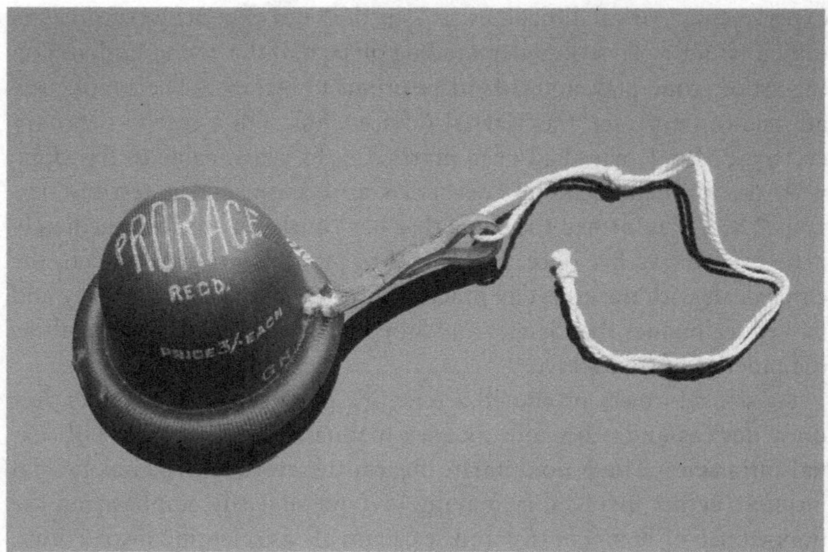

FIGURE 8. Marie Stopes promoted the Prorace pessary (England, 1915–1925) as a contraceptive that would further racial advancement by preventing "unwanted" children. Science Museum, London. Attribution 4.0 International (CC by 4.0).

and the practice of sex as love or mutual fulfillment. Hawthorne noted that her patient, a lady from Woking, would "be all right now + have some peace of mind. She wrote later asking how her husband could delay his orgasm to coincide with her own."[81]

Like Stopes, Sanger also extended her advice on sex to the available technologies for making love possible. The Birth Control Central Research Bureau (BCCRB), directed by Sanger, generated reports on the success or failure of the use of Rantos and lactic acid jelly as birth control methods. These reports specifically noted the way these technologies were intimately entangled in marital relationship dynamics and emotions. The reports between 1928 and 1930 indicate that women refused or discontinued these methods because their husbands objected and because they were "uncertain of the technique," and had a "lack of confidence" in them.[82] At Sanger's BCCRB, doctors provided patients with pessaries as well as marital sex advice and suggested techniques and ideals of sex that resonated with Stopes's and Sanger's descriptions of sex as love in their books. For example, one report of a couple's visit in 1932, noted that the wife was fitted with a pessary but failed to understand how to use it. According to the report, the couple was experiencing marital difficulties, as "she does not experience an orgasm, difficulty due to lack of understanding on part of the young husband on the art of erotic play, and correct positions to assume." The couple was advised to return to "the Marital Advice Clinic." In a case in February of 1932, Mrs. F, who had been married eight years, came to the clinic with the problem that she "never has an orgasm and is terribly nervous." Mrs. F informed the clinic that her "husband erects immediately if he even kisses her once, and then has an ejaculation." As such, the clinic dealt with the everyday practical problems of sexual intimacy and flawed techniques that Sanger and Stopes addressed in their manuals as the practice of sex as love.[83]

As sex reformers promoted a scientific practice of sex as love, they drew devices and other aids like sex manuals into the context of sexual intimacies. These nonhuman objects therefore emerged as crucial intimate actors involved in making love possible. By emphasizing the importance of birth control and sex manuals as scientific instructions, sex reformers disturbed the very naturalness of sex. The intimate engagement between sexual bodies and these new technologies for altering, managing, or transforming them raises the question of whether the technologies or the bodies themselves were engineering sex as love. Moreover, sex reformers suggested that the very capacity to manage these technologies and follow sex manuals introduced a crucial dividing line between the human and the animal. With the advent of new devices, sex reformers promoting birth control drew a distinction between sex as purely natural and refined disciplined sex, which involved applying human intelligence, culture, and invention to reshape or bend nature. It mattered whether a poor immigrant woman or a "lady" with a nervous, frigid disposition toward sex walked into the birth control clinic. In the first case, sex reformers regarded birth control technologies as a solution to the problem of over-sexed lower-class couples breeding irresponsibly, whereas in the second case, sex reformers regarded birth control technologies as devices for enabling middle-class couples to enjoy sex. Through these different framings of the purpose of birth control technologies and the marketing of sex manuals to the middle class, sex reformers created a hierarchy of sex extending from humans deemed closer to the animal to the most evolved civilized humans.

5

Romancing Evolutionary Biology

Darwinism in the Metropolis

Whether navigating bedrooms, workplaces, or the metropolis, sex reformers moved through their everyday lives reliving Darwinian dramas in the present. Neith Boyce and Hutchins Hapgood, for example, navigated New York City as affective voyeurs in a modern incarnation of a Darwinian metropolis. In June of 1898, Boyce wrote to Hapgood that "the people of the 'Quarter' who swarm about the Square day and night now are more dingy and forlorn and utterly sordidly unattractive than ever."[1] She emphasized Hapgood's enjoyment of this spectacle as an observer delighted by "the elemental and the instinctive—how you ought to revel in such a crowd of human creatures who certainly are not overburdened with ideas or complexities!"[2] Like Boyce, Hapgood identified the people of the Quarter with animals, describing them as "commonplace and filthy, bestial human beings." He noted that being "too much civilized" gave him "the power of seeing in them, or in anyone, the 'primal sympathy' for things which to refined persons have an added charm for their very primal quality."[3]

Hapgood and Boyce identified an affective difference from these allegedly "filthy, bestial beings," namely, his capacity to gaze with wonder and appreciation at the instinctive and elemental qualities of other humans who were closer to the animal. Significantly, New York City's Quarter was an immigrant enclave, home to populations deemed nonwhite at a time of rising American nativism and xenophobia. Hapgood and Boyce approached these populations as exotic, racialized others with a lower elemental and instinctive affective character that they also equated with lower intelligence or lack of "complexities." As sex reformers shaped the truths about love in the early twentieth century, these truths were inseparable from evolutionary theories about racial reproduction on an anthropological scale.

The entanglement of Darwinian evolution, sexual practices, and love has a long genealogical thread, beginning with Darwin's interest in sexual selection and mutating over time as multiple scholars in different times and places engaged with Darwin's ideas. Feminist scholars interested in disturbing the naturalness of sex have interrogated Darwinian evolution as the larger foundation for grounding sex in nature.[4] In other words, what counts as human sexual truths have been contingent upon their comparability with animal sexual practices as truths about the body prior to culture, society, technology, invention, and artifice. Feminist scholarship intersects with science studies by drawing attention to how gender and sexual norms inform the construction of evolutionary truths. While interrogating sex and nature has been a site of mutual interest for feminist and science studies scholars, the relationship between love, science, and sex has been less explored. The racial politics of the science of sex cannot be fully grasped without considering how sexology drew upon evolutionary understandings of bodies capable of perfecting sex as love.

By situating sex in an evolutionary context, sex reformers identified love as the pinnacle of sexual evolution, which not only separated the human from the animal but differentiated a superior civilized form of humanity from other humans. From 1890 to 1930, sex reformers extended the lessons of Darwin on the evolutionary significance of mate selection and reproduction to love as a practice of sex among superior human bodies informed by Darwinian ideals of racial advancement. Turning to Darwinian evolutionary theory, sex reformers highlighted the stakes of scientifically managing sex in terms of how sexual attraction, sexual intercourse, fertility control, and sexual reproduction could shape the course of evolution. Sex reformers located the art of love on an evolutionary platform far above animal sex, promiscuous sex, and sex solely for procreative purposes. Grounding love in evolutionary science, sex reformers redefined the racial, class, and sexual differences across the evolutionary spectrum of bodies in terms of the affective potential of those bodies to experience love. By casting love within an evolutionary schema, sex reformers sharpened and refined the meaning of the human in relation to love and sex while radically expanding the margins of the nonhuman.

While the previous chapter focused on the affective potential of two bodies to achieve love at a precise moment, this chapter shows how evolutionary time was an implicit and crucial backdrop to the potential of what these bodies might feel. The shadows of Darwinism and ancestral history hung over these bodies in the intimate moments of mastering techniques of sex as love. Sex reformers recalibrated the anthropological theory of the rise of humans through the use of tools by reinterpreting the modern tools as birth control and sex manuals mastered by tool users with superior capacities for love. As historians and science studies scholars have shown, the rise of Darwinism marked an important development in emerging scientific justifications for racism whereby the exclusion of non-white populations from social and political power could be explained by a failure to evolve or, perhaps worse, degenerate.[5] This chapter focuses on how sex reformers reconfigured love in relation to new scientific thinking on race, extending scientific racism to emotional capacities. In grappling with the significance of this intersection of science, love, and race, there is an important disciplinary convergence across history, feminism, and science studies where the politics of knowledge met the politics of love.

DARWINIAN AFFECT: BIRDS, LOVE, AND EVOLUTION

Feminist science studies draws attention to the importance of how evolution has informed the contemporary experience of women's bodies.[6] The historical emergence of Darwinism, from its inception to the initial rise of its popularity, is significant to consider as a genealogical thread to our present grappling with what counts as knowledge of women's bodies. One advantage to this close historical look at the intersection of Darwinism and the experience of women's bodies is to explore the very moment at which evolutionary truths formed and how these truths intersected with sexual politics. Rather than reflect on how Darwinism as a theory might be linked to contemporary sexism or, alternatively, how Darwinism might be reworked or reinvented for feminist purposes, here the question is about what kinds of conditions and culture informed Charles Darwin's scientific inquiries, observations, questions, and eventual formation of evolutionary theory.[7] By situating Charles Darwin in the social and political context of his research and writing, it is possible to consider how Darwinism was made out of multiple scientific, social, political, economic, and cultural currents, notably sexual science and sex reform.[8]

As sex reformers turned to the subject of love in the late nineteenth century, they situated love in evolutionary narratives of animal courtship, mate selection, reproduction, and emotions. By the late nineteenth century, Darwinism, while debated, had begun to shape the intellectual imagination, scientific methods, and cultural practices of both American and British society. Although Charles Darwin had published the *Origin of Species* in 1859, *On the Descent of Man* in 1871, and *The Emotions of Man and Animals* in 1873, his works continued to profoundly inform sex reformers' practices of love well into the twentieth century. Darwin is typically known for his theory of natural selection, which traces a struggle for existence among species with those who adapt to environmental conditions and reproduce as the survivors. Yet, Darwin also devoted considerable attention to aspects of feeling in the form of attraction, aesthetics, romance, and emotions.[9] Sex reformers seized on the affective dimensions of Darwin's works, which noted that feelings, just like intelligence and physical bodies, were subject to the vicissitudes of evolutionary processes.

While the scientific advances in evolutionary theories shaped sex reform, it was also the case that cultural practices, norms, and debates concerning sex shaped science. In spite of sex reformers' reliance on Charles Darwin's insights into evolution, his personal life was shaped by conservative Victorian moral codes that underpinned the traditional gendered roles of the Darwin household. Charles Darwin, in fact, distanced himself from his grandfather Erasmus Darwin's libertarian sexual ethics, particularly Erasmus's reputation for philandering. In many ways, sex reformers' turn to Darwinism was ironic given Darwin's concerns with respectability, particularly his fears of being associated with social radicals. In his political beliefs, Charles Darwin supported the Whig Party's philosophies, which were consistent with his views of nature as ruthless competition and survival based on individual merit. At the time, Charles Darwin supported a Whig Poor Law Amendment to compel the poor to compete for jobs rather than attain government assistance. Conservative in his sexual politics, Charles Darwin also refused to testify at the notorious Bradlaugh-Besant trial in 1873; a trial venerated by sex reformers for Charles Bradlaugh and Annie Besant's stand against obscenity legislation that included contraceptive information. Furthermore, Darwin's marriage to his first cousin, Emma Wedgwood, was far from the marital ideal envisioned by sex reformers. Emma and Charles had ten children in a household that operated along the Victorian patriarchal lines of Emma's role as caregiver and homemaker rather than intellectual companion. Darwin discouraged Emma from reading scientific works and generally judged women's mental capacity as inferior to men's.[10]

Although more conservative than his grandfather in sexual morals, Charles Darwin reflected on the radicalism of his own work in relation to Erasmus's reputation as a freethinker in religion and writer on transmutation in *Zoonomia*. As Darwin biographers Adrian Desmond and James Moore have contended, "[Charles] Darwin's non-human orientation was a total departure from radical wisdom, let alone religious conviction."[11] This nonhuman orientation persisted in various phases throughout Darwin's life, shifting from obsessions with barnacles to pigeon breeding to orchids to worms. Between the 1860s and 1880s, Darwin's works contributed to an intellectual and political climate that turned attention to the significance of sex in the past, present, and future. Darwin brought humans and nonhumans into greater intimacies, particularly through a kinship in shared capacities for feeling, which made it possible for animal inheritance to be felt within human bodies even while those bodies surpassed their former animalized physiques. Darwin's legacy to sex reform was the profound importance he attributed to sexual reproduction and sexual attraction in the making of the world.

Although Darwin's turn to nonhuman kinship was radical for the period, it was underpinned by concerns for maintaining Victorian respectability and racial supremacy. Darwin's racial investments in British imperial whiteness informed his theory of evolution when, during his S.S. *Beagle* voyage, he took observations of native Fuegians as evidence of animal ancestry.[12] In fact, Darwin preferred to align his ancestry with animals rather than those he deemed to be "savages" or "barbarians."[13] Darwin's own sense of racial superiority led him to presume that tribal societies were much closer to the nonhuman than to "civilized" British subjects. As such, Darwin also provided a foundation for the late nineteenth- and early twentieth-century shaping of the whiteness of love.

Darwin's personal connections to multiple strands of "sex reform" included his relationship with his cousin, Sir Francis Galton. Galton became known as the father of eugenics, also known as the science of better breeding, which informed sex reformers' practices of love. Darwin was fascinated by Galton's essay "Hereditary Talent and Character," which insisted that the essential character of particular races and classes was defined by inherited mental and moral traits.[14] Like sex reformers, Darwin's concerns with sexual reproduction and evolution were influenced by Thomas Malthus's gloomy predictions that population would outstrip food supply. Through a Malthusian perspective, Darwin observed the significance of eugenics in its concerns for the unchecked reproduction of the "unfit," namely, the lower classes and non-white colonized subjects.[15] Like Galton, Darwin was deeply concerned about the selection of mates, inheritance, and the breeding of fitter offspring. Darwin's inquiries into the mysteries of inheritance were informed by personal concerns over the potentially disastrous effects of inbreeding, particularly his own marriage to his cousin. Yet Darwin, the gentleman son of a wealthy physician, rationalized that his economic position advantaged his family in the struggle for existence in modern British society.[16]

In *On the Descent of Man*, where Darwin first addressed human evolution, he introduced romantic evolutions in the form of sexual selection. Darwinian eroticism manifested in Darwin's focus on courtship antics, beauty, and secondary sexual characters that would lead to sexual attraction and the evolutionary reproduction of the species. It was Darwin's story of the birds' courtship antics that later caught the attention of early twentieth-century sex reformers, scientists, eugenicists, and birth controllers. Birds found their way into discussions of perfecting sex in treatises, articles, and publications in periodicals such as the *Eugenics Review*. In *On the Descent of Man*, Darwin noted the elaborate rituals of the birds for which "courtship is, in many instances, a prolonged affair." He detailed both the fighting among male birds for the females and the ornamental bodies of the males to attract the females. Male birds displayed their beauty in "lengthened feathers" and the beak and skin near the head, which were "gorgeously coloured." Darwin insisted that pugnacity and the amorous ornamentation of male birds were important to bird courtship. Not only did the breeding season involve male birds decked out in their most elaborate colors but "the season of love is that of battle." However, Darwin noted that female birds did not always choose the victorious males.[17]

In addition to the ornamentation of wattles, protuberances, plumes, combs, and other parts of the body, male birds also elicited female attraction through a musky odor, songs, and dancing. Songs, too, specifically occurred as part of mating rituals: "The true song, however, of most birds and various strange cries are chiefly uttered during the breeding-season; and serve as a charm, or merely as a call-note to another sex." Darwin concluded that "nearly the same emotions but much weaker and less complex are probably felt by birds when the male pours forth his full volume of song, in rivalry with other males, for the sake of captivating the female. Love is still the commonest theme of our own songs."[18] In doing so, Darwin declared an emotional connection yet a fundamental difference in quality, as earlier traces of love in animals became more complex and stronger as love evolved to "our own songs." These distinctions were important for suggesting varying degrees or capacities for love for different bodies tied to different stages of evolution.[19]

Darwin's *On the Descent of Man* coupled with *On the Expression of Emotions in Man and Animals* in 1873 provided a crucial scientific foundation for sex reformers to configure love as a category for hierarchically sorting out bodies. In 1873, however, the stakes of discussing love as evolution were different for Darwin than they were for sex reformers by the 1890s.[20] For one thing, Darwin did not devote extensive attention to love in *On the Expression of Emotions in Man and Animals*. In terms of feelings equated with civilization, Darwin tended to emphasize sympathy and blushing. Contrary to sex reformers, Darwin's main objective was to show early traces of emotions in human ancestors. When he discussed love, Darwin focused on earlier forms or possible animal origins of love, such as tracing the desire to touch a beloved to maternal love in female animals nursing their young. He insisted that "we probably owe this desire to inherited habit, in association with the nursing and tending of our children, and with the mutual caresses of lovers." Darwin was strangely silent on the subject of romantic love in his 1873 work. In a chapter devoted to positive feelings of joy, love, and "tender feelings," Darwin tracked physical expressions of kissing and touching as ways of capturing earlier forms of love. According to Darwin, "with the lower animals we see the same principle of pleasure derived from contact in association with love." Darwin noted examples of animal expressions of love in cats and dogs that rubbed against their masters or mistresses and monkeys that fondled each other at the Zoological Gardens. It was physical contact linked with expressions of love that Darwin highlighted as the possible bridge for connecting animal and human love.[21]

For sex reformers, Darwin's work not only implied that love changed over time but that it had different forms, degrees, levels of intensity, and complexity contingent on stages of evolution. As sex reformers turned to Darwin's grounding of love in evolution, they framed practices of the highest form of love as the affective potential of only the most evolved eugenically fit bodies. Darwin's own works, however, bore traces of Galtonian notions of manipulating forces of love and attraction toward racial advancement. In a chilly precursor to eugenic debates on marriage, Darwin suggested that "weaker and inferior members of society [should] not [be] marrying so freely as the sound."[22] On the subject of sympathy and philanthropy, Darwin warned that "care wrongly directed, leads to the degeneration of a domestic race, but excepting in the case of man himself, hardly any one is so ignorant as to allow his worst animals to breed."[23] Although Darwin's works emphasized degrees of commonality or traces of love, eugenicists would invoke evolution to redefine love as a mark of racial superiority.

DARWINIAN NARRATIVES OF SEX REFORM AND THE EVOLUTION OF MODERN LOVE

Sex reformers' efforts to revolutionize love by grounding it in a Darwinian science of sex offers an important case study in the rearticulations of scientific truths in response to cultural and political exigencies at a specific moment in time. By grounding love in science, sex reformers entangled the evolution of love with eugenics as a racial science of breeding the fittest populations and weeding out the unfit. Shaped by prevailing fears over high birthrates in immigrant communities and colonized countries, sex reformers construed love as sex practiced according to eugenic principles whereby only the offspring of racially superior parents could be counted as wanted, planned, and loved children. Situating love as a uniquely evolutionary product in highly "civilized" bodies, sex reformers rendered "natural" and "artificial" nonhumans complicit in class, racial, and sexual politics. Sex reformers' re-narration of evolutionary progress as a story of the transformation from promiscuous sex to a science of sex as love is a cautionary tale of how the promises and seductions of science can consolidate, uphold, and facilitate racial, colonial, class, and gender inequalities. In their reconfigurations of love, sex reformers entangled elements of Darwinian sexual selection with eugenics to sanction, advance, and cultivate white romances and racial reproduction with dire consequences for nonhumans and allegedly less evolved humans as resources and raw materials for the production of love.

Between the 1890s and 1920s, sex reformers turned to Darwin's works for mounting a compelling case for the "natural" cultivation of sexual instincts as part of nonhuman kinship. Situating love within an evolutionary process, sex reformers argued that the practice of sex could evolve and become civilized through a series of techniques for mutual pleasure and attentiveness to one's partner to achieve love. By the 1920s, sex manuals that proliferated across Britain and the United States promised instructions in sex as much as love, which implicitly owed a debt to Darwinism for espousing the naturalness of sexual instincts. Radical intellectuals such as Edward Carpenter, Havelock Ellis, Emma Goldman, and Margaret Sanger invoked Darwinism to ground their practices of love in science. What historian Laura Doan has discussed as Edward Carpenter's "utopian evolutionary theories" toward a higher love ultimately relied on the nonhuman not only as a beginning point of sexual passions but as a dangerous potential for degeneration.[24] Similarly, Havelock Ellis, Emma Goldman, and Margaret Sanger situated love as a practice of eugenic reproduction that identified love with strategic mating for the purpose of securing the reproductive future of white middle- and upper-class bodies.

In their specific formulation of modern love, sex reformers situated scientific practices of love in Darwinian evolutionary narratives, extending Darwin's concepts of mate selection and reproductive survival to eugenics as a science of racial reproduction. For sex reformers, there was a powerful linkage between Darwinism and eugenics, namely, eugenics as a modern version of Darwinism with more sophisticated tactics of mate selection. In his 1896 publication *Love's Coming-of-Age*, Carpenter attributed certain capacities of love to "the animal and lower human world—and wherever the creature is incapable of realising the perfect love (which is indeed able to transform it into a god)—Nature in the purely physical instincts does the next best thing, that is, she effects a corporeal union and so generates another creature." Carpenter's work therefore noted that animal and lower human worlds had a lower threshold of affective potential, limited to feelings of lust and sexual passion but incapable of "perfect love." Referring to "nature in her slow evolutions," Carpenter pointed to gradations of emotional bodies to the eventual stage of "the evolution of the human element in love."[25] About twenty years later, Havelock Ellis told a similar evolutionary tale of love in his 1917 *Objects of Marriage*, observing that love "is found, it is true, among some lower races, and it appears that some tribes possess a word for the joy of love in a purely psychic sense. But even among European races the evolution was late."[26] Like Carpenter, Ellis told an evolutionary tale of modern practices of love whereby a "human" experience of love had to be qualified as excluding certain kinds of humans, particularly lower races deemed closer to the animal.

Turning attention to love as modern evolutionary drama of reproductive struggle, sex reformers found common ground with prominent eugenicists who also drew connections between Darwinism, love, and eugenics. In the *Eugenics Review*, British and American authors addressed the subject of love in Darwinian terms as the superior emotional capacity of eugenic heterosexual bodies, grounding love in racial reproduction. American psychologist, J. W. Slaughter, turned to questions of beauty, attraction, and love. In "Selection in Marriage," Slaughter advocated eugenic mate selection as an "integral part of the psychology of love." In the case of human reproduction, Slaughter claimed, "That which renders man the agent of selection is his superior economic position." Slaughter suggested that modern human courtship could learn from female birds as the agents of selection who chose from ornamental male birds. For Slaughter, this practice was instructive in highlighting the primacy of female control over reproducing the future race.[27] In another issue of the *Eugenics Review*, British journalist Caleb Saleeby's "The Psychology of Parenthood" addressed the "parental instinct" as the eugenic basis of love that would inform mate selection, romantic love, and marriage in anticipation of the traits of future offspring. Saleeby, however, qualified who or what was capable of love in the context of eugenics and evolution, claiming that "except in utterly degraded persons, the object of the feelings which are associated with the racial instinct becomes the object of the feelings which are associated with the parental instinct. The object of the emotion of sex becomes also the object of tender emotion. Thus, 'love,' in its lower sense, becomes exalted by Love in the noble sense."[28] By situating love in a modern evolutionary narrative, eugenicists and sex reformers found common ground in addressing love as not only uniquely human but a capacity of those humans occupying the highest echelons of modern civilization, namely, white educated bodies of leading imperial nations.

Far from an innocent benign story about emotional connections to nonhumans, sex reformers seized on Darwinian narratives to inform constructions of love as eugenic mating whereby the experience of love became a crucial dividing line between the fit and the unfit, the human and the less than human, and wanted as opposed to unwanted babies. In Britain and the United States, eugenics organizations developed in tandem with the sex reform movement. The first American national eugenics organization, American Breeders Association, was founded in 1903 followed by the formation of the American Eugenics Society in 1922. In Britain, the Eugenics Education Society formed in 1907. The periodical, the *Eugenics Review* provided eugenicists with an international forum that carried articles by British and American eugenicists on the subject of love and marriage. With the rise of the eugenics movement from the 1880s to the 1920s, sex reformers invoked Darwinism through the lens of contemporary anxieties over the present, particularly the uncertainty of the future in light of proximities to the animal.[29] As sex reformers' fears turned to emotional "atavism" in terms of degeneration into animalistic lust, hypersexuality, and primal passions, they invested their hopes in eugenics by advocating careful mate selection and sex as an expression of love.

Through their entanglements of love with the racial reproduction of a future race, sex reformers devoted crucial attention to the importance of women's bodies and their sexual choices. Ellis and Carpenter's connections to birth control advocates in both the United States and Britain exemplify a growing emphasis on love as vested in the power of women's reproductive bodies and choices. In a letter to Carpenter, dated May 16, 1920, Ellis advocated "intelligent eugenics, working through birth control, as the only now possible way of getting towards that high natural level that you aim at."[30] By referring to this "high natural level," Ellis drew on a prominent theme of birth control advocates who endorsed birth control and, often eugenics, as not simply a mechanical planning for physical bodies but as a tool of love that emotionally invested their racial projects. Ellis promoted birth control in the *Eugenics Review* to "cut off the supply of the unfortunate and to diminish steadily the output of incapables." In "Birth Control and Eugenics," Ellis advocated birth control as a more practical solution to curtailing the births of the unfit in comparison with Francis Galton's claims to prevent procreation by banning dysgenic marriages.[31] In doing so, Ellis insisted on the separation of sex from marriage and procreation. Ellis's advocacy of the joint application of "intelligent eugenics" and "birth control" to prevent the births of unfit children specifically excluded love from the practice of dysgenic as opposed to eugenic marriages and the births of unfit as opposed to fit children. As sex reformers invoked the importance of women's bodies, they differentiated among birth control for the purpose of love in "civilized" bodies of higher classes and higher races as opposed to birth control in the context of promiscuous sex to curtail reproduction among lower classes and lower races.

Led by prominent advocates of sex reform, the birth control movement brought connections between love and eugenics into focus as a critical underlying subtext in managing women's reproductive bodies. Margaret Sanger, for example, began to promote birth control as a tool for both sexual happiness and racial improvement. Sanger's sympathies with eugenics are evoked in her distinction between birth control as the enhancement of love for young professional couples and birth control to prevent the misery of working-class mothers with sexually demanding husbands in loveless homes with unwanted children. Sanger's career as a nurse in the Lower East Side of New York City exposed her to the frequent childbirths of poor immigrant women. In her autobiography, Sanger specifically noted that the case of Jewish immigrant Sadie Sachs's death after a second abortion inspired her birth control activism partly out of the sense of helplessness and guilt at being unable to provide Sadie with birth control instruction when they first met.[32] Sanger's particular concern with the fecundity of poor women informed her choice of the Brownsville district in New York City as the site of her first birth control clinic in 1916. Later expanding her birth control activism on a global scale, Sanger visited East Asia in 1922 and India in 1934.

In addition to Sanger's birth control activism, she also widely published works that drew specific connections between eugenics and birth control in the different objectives of birth control for white middle-class women in contrast to working-class women. In 1922, Sanger's *The Pivot of Civilization* addressed birth control as a solution to the problem of undisciplined sexual instincts among a laboring population "cheated by their desires and ignorance into unrestrained and uncontrolled fertility."[33] Instead of exalting birth control as necessary to love and intimacy, she suggested birth control as way to prevent pregnancy among women having too much sex and too many children.[34] For working-class women, Sanger did not frame the problem as one of bourgeois ladylike repression or frigidity. For Sanger, birth control entailed achieving the goals of positive eugenics, by encouraging healthy, white, middle-class couples to express their sexual instincts to reproduce a better race, and negative eugenics, by preventing the reproduction of allegedly unfit children.

At the intersections of birth control and eugenics, sex reformers situated women's bodies and their capacities for love in the context of early twentieth-century feminist as well as racial politics. From Goldman's revival of primal passions to the future eugenic mother, she situated love's stakes within evolutionary narratives.[35] Goldman shared the concerns of Sanger, Ellis, and Carpenter about the reproduction of the race and, like them, she regarded birth control as a technology of love that ensured the births of wanted children. Goldman published a pamphlet, *Why and How the Poor Should Not Have So Many Children*, which grounded birth control in eugenics, and in "Marriage and Love" she connected marriage, love, and controlled reproduction through the figure of the "woman [who] no longer wants to be a party to the production of a race of sickly, feeble, decrepit, wretched human beings."

This woman, according to Goldman, "desires fewer and better children, begotten and reared in love and through free choice; not by compulsion, as marriage imposes."[36] As she specified this connection between love and reproduction, Goldman entered into the fray of a politics of love shaped by eugenic practices.[37]

When sex reformers told evolutionary tales, they ascribed a distinctive emotional character to women deemed to be at the higher end of the evolutionary spectrum. In these narratives, sex reformers romanticized eugenics as they equated love with socially and economically privileged female bodies deemed fit for reproducing the future race. Contrary to the problem of too much sex and too many pregnancies among lower-class women, sex reformers told the story of love in terms of the need to awaken sexual desires in respectable women whose marriages were suffering from their sexual reticence, coldness, and frigidity. In striking contrast to her characterization of poor women overburdened by sexual demands, Goldman described a very different condition for women who were targets of the sex reform campaign to embrace sexual freedom and scientifically practice sex as love. Goldman's "Marriage and Love," published in 1916, addressed women who needed to cultivate sexual pleasure as love in the following terms: "a healthy, grown woman, full of life and passion, must deny nature's demand, must subdue her most intense craving, undermine her health and break her spirit, must stunt her vision, abstain from the depth and glory of sex experience until a 'good' man comes along to take her unto himself as a wife." For Goldman, this state of marriage requiring woman to suppress "her spirit" marked the "factor of marriage which differentiates it from love."[38] In the *Love Rights of Woman*, Ellis constructed a similar evolutionary tale of love and eugenics by considering women's "love rights" in terms of a new "biological order of the world." Ellis specifically addressed the 'love rights' of only certain types of valued female bodies, namely, the frigid and unresponsive female body "civilized" by oppressive religious morality.[39] Ellis wrote:

> It is true that women whose instincts are not perverted at the roots do not desire to be cold. Far from it. But to dispel that coldness the right atmosphere is needed, and the insight and skill of the right man. In the erotic sphere woman asks nothing better of a man than to be lifted above her coldness, to the higher plane where there is reciprocal interest and mutual joy in the act of love. There-in her silent demand is one with Nature's. For the biological order of the world involves those claims which, in the human range, are the love rights of women.[40]

Ellis's evolutionary narrative of love signifies an important historical moment when sex reformers situated the experience of love within biological limits, racial hierarchies, and the science of sex.[41] By advocating that women cultivate sexual desires as part of broader objectives in making eugenic mate choices, sex reformers specifically sought to nurture the sexual freedom and empowerment of future white middle-class mothers.

Sex reformers' evolutionary narratives on the rights of women to sexual pleasure formed a specific strand of feminism among divergent and contesting early twentieth-century feminist positions.[42] These rights to sexual pleasure, however, must be considered in light of what Louise Michele Newman has addressed as "white women's rights," which presumed a specific white middle-class existence as the starting point for improving women's social and political influence. Sex reformers engaged with and challenged a discourse of white women's rights that manifested in suffragism and the social purity movement as an argument for women's social and political rights on the basis of their chastity, moral influence, and compassion. While Ellis and other feminist sex reformers told evolutionary tales of the evolving cultivation of women's sexual instincts, other feminists, like Charlotte Perkins Gilman, regarded evolution in terms of rendering sex less important to women's place in society.[43] Some historians have, in fact, dismissed these New Feminists as anti-feminists who reinforced a patriarchal advantage of male sexual access to women.[44] This, however, fails to consider the importance of an early twentieth-century feminist critique of sexual pleasure as a male entitlement to certain affective experiences. At the time, New Feminists asserted that greater sexual expression departed from earlier Victorian free lovers such as Victoria Woodhull, Moses Harmon, and Angela and Ezra Heywood, who were part of a tradition of free love that espoused the rights of women to refuse sex as opposed to their rights to enjoy sex.[45] Drawing particular attention to women's sexual experience and reproductive bodies, sex reformers also advocated the eugenic importance of white women's sexuality to evolutionary destiny.

Sex reformers' new ethic of love as a disciplined scientific practice of sex was informed by a mélange of socialist, feminist, and eugenic principles for shaping the future of civilization. For sex reformers, a new world based on love entailed an upheaval of traditional gender relations that were inextricably tied to capitalist investments in private property and sexual as much as economic ownership. In *Love's Coming-of-Age*, Carpenter told an evolutionary story of the white middle-class family that emerged through the emotions of the male's "greed of Private Property" and overwhelming "sex-passion." In Carpenter's framing of evolution, affects ranging from impulses to emotional states underpinned the capitalist and patriarchal order of the family. According to Carpenter, possessive impulses leading to private property "rose and spread with a kind of contagion over the advancing races of mankind, the human Male, bitten by it, not only claimed possession of everything he could lay his hands upon, but ended by enslaving and appropriating his own mate." Carpenter concluded that such a family arrangement reduced woman to "a mere chattel, a slave, and a plaything." He worried that Man had alienated love from these movements toward civilization.[46] As a pivotal work to shaping the sex reform movement, Carpenter's *Love's Coming-of-Age* put both gender as well as class relations into anthropological perspective. In doing so, however, Carpenter highlighted the white middle-class family as the target for sex reformers' efforts to bring sexual pleasure, love, and vigor to the bodies bearing the burden of civilization.

Seizing on the importance of furthering reproduction for those women at the highest stage of modern evolutionary progress, Carpenter addressed the significance of returning to a female-driven mate selection process resembling Darwin's narrative of bird courtship. He challenged the current condition of contemporary white middle-class families based on "a kind of false sexual selection" that robbed women of the reproductive agency of selecting males on the basis of the health of future offspring. As a sex reformer, Carpenter saw the emphasis on women's sexual modesty as particularly harmful for creating "the civilised girl [who] is led to the 'altar' often in uttermost ignorance." Like other feminists and sex reformers, Carpenter saw important possibilities for women's sexual expression in stories of the nonhuman "natural" world but firmly identified love as an evolutionary achievement of white middle-class couples affectively advancing from stages of greed and sex-passion to a potential higher stage of love.[47]

Associating love with a carefully orchestrated heterosexual performance that only resulted in wanted or loved children, sex reformers also excluded the possibility of love arising from any perverse nonnormative desires. As historians of eugenics have shown, in Britain and the United States, eugenics took hold as a powerful "new morality" that governed and politicized heterosexual romantic relationships.[48] Nancy Ordover's *American Eugenics* specifically noted how eugenics targeted homosexual, lesbian, and other nonnormative sexual orientations as signs of racial unfitness that should be strategically weeded out of future populations.[49] Historian Jennifer Terry specifically notes that this period witnessed intense research among "scientific sex reformers" who, "through the scientific exploration of nonreproductive sexual desires and practices, [constructed] a modern idealized reproductive family," defined in opposition to both Victorian repression and sexual perversity.[50] In this period, sex reformers shaped an important emotional subtext of sex as love that excluded and dehumanized other forms of sexual practices as unnatural, perverse, and lustful passions.

While sex reformers raised awareness of the plethora and diversity of sexual desires and practices, they formulated love as an exclusively heterosexual practice of sex and thus relegated bodies drawn to sexual perversions as less evolved. Although Edward Carpenter wrote of "homogenic love," he refused to associate homosexual practices with this love and, instead, emphasized that "the relation is not distinctively sexual at all, tho' it may be said to be physical in the sense of embrace + endearment." Carpenter privileged heterosexual sex when discussing love as an expression of sex, he noted that "in the homosexual love—whether between man + man or between woman + woman—the physical side, from the very nature of the case, can never find expression so freely + perfectly as in the ordinary heterosexual love." Moreover, Carpenter positioned homogenic and heterosexual love within an evolutionary schema, insisting that in all cases "sensuality apart from love is degrading + something less than human."[51] Although many sex reformers were considered advocates for ending the persecution of homosexuality, their constructions of love continued to marginalize bodies with desires falling outside of normative heterosexuality.

Sex reformers' heterosexualization of love occurred in the context of privileging the critical importance of eugenic mate selection and women's reproductive bodies for securing the future of white civilization. This marks a significant historical episode in a genealogy of love as an early instance of a trajectory that Lee Edelman has described as "reproductive futurism" with heterosexuality privileged through the association of the future with reproducing the next generation.[52] This "reproductive futurism" has shaped scientific understanding of nonhuman practices in evolutionary theory that has, since Darwin, ignored the diversity of sexual practices in nonhuman communities.[53] Like Carpenter, Emma Goldman's sex reform activities included her defense of homosexuality against state persecution, but her writings on love focused on heterosexual sex as the mutual fulfillment of man and woman. Historian

Terence Kissack's *Free Comrades* emphasizes Emma Goldman as part of a coterie of Greenwich Village radicals who promoted new sexological literature to advocate an end to the persecution of homosexuality.[54] Yet, Kissack's evidence suggests that these radicals emphasized tolerance for homosexuality but did not promote homosexual practices or techniques as love. Goldman, in fact, had a same-sex relationship with Almeda Sperry but distanced herself from associations with Sperry. Moreover, Goldman was deeply disturbed to find that French radical Louise Michele of the 1871 Paris Commune had been placed in sex reformer Magnus Hirschfeld's collection of homosexuals. Goldman wrote "I am so anxious that Louise Michel should be saved the unfounded charge of Homo-sexuality."[55] Much of Goldman's work in sex reform activism involved the advocacy of sex as creative energy for reproducing a new race of wanted children; thus, diminishing the importance of homosexuality to "civilization." While sex reformers such as Carpenter, Ellis, and Goldman were well known for acknowledging the diversity of sexual desires and the freedom to pursue those desires, the category of love held a very particular status of racial, heterosexual, and class privilege.

"Varietist" experiments were part of the privileged position of sexual freedom for couples deemed to be at the forefront of evolutionary advancement as the architects of a new evolutionary future. While sex reformers turned to varietist marriage as new social experiments to foster love, they engaged in these new trials of intimacy through an anthropological lens and consciousness of being at the apex of modern evolutionary progress. Havelock Ellis, for example, drew on Darwinian tales of bird courtship in addition to the anthropological work of his friend, Bronislaw Malinowski, which put modern social conditions into a modern evolutionary perspective. At the time of the rise of the sex reform movement, Malinowski and Edward Westermarck had published popular works on sexual customs in an anthropological context.[56] Ellis developed his knowledge of love, marriage, and sex through his relationships with Olive Schreiner and his wife Edith Lees. Ellis and each of these women believed in reforming marriage along the lines of love, which entailed sexual freedom to pursue affairs beyond marriage and the treatment of both partners as individuals rather than property.[57]

Although Olive Schreiner was Ellis's first love relationship, it was his marriage to Edith Lees that showed the complex negotiations and emotional challenges in applying abstract ideals of love, mutual understanding, and sex to a new radical form of marriage. Ellis met Edith Lees in 1890 when she was working as a secretary for the Fellowship of New

FIGURE 9. Edith Lees and Havelock Ellis at the time of their involvement in free love experiments. Photograph dated prior to 1916. Unknown author and unknown source. Image is in the public domain.

Life. When Ellis married Lees, they decided to experiment with a new form of marriage by living in separate residences for part of the year and permitting affairs beyond the marriage. While it has been debated whether Ellis knew of Edith's lesbianism upon marriage, she soon told him about her lover, Claire.[58] Havelock and Edith's marriage took a similar pattern to other sex reformers' experiments with varietism, even though sex played a small part in what they considered to be a passionate loving relationship.[59] Many of the characteristic features of varietist marriage experiments were present in the Havelock Ellis/Edith Lees marriage: namely, the open discussion of lovers, the efforts to overcome jealous feelings, and the insistence that their lovers should not disrupt their household and commitment to one another. Ellis's varietist practices must be situated in the broader context of a new ethic of love that sex reformers considered as the modern evolutionary progress of women's love rights, eugenics, and equality in marriage.

Although Carpenter also shared a feminist vision of more egalitarian sexual relations between men and women as the direction for the future course of evolution, his own varietist practices occurred among male lovers outside of the context of marriage and heterosexual sex. Carpenter began writing on love and sex in the 1890s and, while he influenced many American Greenwich Village bohemians, he was not on good terms with the Bloomsbury Group, with the exception of artist Roger Fry.[60] Carpenter practiced living the simple life at his commune, Millthorpe, which he created as an oasis outside of "modern time" and normative codes, where he became a market gardener, wore sandals, and built a long-term romantic relationship with George Merrill. Carpenter's international notoriety occurred in tandem with the growth of the sex reform movement from 1900 to 1919. As biographer Sheila Rowbotham notes, Carpenter considered sex to be at the root of his varied projects of social activism in terms of change through liberating human feelings.[61] Yet, for Carpenter, it was more precisely a scientific and political practice of sex as love that would be socially transformative. According to Rowbotham, Carpenter was "inclined to the view that structures of feeling peculiar to different races were passed on" and held England at the center of a humanitarian world order. In other words, Carpenter's practices of love and sex were informed by the prevailing racial politics of eugenics, which hierarchized bodies along racial lines of intelligence, physical fitness, beauty, and emotional maturity. By projecting modern practices of love as the evolutionary future of humanity, Carpenter identified with a common narrative of love as the capability of a "civilized" body.

Carpenter's *Love's Coming-of-Age* shows how his work mirrored the entanglement of socialism, feminism, and evolutionary theory in his own life and practices. Like a number of other sex reformers, Edward Carpenter became familiar with Darwinian theories of evolution early on in his life. From 1844 until his death in 1929, Carpenter witnessed the controversies surrounding the publication of Darwin's works, the first phase of the free love movement spanning the 1830s to the 1880s, and the rise of the sex reform movement from the 1890s to the 1920s. He was influenced by American poet Walt Whitman's erotic expressions of love between men. In 1877, when Carpenter met Whitman, he was particularly impressed by Whitman's relationships with working-class men. Throughout his life, Carpenter was attracted to working class men, a common cross-class appeal, which historians of homosexuality have explained as the appeal of less restrictive codes of sexual morality among the working class.[62] In the 1880s, Carpenter became actively involved in socialism. He was a member of the Fellowship of New Life, which split the socialist movement and its competing philosophies between Fabian Socialists who regarded socialism primarily in economic terms and New Lifers who regarded socialism as a blueprint for an alternative way of life, with the body as a site of reform through simpler diets, physical labor, and freer sexual relations.[63]

Ellis and Carpenter, both proponents of free love, had direct connections to sex reformers in the United States who also identified love with radical transformations in gender as well as economic relations. Emma Goldman, an anarchist-feminist as well as free lover, exemplified the entanglement of socialism and feminism in an evolutionary vision of the future of motherhood. Ellis, in fact, corresponded with Emma Goldman, who emigrated from Kovno in the Russian Empire to the United States in 1885. One of Goldman's biographers has claimed that she was likely deported to Russia in 1919 and exiled from the United States as much for her sexual radicalism as for her militant labor politics.[64] When Goldman first moved to New York City, she primarily associated with Jewish, German, and Russian labor radicals, notably Alexander Berkman, Goldman's lifelong best friend.[65] In the 1910s, Goldman found a receptive and encouraging audience for her sex radicalism among Greenwich Village bohemians, a privileged set of young professional men and women. According to Goldman, marriage amounted to little more than legalized and church-sanctioned prostitution, a contract whereby the husband owed the wife financial support and the wife owed him sexual services. In one essay, Goldman regarded the preparation of women for marriage as "the mute beast fattened for the slaughter." For Goldman, love should be privileged as the only binding tie in a marriage. She challenged the principle of monogamy by claiming that women as well as men could be "varietist" in being attracted to a variety of partners to meet their sexual needs.[66] She was among the earliest advocates of birth control in the United States, preceding Margaret Sanger who opened the first American birth control clinic in 1916. In 1895, Goldman attended one of Freud's lectures in Vienna Austria. Goldman also visited Edward Carpenter's Millthorpe commune in England. She had read both Carpenter's *Love's Coming-of-Age* and Havelock Ellis's

1897 work on *Studies in Psychology of Sex*. Goldman was also familiar with Darwinian evolutionary theory and embraced Peter Kropotkin's critique of Darwin that evolution should not be based on individualistic competition but cooperation and mutual aid. This amounted to a socialist rereading of Darwin.[67] As such, this period witnessed important convergences between science, sex reform, love, and politics that often mutually informed and justified each other.

Goldman situated sexual experience within both the evolutionary narrative of primal passions and the popular fad of "primitivism," which white middle-class bohemians fetishized as an earlier era of intense sexual intimacies in the absence of rigid moral codes.[68] Goldman's intimate relationship with her tour manager, Ben Reitman, illustrates how Goldman intensely felt these connections between evolution, love, and sex.[69] Reitman's relationship with Goldman began in 1908 and ended in 1917 when he decided to marry his lover, who was pregnant. Throughout their turbulent relationship, Goldman and Reitman endeavored to adhere to their beliefs in free love and socialism, abandoning the notion of fidelity as claims to ownership over another body. Both Goldman and Reitman nostalgically drew on evolutionary stories of earlier phases of human development as an alternative discourse of affections, lying outside current "civilized" frames of marriage and possession. In 1908, Goldman wrote to Reitman, "I have tasted the invigorating breeze at your primitive, and trammeled nature." In a subsequent letter, she referred to Reitman as "darling savage mine."[70] She confided to him that he was "the most beautiful type of an elemental being, all instinct all elemental force" and "all nature wild and savage and beautiful."[71] Goldman's references to Reitman as "savage," "elemental," "primitive," and "trammeled nature" presupposed a body carrying an evolutionary and affective history of ancestors from animals to earlier forms of humanity to the allegedly highest form of modern "civilized" humanity. Goldman and Reitman's experience of love therefore replayed evolutionary dramas within the present.

ANTHROPOLOGIES OF LOVE AND THE FUTURE OF MARRIAGE

During the 1930s, Edward Westermarck, a Finnish anthropologist, captured how the work of sex reformers in their efforts to reform marriage raised crucial questions about the implications of changing the practice of love for the future of civilization. Westermarck's three-volume study, *The History of Marriage*, was recommended by some sex reformers who looked to the transformations of marital customs across societies, ranking them within evolutionary time as backward or progressive. By 1936, sex reformers' radical revisioning of marriage was sufficiently popular to earn them their own place within an anthropological work that took account of the present and future. In his anthropological narrative of *The Future of Marriage*, Westermarck speculated how sex reformers' changes to marriage would influence the future evolutionary stages of love and civilization.

Making a case for the timeliness of his book, Westermarck noted that marriage as an institution seemed to be in trouble. Sex reformers' challenges to marriage from the 1890s through the 1920s had been felt with a mixture of anxiety, excitement, and fear. Westermarck claimed that "Marriage is said to be facing a crisis; and some writers even speak of its collapse or 'bankruptcy,' and of 'free love' taking its place."[72] While Westermarck conceded that marriage, even chastity, existed among so-called "lower stages" of civilization, he drew the line at love. He remarked that "however different the love of a savage may be from that of a civilised man, we discover in it traces of the same ingredients."[73] Tracing the genealogy of love, Westermarck took the standard of the Western, white, professional, heterosexual couple as the culminating point of love's evolution. Westermarck wrestled with questions then at the heart of much social and political concern over new radical experiments in family life.[74] For Westermarck and many others, the pressing question was whether these new experiments signaled the end of marriage as it was traditionally known or simply marked a passing phase that would eventually end with the triumph of traditional monogamy.

Although Westermarck allowed for a broader concept of marriage to include people at lower stages of evolution, he sharply differentiated the affective nature of those marriages. Admitting that affectionate ties existed at all stages, Westermarck nonetheless posited a higher standard of romantic love as a product of civilization. In *The Future of Marriage in Western Civilisations*, Westermarck's focus on a number of influential white sex reformers recognized their importance not only as authorities on marriage, love, and sex but as the vanguard of the future. It was white sex reformers who were seen as leaders in defining new standards of love and expectations of sex as the sensual and spiritual basis of marriage.[75] Westermarck gave considerable credit to prominent American and British white sex reformers such as Margaret Sanger, Marie Stopes, H. G. Wells, Havelock Ellis, Bertrand Russell, and Edward Carpenter.[76] He, in fact, dedicated his book to Havelock Ellis. In their efforts to reform marriage, sex reformers took love as their primary concern to change the form of marriage. They argued for new practices of marriage such as "varietist" marriage, "trial" marriage, or "companionate" marriage, which acknowledged marriage as an uncertain provisional condition where sexual desires did not necessarily abide by the duty of fidelity. Westermarck pointed out that current marriages struggled with a "desire for variety," predominantly in men but also found in women.[77]

On the subject of love, Westermarck told an evolutionary tale. He recounted his "theory of the origin of marriage," arguing that "like the sexual impulse, the other essential elements in marriage have a deep foundation in human and even pre-human instincts."[78] Westermarck, however, noted that the ideal form of love then being articulated by sex reformers had to wait for civilization. For Westermarck, the existence of marriage among past ancestors did not signify the same forms or bodily capacities for affection. Westermarck claimed that "combined with that impulse, there must from the beginning have been some degree of attachment which kept the individuals of different sex together till after the birth of the offspring."[79] Only gradually did the present ideal of sex reformers' practice of love emerge out of "the germ of that unity and intermingling of the spiritual and sensual elements in sexual love which characterizes the normal relations between husband and wife among ourselves."[80] It is significant that Westermarck, a Finnish anthropologist, noted this highly evolved form of love as "among ourselves," a testament to the distance between affections of the "savage" and the love of the "civilized." Westermarck lent the disciplinary and scientific weight of anthropological "truth" to evolutionary capacities for the practice of love that differentiated humans from nonhumans.

While sex reformers turned to love as an evolutionary mark of the emotional distance between the sexual passions of the nonhuman and the expression of sexual instincts in the civilized, they also drew on the evolutionary history of the trajectory of the nonhuman to the human to anticipate the future. Anticipating the future stage of evolution, sex reformers co-opted Darwinism into a millennial narrative that spiritualized sex and drew sex reformers into new intimacies with nonhuman occult forces. Thus, sex reformers' turn to love entangled sexual science, eugenics, and new forms of spirituality. While Darwin wrestled with the contentious implications of a theory that undermined the spiritual status of the human as part of the family of nonhuman animals, sex reformers not only invoked new evolutionary narratives focused on love, but, like Galton's view of eugenics, turned to sex as a religion of the future with love as its cardinal principle. In the sex reform campaign that put love in an evolutionary framework, the lessons from Darwin were as much about a look backward to the nonhuman inheritance of sexual instincts as about a look forward to the millennial and divine potential of sex as love to craft an imagined new race of supermen and superwomen.

Conclusion

Genealogies of Love: Darwinian Romances in Reproductive Sciences

To explore the genealogy of contemporary advances in reproductive science necessarily entails grappling with the Darwinian past of genetics and the nonhuman actors in love's evolutions. Early Darwinian contributions to genetics involved Darwin and his followers' concerns with the evolution of love through observations of attraction, desire, and affection among animals as well as plants. How scientists like Darwin have investigated the relationship between sex and love has been integral to the development of reproductive sciences and the politics of who or what can love. On the one hand, Darwin's critical insights into the selection of traits to further reproductive advantage involved a vertical hierarchical ordering informed by Victorian racial theories, which associated lower races with animals. On the other hand, Darwin's works addressed a horizontal relationship across humans and nonhumans, expanding the array of nonhuman actors in shaping human bodies and emotions. This radically opened possibilities for addressing the network of actors involved in furthering the evolution of human love while, at the same time, denying the capability of nonhumans to experience love. Scientists and more broadly, sex reformers construed the relationship between sex and love as a new level of ontological as well as racial politics in the early twentieth century.

TIME, SCIENCE, AND THE POLITICS OF LOVE: H. G. WELLS AND THE TIME MACHINE

From cloning to in vitro fertilization to stem cell research, reproductive technologies have been invested with millennialism characterized by the hopes and fears of the possible future of sex, bodies, and love.[1] In contemporary debates over the direction of reproductive technologies, social commentators on the right suggest a pervasive threat to cultural and moral values, whereas leftist social commentators point to the expansion of reproductive choices as well as parental and marital love among marginalized populations. These contemporary associations of millennialism and reproductive science as well as the contentious sentiments surrounding reproductive choice are informed by a historical legacy of eugenics, evolution, and sex reform. In projecting the reproductive futures of bodies in contemporary society, scientists necessarily grapple with the past or evolutionary history of those bodies to anticipate their futures.

Much like the story told here of sex reformers, sexual science, and nonhuman involvement in love, science studies scholars have highlighted how reproductive technologies can advance a promising agenda of inclusive kinship that encompasses animals, plants, and other organisms. At the same time, this vision of kinship also works in tension with what scholars have also addressed as the vertical and hierarchical ordering of bodies along the lines of evolutionary superiority and inferiority or evolutionary advance and atavism. What unites both the early twentieth century and current debates on reproductive science is the importance of grappling with a long legacy of privilege, exclusionary practices, and the material effects on inequalities that come to bear on how reproductive futures are defined, enacted, and projected.

Sex reformer and novelist, H. G. Wells's *Time Machine* is instructive for how sexual science as a reproductive science in an earlier form anticipated much of the current debates, hopes, and fears that shape current reproductive science and technologies. Although Wells's *Time Machine* is a work of fiction, Wells constructed the narrative out of the contemporary scientific and political issues captivating the attention of sex reformers. Wells's contrasting worlds of the Eloi and the Morlocks illustrate the imagined utopian and dystopian futures that haunted sex reformers' efforts to productively interweave a new scientific practice of sex with love in the interests of reproducing an evolutionary superior race. As a futuristic novel profoundly rooted in early twentieth-century social and political conditions, Wells's novel lies at the crossroads of how sex reformers anticipated future worlds based on an eventual mainstream practice of sex as love and how current reproductive sciences must grapple with the darker eugenic legacies of sex reform as a genealogical moment.

H. G. Wells's novel *The Time Machine*, published in 1895, illustrates how sex reformers apprehended time as the embodiment of genealogies projected backwards and forwards, across humans and nonhumans. Wells told a story that conveyed how sex reformers practiced love in the shadow of utopic and dystopic projections, at the edges of the past, present, and future. As Wells revealed two very different worlds in the *Time Machine*, he illustrated how sex reformers were deeply concerned about matters of genealogy, shaping a politics of love out of concerns for selectively drawing on a Darwinian past and present, and projections of future bodies evolving beyond the human. Of course, for Wells and sex reformers more broadly, charting future worlds required confronting a past. Wells's *Time Machine*, as a commentary on the stakes of reproduction across temporalities, is also useful for reflecting on the time machines that we construct out of contemporary advances in reproductive science. As we critique the problems of the futures anticipated by sex reformers, we must also grapple with the genealogical ties of reproductive science to sex reformers, with particular attention to the place of love and nonhumans. In light of the legacies of biotechnology and the persistence of evolutionary thought, genealogies today are no less hybrid than they were in Wells's time, but they are informed by a very different politics of love with different hopes and fears.

Wells's *Time Machine* and contemporary time machines constructed out of current reproductive science are entangled in the theme of highlighting the malleability of bodies and the disturbance of fixed ontological boundaries through intensified human and nonhuman intimacies. In the *Time Machine*, the Time Traveler exemplifies how sex reformers treated their own bodies as fleshy time machines, reviving latent ancestral impulses and gauging latent potentialities in anticipation of the next stage of evolution. For the Time Traveler, it is the affective capacities of a particular kind of body that enable connections across time and the reconstruction of genealogical lines of descent and ascent. It is significant that Wells's Time Traveler is a white educated British mathematician interested in the fourth dimension, a mathematical as well as spiritual concept associated with new relations of sex, science, and religion.[2] Wells's Time Traveler, in fact, approximated the class, racial, and evolutionary status of prominent sex reformers, enabling the Time Traveler to both look back to a purportedly buried ancestral past and anxiously look forward to the dual possibilities of an evolutionary superior form or an atavistic one. These evolutionary intimacies reverberate in contemporary cultural reactions to reproductive science whether social commentators regard reproductive science as a threat to the godly integrity of the human body or as a positive challenge to reconsidering the transformative possibilities of a human body entangled in its relations with the world. In contemporary white Western cultures, the trend in tracing ancestral blood connections through new agencies like Ancestry.com highlights how evolutionary racial politics continue to haunt our present.

Wells's Time Traveler is also a productive lens for considering the genealogy of current academic trends in the turn to affect, particularly in the context of how affect has recently informed feminist science studies. As previous chapters have shown, sex reformers' politics of love unsettled ontological boundaries between the human and the nonhuman, exposing their malleability through intimate encounters with one another. In addition to showing how sex reformers addressed the permeability of bodies to one another, previous chapters have also shown how sex reformers treated love and, more broadly, affective nuances as vehicles for bodily transformation. Wells, in fact, situated the Time Traveler's possibilities for time travel within the higher affective potential of "civilized" bodies. As the Time Traveler moved through temporal dimensions, he relied on his body as a sensitive instrument to apprehend time travel. Traveling through time, the mathematician referred to "the peculiar sensations of time travelling," giving the specific details of "gaining velocity," feeling "the palpitation of the night," observing "luminous color," "jamming myself, molecule by molecule," and "bringing my atoms into such intimate contact."[3] This capacity for time travel exemplifies what we have seen in previous chapters as late nineteenth- and early twentieth-century constructions of the unique sensitivity of white bodies to their surroundings. While science studies scholars and feminist theory scholars more broadly have turned to affect as a lens for considering the liveliness, mobility, and transformation of reproductive bodies, this story of the history of love in relation to the formation of sexual science also highlights a dark side of affect in the colonial racial politics of evolutionary narratives shaping reproductive science.[4]

H. G. Wells's *Time Machine* offers a glimpse of the hopes that, in our present political climate, continue to be invested in possibilities for reproductive science to reshape the world in terms of human and nonhuman intimacies. For Wells, the scientific management of reproduction was capable of fostering greater love among humans as well as between humans and nonhumans, reshaping eating habits, environmental conditions, and labor. Arriving in the year 802,701 AD, the Time Traveler observes an Edenic Paradise populated by Eloi, whom the Time Traveler readily identifies as future evolutionary kin beyond the human. In this world of the future, the Time Traveler notes that human scientific and industrial endeavors had reached their climax. In this place, "the whole earth had become a garden" where no property rights and no agricultural labor existed. The Eloi, the human of the future, appeared white, rosy, childlike, peaceful, happy, healthy, and leisured. They were dressed in brightly colored robes with gleaming white limbs and talked in "laughing speech." The Eloi embodied the future human species, a "beautiful race" that had reached the pinnacle of evolutionary achievement and, consequently, ended evolutionary struggle. As the Time Traveler observed this new world, he noted that the disappearance of such struggle must have eliminated the need for intelligence as a skill for survival. In this world, there were no signs of work, no signs of the traditional family, and no signs of meat eating. The Time Traveler observed that the Eloi were fruitarians and vegetarians who played, made love, slept, and bathed in the river every day. This exquisite harmonious world also rendered the sexes much less distinct. The Time Traveler observed that: "seeing the ease and security in which these people were living, I felt that this close resemblance of the sexes was after all what one would expect; for the strength of a man and the softness of a woman, the institution of the family, and the differentiation of occupations are mere militant necessities of an age of physical force." Given sex reformers' Malthusian and eugenic fears of a world without responsible racial reproduction, Wells suggested that the well-managed population growth of the Eloi made this utopic world possible. The Eloi, in fact, did not need to worry about child-bearing with its abundant and well-balanced population. While the Eloi were a much different incarnation of the "human," what made them seem most human was their affection. It was this capacity for affection that not only racially bonded the Eloi but shaped how the Time Traveler identified genealogical connections to the human.[5] As such, the Time Traveler's affinities to the Eloi influenced historical linkages across time through sex and reproduction. Wells's depiction of the Elois not only highlights the optimism characteristic of a pivotal historical moment in the shaping of reproductive science but, in fact, raises the question of how love is situated and constructed in contemporary discourses, institutions, and research in reproductive science.

Wells's striking juxtaposition of the world of the Elois with the underground world of the Morlocks highlights what Edward Chamberlain and Sander Gilman's collection of works has shown as the dark side of progress.[6] Although written in 1896, Wells's depiction of the world of the Morlocks offers a strong visual image of a messy Latourian ANT-like world of relations on the ground as the Morlocks perform the gritty, undesirable work underground that is crucial to maintaining the Eloi world.[7] While Latour maintains that sociologists have a tendency to operate like angels in discussing the abstract world while neglecting the messy relations of nonhumans on the ground, Wells's Eloi embody the highest form of evolution while relying on the atavistic sub- or nonhuman Morlocks. To Wells, the Morlocks embodied the worst fears of human atavism and an unsettling reminder of the animal within. Choosing to affiliate with the Eloi, the Time Traveler drew human/nonhuman distinctions of kinship, disavowing the Morlocks with whom "it was impossible, somehow to feel any humanity in the things." Wells described the Morlocks as fierce, meat-eating, dirty, ant-like, and cannibalistic. Yet, in spite of these reprehensible qualities of the Morlocks, they performed the labor that was necessary to the functioning of the Eloi paradise. Far from a docile working-class species, the Morlocks preyed upon the Eloi and likely engineered their breeding. Reflecting on "the Great Fear" between the two species, the Time Traveler shuddered at "the clear knowledge of what the meat I had seen might be." He admitted sharing the Eloi disgust of "this new vermin that had replaced the old." The Upperworld Eloi pursued pleasure and comfort while the Underworld Morlocks worked below as the new servant class. In this future, the two species of the Eloi and Morlocks embodied utopic and dystopic visions of two different worlds that amplified class and racial distinctions. These two worlds were defined by two very clearly different emotional climates: the Eloi one of love, happiness, and peace, the Morlocks one of hatred, depression, and violence.[8] Through the sympathy with the Eloi, the Time Traveler constituted his own genealogy, suggesting the difficulty of acknowledging the Morlocks as kin. As a world that resonates with academic turns to the crucial participation of the nonhuman in enabling human worlds and privileges, the place of love as a force pervading and underlying Eloi/Morlock distinctions begs the question of what might be the significance of a reproductive science that promotes the control of reproduction and prevention of unwanted births in colonized or impoverished areas while promoting love and romance in white affluent areas. Wells's Eloi/Morlock worlds prompt the question of the politics of love underlying reproductive science and technologies in the time machines or future worlds we construct in the present.

ENTANGLEMENTS OF AFFECT AND SCIENCE STUDIES: THE STAKES OF NONHUMAN LOVE STORIES

By exploring how the politics of love informed sex reformers' early influence in shaping reproductive science, this book contributes to the critical juncture of affect studies and science studies. As one of the pioneers of this juncture, Patricia Clough has provided crucial insights into the role of affect in bio-political regimes that draw on scientific and technological knowledge of bodies to politically manage a population.[9] Yet, while Clough and other scholars in the anthology *The Affect Theory Reader* have discussed a politics of fear shaping contemporary geopolitical climates, there is a notable silence on the subject of a politics of love.[10] As shown through the story of sex reformers, the politics of love is worth exploring to deepen our understanding of the entanglements of reproductive science and political regimes.

Although far from a comprehensive genealogy of the place of love in shaping reproductive science, this book focuses on a very specific yet prominent strand of that genealogy to raise awareness of the role of affect in the early formation of reproductive science. Indeed, a different book might explore the genealogical strand of affect in relationship to a politics of fear with different actors, events, practices, and connections to our present. Arguably, historians who have written on eugenics and sterilization have highlighted this politics of fear as a dark side of the birth control movement.[11] This historical moment of the early formation of reproductive science highlights the need for further exploration of how assumptions about who or what can love shape the roles of nonhumans in scientific practices. By moving beyond questions of sex and turning toward what love had to do with reproductive science, the entanglements of affect studies and sciences studies can be brought into mutually productive interdisciplinary conversations.

In the contemporary academic turn to affect across disciplines, scholars have given little attention to the historical entanglement of affect with the rise of psychology as a science of emotions. For instance, science studies scholars have made an important contribution to affect studies by addressing the ways scientific inquiries, subjects, and experiments in areas like psychology and sociology have profoundly influenced how affect is defined, experienced, and culturally circulated. This study of the early twentieth-century moment of sex reformers' politics of love at a time when psychology was developing as a discipline highlights the intimate and mutual shaping of the cultural value of emotions at a time of the framing of legitimizing scientific discourses of those emotions.

In making the case of historicizing affect and its relationship to psychology as a science of emotions, it is important to note that Darwinian evolutionary theory informed psychology as a discipline that drew on affects as forces that connected as well as hierarchically separated bodies. Although it is true that Darwinian evolution situated the human within an expanded network of nonhuman kin, Darwinian evolution emphasized different repertoires of emotional experience. This strand of Darwinian evolutionary thought, tied to essentialized understandings of biological capacities for love, persists in the present. In a recent collection of essays, *The New Psychology of Love*, scholars address new shifts in understanding love since the late 1980s that are currently informed by Darwinian evolutionary theory.[12] Throughout the collection, scholars emphasize love as an evolved emotion tied to reproduction and species survival, privileging heteronormativity as the appropriate context for love. Within affect theory, there is a strand of theorists such as Paul Ekman, Silvan Tomkins, and Antonio Damasio who have turned to affect to differentiate human from nonhuman kin.[13] This particular strand of affect theorists reinforces human exceptionalism, unlike the Deleuzian strand of affect theorists who invoke Darwin for the hopeful possibilities of engaging in new intimacies that challenge the boundaries of the human. As affect studies grows, it becomes more pressing for affect scholars to be mindful of the genealogical relationship between affect, psychology, and reproductive science, particularly as the strands of affect theory multiply with potentially conflicting politics and divergences among affect theorists.

As a genealogical episode illustrating the intimate entanglements of affect and reproductive science, the narrative of sex reformers' politics of love highlights the historical legacy of this relationship for leftist political movements shaped by scientific understandings of the body and cultural practices of love. More specifically, my turn to sex reformers' politics of love in relation to shaping sexual science is informed by how feminist, queer, anti-colonial, and anti-racist activists have turned to love as a promising lens for furthering social justice. As many affect theorists have noted their intellectual debts to feminism and queer theory, it is specifically the politics of love in leftist social movements that shaped the affective turn. Moreover, many affect theorists across disciplines have also drawn on feminist critiques of scientific representations of the reproductive body as natural, inert, and fixed. While I have focused on the 1920s as a significant moment in the genealogy of affect, this politics of love certainly did not stop in 1930 but took new forms in the 1960s, 1980s, and in the present. Whether we look to Luce Irigaray's *The Way of Love* or cultural feminists' insistence on the special feminine capacities for love, the hopeful turn to love on the left as a promising direction for a better future bears a particularly close genealogical tie to affect studies, perhaps more than any other emotion.[14] In the enthusiastic embrace of affect as an analytical lens for furthering critiques of power and efforts to differentiate affect from emotion, affect theorists seem to have lost sight of how the politics of love and reproductive science shape affect studies. In what Nigel Thrift has discussed as a focus on affect to attend to the background, affect theorists seem to have created another background where the politics of love and its relationship to scientific theories on bodily capacities for emotion permeate the atmosphere of our affective turn.[15] As the case of sex reformers' politics of love suggests, it is imperative to remind ourselves of how a changing politics of love and a changing science of what a body can do can shape transformations of affect and political futures.

More than simply highlighting academic entanglements of affect studies and science studies, this book's focus on nonhuman love stories also aims to inform our everyday cultural practices with nonhumans. Nonhuman love stories show how the politics of love underpinning reproductive science has shaped an agricultural industry that dismisses nonhuman love in its exploitation of plant and animal breeding. What or who could be admitted as kin emerged as a pressing question among sex reformers who drew on Darwinian evolution and new technologies of reproduction to perfect sex as a practice of love. Wells's *Time Machine* showed how a politics of love mattered on the scales of making new worlds by making new genealogies. This entanglement of affect, reproductive science, kinship, and world making has persisted into the present. Affect theorists turned to Darwinian evolution for its promises in stretching the parameters of kinship across human and nonhuman divides; thus challenging lines of descent that restrict who or what counts as kin.[16] Yet, as the story of sex reformers' politics of love has shown, Darwinian kinship ties with nonhumans did not erase inequalities between humans and nonhumans but created a new axis of power in terms of the affective potential of bodies along an evolutionary scale from nonhumans to "primal" humans to "civilized" humanity. This marks a cautionary tale in how love is deployed, by whom, for what purpose, and with what consequences.

Notes

INTRODUCTION. LOVE STORIES FOR THE NONHUMAN

1. Neith Boyce to Mabel Dodge, 22 January 1920, Mabel Dodge Luhan Papers, Beinecke Library, Yale University, Box 3, Folder 93.

2. Historians have shown how affection, sentiment, and emotions can be sites of asserting racial and imperial power as a form of normative violence. See for example, Laura Wexler, *Tender Violence: Domestic Visions in an Age of U.S. Imperialism* (Chapel Hill: University of North Carolina Press, 2000) and Ann Laura Stoler, *Carnal Knowledge and Imperial Power: Race and the Intimate in Colonial Rule* (Berkeley: University of California Press, 2002).

3. George Beard, *American Nervousness* (New York: G.P. Putnam's Sons, 1881), 28.

4. See for example, Timothy Gilfoyle's discussion of Anthony Comstock's New York and the moral reformers seeking to clean up sexual immorality in *City of Eros: New York City, Prostitution, and the commercialization of sex, 1790–1920* (New York: Norton, 1992). On the Progressive movement and women's political activism through social welfare, see Robyn Muncy, *Creating a Female Domain in American Reform, 1890–1935* (New York: Oxford University Press, 1994).

5. For a discussion on how colonizers framed colonialism as a duty and burden, see Antoinette Burton, *Burdens of History: British Feminists, Indian Women, and Imperial Culture, 1865–1915* (Chapel Hill: University of North Carolina Press, 1994).

6. Katrina Irving discusses Lothrop Stoddard's 1920 publication on *The Rising Tide of Color against White World Supremacy* in the context of how it shaped discourses on the fecundity of immigrant mothers and eugenics. See Katrina Irving, *Immigrant Mothers: Narratives of Race and Maternity, 1890–1925* (Urbana: University of Illinois Press, 2000), 36.

7. Gilles Deleuze and Felix Guattari, *A Thousand Plateaus: Capitalism and Schizophrenia*, translated by Brian Massumi (Minneapolis: University of Minnesota Press, 1987).

8. Gregory J. Seigworth and Melissa Gregg, "An Inventory of Shimmers," in *The Affect Theory Reader* (Durham, NC: Duke University Press, 2010), 1; Nigel Thrift, *Non-representational Theory: Space, Politics, Affect* (London: Routledge, 2008), 175; Brian Massumi, *Parables for the Virtual* (Durham, NC: Duke University Press, 2002), 27–28, 35; Clare Hemmings, "Invoking Affect: Cultural Theory and the Ontological Turn," *Cultural Studies* 19, no. 5 (September 2005): 548–67; Sara Ahmed, *The Cultural Politics of Emotion* (New York: Routledge, 2004); Rei Terada, *Feeling in Theory: Emotion after the "Death of the Subject"* (Cambridge, MA: Harvard University Press, 2001), 82.

9. Rosi Braidotti, *Metamorphoses: Towards a Materialist Theory of Becoming* (Cambridge: Polity Press, 2002); Patricia Ticineto Clough, *Autoaffection: Unconscious Thought in the Age of Teletechnology* (Minneapolis: University of Minnesota Press, 2000).

10. See for example, early twentieth century psychologists' references to affect. William James, *Principles of Psychology*, Vol. 2 (Cambridge, MA: Harvard University Press, 1981), 1027, 1030, 1032, 1053; William McDougall, *An Introduction to Social Psychology* (Boston: John W. Luce & Co., 1910), 5, 23, 47, 219.

11. Bruno Latour, *Reassembling the Social: An Introduction to Actor-Network Theory* (New York: Oxford University Press, 2005).

12. On the ghosts that haunt Darwinian narratives, see Banu Subramaniam, *Ghost Stories for Darwin: The Science of Variation and the Politics of Diversity* (Urbana: University of Illinois Press, 2014).

13. Donna Haraway, *Modest_Witness@Second_Millennium. FemaleMan_Meets_OncoMouse: Feminism and Technoscience* (New York: Routledge, 1997); Sarah Franklin, *Dolly Mixtures: The Remaking of Genealogy* (Durham, NC: Duke University Press, 2007); Myra Hird, *The Origins of Sociable Life: Evolution after Science Studies* (New York: Palgrave MacMillan, 2009); Luciana Parisi, *Abstract Sex: Philosophy, Bio-technology and the Mutations of Desire* (London: Continuum, 2004).

14. Charis Thompson, *Making Parents: The Ontological Choreography of Reproductive Technologies* (Cambridge, MA: MIT Press, 2005); Franklin, *Dolly Mixtures*; Hird, *The Origins of Sociable Life*; Parisi, *Abstract Sex*.

15. See for example, Jan Lewis and Peter Stearns, "Introduction," in *An Emotional History of the United States*, ed. Peter Stearns and Jan Lewis (New York: New York University Press, 1998), 7.

16. Sandra Harding, "Chapter 2: Stronger Objectivity for Sciences from Below," in *Objectivity and Diversity: Another Logic of Scientific Research* (Chicago: University of Chicago Press, 2015), 26–51; Helen Longino, "Chapter 4:

Values and Objectivity," in *Science as Social Knowledge: Values and Objectivity in Scientific Inquiry* (Princeton, NJ: Princeton University Press, 1990), 62–82.

17. Thomas Kuhn, *Structures of Scientific Revolutions* (Chicago: University of Chicago Press, 1970); Ian Hacking, *Historical Ontology* (Cambridge, MA: Harvard University Press, 2002).

18. Bernard Lightman, *Victorian Popularizers of Science: Designing Nature for New Audiences* (Chicago: University of Chicago Press, 2007); Theodore Porter, *Trust in Number: The Pursuit of Objectivity in Science and Public Life* (Princeton, NJ: Princeton University Press, 1995).

19. See for example, Michel Foucault, *History of Sexuality, Vol. 1: An Introduction* (New York: Random House, 1978); Michel Foucault, *Madness and Civilization: A History of Insanity in the Age of Reason*, translated by Richard Howard (New York: Pantheon Books, 1965).

20. See Donna Haraway, *When Species Meet* (Minneapolis: University of Minnesota Press, 2008); Franklin, *Dolly Mixtures*; Haraway, *Modest Witness.*

21. Michel Foucault, "Nietzsche, Genealogy, History," in *Language, Counter-Memory, Practice: Selected Essays and Interviews*, ed. Donald F. Bouchard and Sherry Simon (Ithaca, NY: Cornell University Press, 1977), 139–64.

22. Feminist and queer theorists have explored alternative conceptions of time that disturb linearity. See for example, Judith Halberstam, *In a Queer Time and Place: Transgender Bodies, Subcultural Lives* (New York: New York University Press, 2005); Elizabeth Grosz, *Time Travels: Feminism, Nature, Power* (Durham, NC: Duke University Press, 2005); Rita Felski, *Doing Time: Feminist Theory and Postmodern Culture* (New York: New York University Press, 2000).

23. Dana Seitler, *Atavistic Tendencies: The Culture of Science in American Modernity* (Minneapolis: University of Minnesota Press, 2008), 25, 29, 130, 171, 180, 200.

24. See for example, Darwin's discussion of tender feelings compared to rage and fear. Charles Darwin, *The Expression of Emotions in Man and Animals*, 3rd ed. (Oxford: Oxford University Press, 1998), 18–19, 78, 144, 214–16.

1. "BECOMING-ANIMAL": EVOLVING LOVE IN ANIMAL SEX EXPERIMENTS

1. Robert Richardson, *William James: In the Maelstrom of American Modernism* (Boston: Houghton Mifflin Company, 2006), 166.

2. Richardson, 199.

3. Donna Haraway, "The Promises of Monsters: A Regenerative Politics for Inappropriate/d Others," in *Cultural Studies*, ed. Lawrence Grossberg, Cary Nelson, and Paula Treichler (New York: Routledge, 1992), 297, 300; Luciana Parisi, *Abstract Sex*, 13, 22–26, 31, 46, 60–83; Adele Clarke, *Disciplining Reproduction: Modernity, American Life Sciences, and the Problems of Sex* (Berkeley: University of California Press, 1998).

4. Franklin, *Dolly Mixtures.*

5. Clough, *Autoaffection*, 28.

6. On mental evolution and class status, see Charles Gross, "Alfred Wallace and the Evolution of the Human Mind," *The Neuroscientist* 16, no. 5 (September 2010): 496–507.

7. Gail Bederman, *Manliness and Civilization* (Chicago: University of Chicago Press, 1995), 81–83.
8. Granville K. Stanley Hall, *Adolescence* (New York: Appleton, 1907), xiii.
9. Hall, 412.
10. Hall, xiv.
11. James, *Principles of Psychology*, 22.
12. James, 320.
13. Havelock Ellis, Diary, 6 August 1876. Havelock Ellis Papers, BL, London, Item 70525.
14. Ellis.
15. Gross, "Alfred Wallace and the Evolution of the Human Mind," 496–507.
16. Celia Brickman, *Aboriginal Populations in the Mind: Race and Primitivity in Psychoanalysis* (New York: Columbia University, 2003); Eliza Slavet, *Racial Fever: Freud and the Jewish Question* (New York: Fordham University Press, 2009), 70, 99, 103.
17. Mari Jo Buhle has shown the patriarchal dimensions of psychoanalysis as a controversial and ambivalent practice for female analysts and analysands. See Mari Jo Buhle, *Feminism and Its Discontents* (Cambridge, MA: Harvard University Press, 1998).
18. On the influence of Darwinism in American culture, see Richard Hofstadter, *Social Darwinism in American Thought* (Boston: Beacon Press, 1992); Ronald L. Numbers, *Darwin Comes to America* (Cambridge, MA: Harvard University Press, 1998). On the influence of Darwinism in British culture, see Bernard Lightman, *Victorian Popularizers of Science.*
19. McDougall, *An Introduction to Social Psychology*, 5.
20. McDougall, 1013.
21. James, *Principles of Psychology*, 1027, 1030, 1032, 1053.
22. Havelock Ellis, *Man and Woman: A Study of Human Secondary Sexual Characters* (London: Walter Scott, Ltd., 1894), 19.
23. Ellis, 54.
24. Ellis, 67–68.
25. Ellis, 47, 219.
26. William McDougall, "Psychology in the Service of Eugenics," *Eugenics Review* 5 (April 1913): 295–308.
27. McDougall, *An Introduction to Social Psychology*, 19.
28. McDougall, 19, 20.
29. See for example, Darwin, *The Expression of Emotions in Man and Animals*, 296–97.
30. Josef Breuer and Sigmund Freud, *Studies in Hysteria*, trans. James Strachey (New York: Basic Books Inc., 1957), 91.
31. Gwen Berger, *Taboo Subjects: Race, Sex, and Psychoanalysis* (Minneapolis: University of Minnesota Press, 2005), xix–xx.
32. On animal experimentation among early twentieth-century psychologists, see Anne C. Rose, "Animal Tales: Observations of the Emotions in American Experimental Psychology, 1890–1940," *Journal of the History of Behavioral Sciences* 48, no. 4 (Fall 2012): 301–17; Michael Pettit, "The Problem of Raccoon Intelligence in Behaviourist America," *The British Journal* for *the History*

of Science 43, no. 3 (September 2010): 391–421; Cheryl Logan, "The Altered Rationale for the Choice of a Standard Animal in Experimental Psychology: Henry A. Donaldson, Adolf Meyer, and 'the Albino Rat,'" *History of Psychology* 2, nos. 1–3 (February 1999): 3–24.

33. William James, "What Is an Emotion?," in *The Emotions* (Baltimore, MD: Williams & Wilkins Co., 1922), 13.

34. Lorraine Daston and Gregg Mitman, *Thinking with Animals: New Perspectives on Anthropomorphism* (New York: Columbia University Press, 2005); Haraway, *When Species Meet.*

35. Breuer and Freud, *Studies in Hysteria*, 14, 51, 58, 62.

36. Sigmund Freud, *Psychopathology of Everyday Life* (Harmondsworth, UK: Penguin Books Limited, 1939), 28.

37. Breuer and Freud, *Studies in Hysteria*, 8.

38. Kim Townsend, *Manhood at Harvard* (New York: W.W. Norton, 1996), 28, 38, 41–42, 114.

39. Hutchins Hapgood, "Husbands and Wives." Hapgood Family Papers, Beinecke, Box 26, File 727.

40. Mathew Thomson, *Psychological Subjects: Identity, Culture and Health in Twentieth-Century Britain* (Oxford: Oxford University Press, 2006), 60.

41. Thomson, 55, 74.

42. Richardson, *William James*, 119, 126, 259–64, 275.

43. Thomson, *Psychological Subjects*, 65.

44. Bonnie Haaland, *Emma Goldman: Sexuality and the Impurity of the State* (New York: Black Rose Books, 1993), 132.

45. Hall, *Adolescence*, 6, 51, 59, 60.

46. Joel Pfister, "Glamorizing the Psychological," in *Inventing the Psychological*, ed. Joel Pfister and Nancy Schnog (New Haven, CT: Yale University Press, 1997), 167–213; Nathan Hale, "Chapter 4: Culture and Rebellion, 1912–1920," in *The Rise and Crisis of Psychoanalysis in the United States* (Oxford: Oxford University Press, 1995), 57–73.

47. Pfister, "Glamorizing the Psychological," 167, 170, 189, 200.

48. Perry Meisel and Walter Kendrick, eds. *Bloomsbury/Freud: The Letters of James and Alix Strachey, 1924–1925* (London: Chatto & Windus Ltd., 1986).

49. Deleuze, *A Thousand Plateaus*, 26.

50. Dr. M. Deddow Bayly, "Voronoff and His Rejuvenation Experiments" (lecture, 17 October 1925, Constructive Birth Control Society Meeting at Queen's Hall, London). Marie Stopes Papers, BL, London, 58589.

51. See for example, Laura Davidow Hirshbein, "The Glandular Solution: Sex, Masculinity, and Aging in the 1920s," *Journal of the History of Sexuality* 9, no. 3 (1999): 277–304.

52. Bayly, "Voronoff and His Rejuvenation Experiments."

53. Bayly.

54. Bayly.

55. Bayly.

56. See Kirill Rossiianov, "Beyond Species: Il'ya Ivanov and His Experiments on Cross-Breeding Humans with Anthropoid Apes," *Science in Context* 15, no. 2 (2002): 277–316.

57. Donna Haraway, "A Cyborg Manifesto: Science, Technology, and Socialist-Feminism in the Late Twentieth Century," in *Simians, Cyborgs, and Women: The Reinvention of Nature* (New York: Routledge, 1991), 149–81.

58. Thompson, *Making Parents*, 8.

59. H. G. Wells, *The Island of Dr. Moreau: A Critical Text of the 1896 London First Edition, with an Introduction and Appendices*, ed. Leon Stover (Jefferson, NC: McFarland & Company, 1996), 89.

60. H. G. Wells, *Experiment in Autobiography* (New York: The MacMillan Company, 1934), 160–61.

61. Marie Stopes to Professor Hill, 31 March 1920. Marie Stopes Papers, BL, London, Item 58482.

62. F. H. A. Marshall's two volume work, *Physiology of Reproduction*, 3rd ed. (London: Longmans Green & Co., 1952) contains a compilation of essays written by a number of scientists, including animal geneticist F. A. E. Crew. See for example, Marshall, "Chapter 19: Parturition," 2:496–524, and Crew, "The Factors Which Determine Sex," 2:741–92.

63. Coral Lansbury, *The Old Brown Dog: Women and Vivisection in Edwardian England* (Madison: University of Wisconsin Press, 1985), 10–12.

64. Marie Stopes to George Jones, 23 October 1922. Marie Stopes Papers, BL, London, 58561.

65. William Bayliss to Marie Stopes, 21 January 1922. Marie Stopes Papers, BL, London, 58483.

66. William Bayliss to Marie Stopes, 17 October 1920. Marie Stopes Papers, BL, London, 58482.

67. William Bayliss to Marie Stopes, 3 August 1922. Marie Stopes Papers, BL, London, 58483.

68. Lynda Birke, *Feminism, Animals, and Science* (Philadelphia: University of Pennsylvania Press, 1998), 46.

69. Gideon Diedrich, "Biological Reasons for Family Limitation," *Birth Control Review* 2, no. 2 (February 1920): 18.

70. L. J. Cole, "Animal Aristocracy and Human Democracy," *Birth Control Review* 3, no. 1 (January 1924): 20–21.

71. Donald Hooker, "The Effect of X-Ray upon Reproduction in the Rat," *Birth Control Review* 6, no. 9 (September 1922): 219–20.

72. Hooker, 219–20.

73. Hooker, 219.

74. Hooker, 219.

75. Hooker, 219.

76. This suggests an early historical episode of what some scholars have seen as the material traffic of bodily matter in transnational networks of biotechnological developments, capitalism, and politics. See Catherine Waldby and Robert Mitchell, *Tissue Economies: Blood, Organs, and Cell Lines in Late Capitalism* (Durham, NC: Duke University Press, 2006).

77. Diedrich, "Biological Reasons for Family Limitation," 18.

78. This suggests an early investigation into male birth control, although far from mainstream. Historian Nelly Oudshoorn has written on male birth

control as a late twentieth-century technology investigated with far more care and caution of physical risks than the birth control pill for women. See Nelly Oudshoorn, *The Male Pill: A Biography of a Technology in the Making* (Durham, NC: Duke University Press, 2003).

79. Hooker, "The Effect of X-Ray upon Reproduction in the Rat," 220.

80. On methodological discussions across the social sciences and humanities on the problem of giving the animal a voice, see Linda Kalof and Georgina Montgomery, eds., *Making Animal Meaning* (East Lansing: Michigan State University Press, 2011).

81. Hooker, "The Effect of X-Ray upon Reproduction in the Rat," 220.

82. Hooker, 220.

83. Hooker, 220.

84. Hooker, 220.

85. Hooker, 220.

86. Karen Rader, *Making Mice: Standardizing Animals for American Biomedical Research, 1900–1955* (Princeton, NJ: Princeton University Press, 2004).

87. On the subject of how eugenics shaped ideas of love as the sexual reproduction of racially fit bodies, see Angelique Richardson, *Love and Eugenics in the Late Nineteenth Century: Rational Reproduction and the New Woman* (Oxford: Oxford University Press, 2003).

88. Chandak Sengoopta, *The Most Secret Quintessence of Life: Sex Glands, Hormones, 1850–1950* (Chicago: University of Chicago Press, 2006), 4, 70. Historian Elizabeth Watkins has indicated that women were largely excluded from the early rejuvenation craze. According to Watkins, ovarian therapy, beginning in the 1890s, was tied to the medicalization and pathologization of women's reproductive bodies. See Elizabeth Watkins, *The Estrogen Elixir: A History of Hormone Replacement Therapy in America* (Baltimore: Johns Hopkins University Press, 2007), 16–17.

89. On the enthusiasm of white middle-class men seeking to restore sexual energies through rejuvenation, see Hirshbein, "The Glandular Solution," 277–304.

90. Norman Haire to Havelock Ellis, 7 February 1922. Havelock Ellis Papers, British Library, London, Item 70540.

91. Norman Haire to Havelock Ellis.

92. See for example, Vern Bullough, *Science in the Bedroom: A History of Sex Research* (New York: Basic Books, 1994); Jennifer Terry, "The United States of Perversion," in *An American Obsession* (Chicago: University of Chicago Press, 1999), 74–119.

93. John R. Baker, *Sex in Man and Animals* (London: George Routledge & Sons, Ltd., 1926), 19.

94. Baker, 19.

95. Baker, 65.

96. Baker, 66.

97. Baker, 66–68.

98. Baker, 69–70.

99. Baker, 69–70, 76.

100. Baker, 87–90, 91.

101. Carlos Paton Blacker to Marie Stopes, 13 February 1931. Marie Stopes Papers, BL, London, 58645.

102. Carlos Paton Blacker to Marie Stopes.

103. Marie Stopes, "Present Day Technique and Clinical Results of Contraception" (lecture, Royal Institute of Public Health, London, 13 November 1930). Marie Stopes Papers, BL, London, Item 58636.

104. Susan Lederer claims that scientists' self-experimentation was common in this period. Lederer discusses this in the larger context of how vivisection encompassed both animal and human experimentation. See Susan Lederer, *Subjected to Science: Human Experimentation in America before the Second World War* (Baltimore, MD: Johns Hopkins University Press, 1995).

105. Stopes, "Present Day Technique."

106. Stopes.

107. Baker, *Sex in Man and Animals*, 90.

108. Oliver Hochadel, "Darwin in the Monkey Cage: The Zoological Garden as a Medium of Evolutionary Theory," in *Beastly Natures: Animals, Humans and the Study of History*, ed. Dorothee Brantz (Charlottesville: University of Virginia Press, 2010), 98.

109. *The Second International Congress for Sex Research* (International Society for Sex Research, London, 3–9 August 1930). Margaret Sanger Papers, Sophia Smith Collection, Northampton, Box 53, File 4.

110. C. Ceni, "Experimental Studies on the Transformation of the Sexual Instinct into the Maternal Instinct in the Female and in the Male," in *The Second International Congress for Sex Research* (abstract, London, 3–9 August 1930); Margaret Sanger Papers, Sophia Smith Collection, Northampton, Box 53, File 4.

111. Ceni, "Experimental Studies."

112. Sigmund Freud, *Civilization and Its Discontents*, trans. David McLintock (London: Penguin Books, 2004), 45.

113. Freud, *Civilization and Its Discontents.*

114. On the beginning of psychology as a discipline, see Edith Kurzweil, *The Freudians: A Comparative Perspective* (New Haven, CT: Yale University Press, 1989).

115. Ernest Jones, *On the Nightmare* (London: Hogarth Press and the Institute of Psychoanalysis, 1931), 64.

116. Jones, 68.

117. Jones, 148.

118. Jones, 132, 137.

119. Jones, 151.

120. Chrysanthi Nigianni, "The Taste of Living," in *The Animal Catalyst: Towards Ahuman Theory*, ed. Patricia MacCormack (New York: Bloomsbury Academic, 2014), 125.

121. Craig Buettinger, "Antivivisection and the Charge of ZooPhil-Psychosis in the Early Twentieth Century," *The Historian* 55, no. 2 (Winter 1993): 277–88.

2. ECO/ONTOLOGIES: LOVE, SEX REFORM, AND ENVIRONMENTAL SCIENCES

1. See for example, a discussion on plants as models for population growth, Sharon Kingsland, *Modelling Nature: Theoretical and Experimental Approaches to Population Ecology, 1920–1950* (Chicago: University of Chicago Press, 1995), 17–18.

2. Latour, *Reassembling the Social*, 25

3. See for example, Luciana Parisi, "Nanoarchitectures: The Synthetic Design of Extensions and Thoughts," in *Digital Cultures and the Politics of Emotion: Feelings, Affect and Technological Change*, ed. Athina Karatzogianni and Adi Kuntsman (London: Palgrave MacMillan, 2012), 33–51; Carla Hustak and Natasha Myers, "Involutionary Momentum: Affective Ecologies and the Sciences of Plant/Insect Encounters," *differences* 23, no. 3 (2012): 74–118; Clough, *Autoaffection*.

4. Peter J. Bowler, *Life's Splendid Drama: Evolutionary Biology and the Reconstruction of Life's Ancestry, 1860–1940* (Chicago: University of Chicago Press, 1996).

5. See for example, Richard Doyle, *Darwin's Pharmacy: Sex, Plants, and the Evolution of the Noösphere* (Seattle: University of Washington Press, 2011); Michael Boulter, *Darwin's Garden: Down House and the Origin of Species* (London: Constable & Robinson Ltd., 2008); Frederick Burkhardt, "Darwin and the Copley Medal," *Proceedings of the American Philosophical Society* 145, no. 4 (December 2001): 510–18.

6. See for example, Elizabeth Grosz, *Becoming Undone: Darwinian Reflections on Life, Politics, and Art* (Durham, NC: Duke University Press, 2011); Joan Roughgarden, *Evolution's Rainbow* (Berkeley: University of California Press, 2009); Bert Bender, *The Descent of Love: Darwin and the Theory of Sexual Selection in American Fiction, 1871–1926* (Philadelphia: University of Pennsylvania Press, 1996).

7. Charles Darwin, *On the Origin of Species* (1859; Cambridge, MA: Harvard University Press, 1964), 8, 37, 43.

8. Charles Darwin, *The Effects of Cross and Self Fertilisation in the Vegetable Kingdom* (New York: D. Appleton and Company, 1877), 1, 15, 58, 56, 103.

9. Charles Darwin, *The Different Forms of Flowers* (London: John Murray, 1877), 24, 29.

10. On the agency of plants in shaping human bodies, see Doyle, *Darwin's Pharmacy*; Gregg Mitman, *Breathing Space: How Allergies Shape Our Lives and Landscapes* (New Haven, CT: Yale University Press, 2007); Linda Nash, "The Fruits of Ill-Health: Pesticides and Workers' Bodies in Post-World War II California," in *Landscapes of Exposure: Knowledge and Illness in Modern Environments*, ed. Gregg Mitman, Michelle Murphy, and Christopher Sellers (Chicago: University of Chicago Press, 2004), 203–19; Michael Pollan, *Botany of Desire: A Plant's Eye View of the World* (New York: Random House, 2001).

11. Benjamin Johnson, "Wilderness Parks and Their Discontents," in *American Wilderness: A New History*, ed. Michael Lewis (Oxford: Oxford University

Press, 2007), 115; Alexandra Minna Stern, "Chapter 4: California's Eugenic Landscapes," in *Eugenic Nation: Faults and Frontiers of Better Breeding in Modern America* (Berkeley: University of California Press, 2005), 119; John Sheail, *Nature Conservation in Britain: The Formative Years* (London: The Stationery Office, 1998); William H. Wilson, *The City Beautiful Movement* (Baltimore: Johns Hopkins University Press, 1989).

12. Peter Thorsheim, "Green Space and Class in Imperial London," *The Nature of Cities*, ed. Andrew Isenberg (Rochester, NY: University of Rochester Press, 2006), 24–37.

13. S. B. Sutton, ed. *Civilizing American Cities: A Selection of Frederick Law Olmsted's Writings on City Landscapes* (Cambridge, MA: The MIT Press, 1971), 175.

14. Frederick Law Olmsted, *Public Parks and the Enlargement of Towns* (Cambridge, MA: Riverside Press, 1870), 32.

15. Robert Engberg and Donald Wesling, eds. *John Muir: To Yosemite and Beyond* (Madison: University of Wisconsin Press, 1980), 51.

16. Stephen Fox, *The American Conservation Movement: John Muir and His Legacy* (Madison: University of Wisconsin Press, 1985), 120.

17. Thrift, *Non-Representational Theory*, 35–38, 71–73. Also see Nigel Thrift, *Knowing Capitalism* (London: Sage, 2005).

18. Martin Melosi, *Garbage in the Cities* (Pittsburgh: University of Pittsburgh Press, 2005), 17, 22.

19. Olmsted, *Public Parks and the Enlargement of Towns*, 32.

20. Olmsted, 15.

21. Olmsted, 118.

22. On national parks as places for white tourists and the removal of Native Americans, see Johnson, "Wilderness Parks and Their Discontents," 115; Carolyn Merchant, *American Environmental History* (New York: Columbia University Press, 2007), 152, 162–63.

23. Stern, "Chapter 4: California's Eugenic Landscapes," 115–49.

24. Phyllis Grosskurth, *Havelock Ellis: A Biography* (London: Allen Lane, 1980), 107, 135-136, 157, 237.

25. Sheila Rowbotham, *Edward Carpenter: A Life of Liberty and Love* (London: Verso, 2008), 60, 185.

26. Bertrand Russell, *The Autobiography of Bertrand Russell: 1872–1914* (London: George Allen and Unwin Ltd., 1967), 20–31, 38–43.

27. Edith Ellis to Edward Carpenter, 20 April 1896, Havelock Ellis Papers, BL, Item 70536.

28. See for example, Lucy Bland and Laura Doan, eds., *Sexology in Culture: Labelling Bodies and Desires* (Chicago: University of Chicago Press, 1998); Bullough, *Science in the Bedroom.*

29. Luther Burbank, John Whitson, Robert John, and Henry Smith Williams, *Luther Burbank: His Methods and Discoveries and Their Practical Application*, vol. 4 (New York: Luther Burbank Society, 1914), 8.

30. On the increasing emphasis on scientific precision in the rise of ecology in relation to questions of reproduction, eugenics, and population levels, see Thomas Dunlap, *Nature and the English Diaspora* (Cambridge: Cambridge

University Press, 1999), 139, 142, 146; Sharon Kingsland, *The Evolution of American Ecology, 1890–2000* (Baltimore: Johns Hopkins University Press, 1998), 5, 63, 72–75, 78, 87, 99; Joel B. Hagen, *An Entangled Bank* (New Brunswick, NJ: Rutgers University Press, 1992), 1–3, 15, 60.

31. Kingsland, *The Evolution of American Ecology*, 99.

32. See for example, how agricultural experiment stations turned to Mendelian genetics to draw conclusions across animal, plant, and human bodies, Barbara Kimmelman, "The American Breeders' Association: Genetics and Eugenics in an Agricultural Context, 1903–13," *Social Studies of Science* 13 (1983): 163–204.

33. On Stopes as a botanist, see Howard Falcon-Lang, "Marie Stopes: The Discovery of Pteridosperms and the Origin of Carboniferous Coal Balls," *Earth Sciences History* 27, no. 1 (2008): 78–99; W. G. Chaloner, "The palaeobotanical work of Marie Stopes," in *History of Palaeobotany: Selected Essays* (London: The Geological Society, 2005). Historians of sexuality have acknowledged Stopes's botanical work but do not integrate it with their primary focus on her interests and contributions to the field of human sexuality. See for example, Richard Soloway, "The Galton Lecture 1996: Marie Stopes, Eugenics and the English Birth Control Movement," in *Marie Stopes, Eugenics, and the English Birth Control Movement: Proceedings Organized by the Galton Institute London 1996*, ed. Robert A. Peel (London: The Galton Institute, 1997); Lesley Hall, "Uniting Science and Sensibility: Marie Stopes and the Narratives of Marriage in the 1920s," in *Rediscovering Forgotten Radicals: British Women Writers, 1889–1939*, ed. Angela Ingram and Daphne Patal (Chapel Hill: University of North Carolina Press, 1993): 118–36.

34. June Rose, *Marie Stopes and the Sexual Revolution* (Stroud, UK: Tempus Publishing Ltd., 2007); Ruth Hall, *Marie Stopes: A Biography* (London: André Deutsch Limited, 1977).

35. On botany's transition from a popular natural history pastime for women to a male-dominated scientific discipline, see Sam George, *Botany, Sexuality, and Women's Writing, 1760–1830: From Modest Shoot to Forward Plant* (Manchester: Manchester University Press, 2007); Ann Shteir, *Cultivating Women, Cultivating Science* (Baltimore: Johns Hopkins University Press, 1996); Elizabeth Keeney, *The Botanizers* (Chapel Hill: University of North Carolina Press, 1992).

36. On the transnational trajectories of plant-breeding science, see Noel Kingsbury, *Hybrid* (Chicago: University of Chicago Press, 2009). Jack Kloppenburg, *First the Seed*, 2nd ed. (Madison: University of Wisconsin Press, 2004). On Gregor Mendel, see Orel Vĕtslav, "History of Plant Hybridization According to Mendel's Contemporary Rudolf Geschwind," *History & Philosophy of the Life Sciences* 8, no. 2 (1986): 251–63.

37. Paul White, "The Experimental Animal in Victorian Britain," in *Thinking with Animals*, ed. Lorraine Daston and Gregg Mitman (New York: Columbia University Press, 2005), 70.

38. Marie Stopes, *Ancient Plants* (London: Blackie and Son, 1910), 174.

39. Marie Stopes, *Botany; or, the Modern Study of Plants* (London: T.C. and E.C. Jack, 1912), 70.

40. On Burbank's record keeping, see Philip Thurtle, *The Emergence of Genetic Rationality* (Seattle: University of Washington Press, 2007), 272–73, 276–78.

41. Liberty Hyde Bailey, *Plant Breeding: Being Six Lectures upon the Amelioration of Domestic Plants* (New York: The Macmillan Company, 1906), 239–46.

42. W. S. Harwood, *New Creations in Plant Life* (New York: The Macmillan Company, 1905), 4.

43. Harwood, 9.

44. Burbank et al., *Luther Burbank*, vol. 1, 111.

45. On Luther Burbank's rise to fame as a plant breeder and the wider cultural enchantment with plant breeding, see Smith, *The Garden of Invention*; Katherine Pandora, "Knowledge Held in Common: Tales of Luther Burbank and Science in the American Vernacular," *Isis* 92, no. 3 (September 2001): 484–516; Paolo Palladino, "Wizards and devotees: On the Mendelian theory of inheritance and the professionalization of agricultural science in Great Britain and the United States, 1880–1930," *History of Science* 32, no. 98 (December 1994): 409–44; Peter Dreyer, *A Gardener Touched with Genius*, rev. ed. (Berkeley: University of California Press, 1985).

46. Luther Burbank, *The Training of the Human Plant* (New York: Century, 1907), 3.

47. Burbank, 16.

48. Stopes, *Ancient Plants*, 51.

49. Marie Stopes, *The Human Body and Its Functions* (London: The Gill Publishing Co. Ltd., 1926), 165.

50. Stopes, 165.

51. Marie Stopes, *Married Love; or, Love in Marriage* (1918; New York: Eugenics Publishing Co., 1927), 44. Stopes discusses "simple physiological laws of life" in *The Human Body and Its Functions*, 173. She discusses numerical laws, laws of hereditary transmission and evolution in *Botany*, 70.

52. Burbank et al., *Luther Burbank*, vol. 3, 47.

53. Luther Burbank, "Some of the Fundamental Principles of Plant Breeding," *Proceedings: International Conference on Plant Breeding and Hybridization* (New York: Horticultural Society, 1902–1907), 38, 39.

54. Burbank, 17.

55. Burbank, 9.

56. Stopes, *Ancient Plants*, 175.

57. Stopes, 72.

58. Stopes, 52.

59. On the intersection of science and the politics of enforcing normative sexuality, see Nancy Ordover, *American Eugenics: Race, Queer Anatomy, and the Science of Nationalism* (Minneapolis: University of Minnesota Press, 2003); Terry, *An American Obsession.*

60. Patricia Ticineto Clough and Jean Halley, *The Affective Turn: Theorizing the Social* (Durham, NC: Duke University Press, 2007), 25.

61. Clough and Halley, 25.

62. Several scholars have discussed the particular conditions, commitments, and experiments at individual agricultural experiment stations and land grant colleges. See for example, Stuart McCook, "'The World Was My Garden': Tropical Botany and Cosmopolitanism in American Science, 1898–1935," in *Colonial Crucible: Empire in the Making of the American State*, ed. Alfred McCoy and Francisco Scarano (Madison: University of Wisconsin Press, 2009), 499–507; Alan Olmstead and Paul Rhode, *Creating Abundance: Biological Innovation and American Agricultural Development* (Cambridge: Cambridge University Press, 2008); Richard Sawyer, *To Make a Spotless Orange: Biological Control in California* (Ames: Iowa State University Press, 1996); Richard Overfield, "The Agricultural Experiment Station and Americanization: The Hawaiian Experience, 1900–1910," *Agricultural History* 60, no. 2 (Spring 1986): 256–66; Alan Marcus, *Agricultural Science and the Quest for Legitimacy: Farmers, Agricultural Colleges, and Experiment Stations, 1870–1890* (Ames: Iowa State University Press, 1985); Charles E. Rosenberg, "Science, Technology and Economic Growth: The Case of the Agricultural Experiment Station Scientist, 1875–1914," *Agricultural History* 45, no. 1 (January 1971), 1–20; Vernon Carstensen, "The Genesis of an Agricultural Experiment Station," 34, no. 1 (January 1960): 13–20.

63. On the British station in the West Indies, see Sir Daniel Morris's paper presented at the plant science conference in New York. Daniel Morris, "Improvement of the Sugar Cane by Selection and Cross-Fertilization," *Proceedings: International Conference on Plant Breeding and Hybridization*, 80–81. See William Storey, "Plants, Power, and Development Founding the Imperial Department of Agriculture for the West Indies, 1880–1914," in *States of Knowledge: The Co-production of Science and Social Order*, ed. Sheila Jasanoff (New York: Routledge, 2004): 109–30.

64. On botany in Germany, see Eugene Cittadino, *Nature as the Laboratory* (Cambridge: Cambridge University Press, 1990).

65. Early twentieth-century conferences devoted to plant sexuality highlight the network of botanists. See for instance, Horticultural Society of New York: *Proceedings: International Conference on Plant Breeding and Hybridization* (New York: Horticultural Society, 1902–1907) and B. M. Duggar, ed. *Proceedings of the International Congress of Plant Sciences, Ithaca, New York, August 16–23, 1926* (Menasha, WI: Banta, 1929).

66. Catriona Sandilands and Bruce Erickson draw attention to the synchronicity between sexology and environmentalism: "Introduction: A Genealogy of Queer Ecologies," in *Queer Ecologies*, ed. Catriona Sandilands and Bruce Erickson (Bloomington: Indiana University Press, 2010), 7.

67. Isabelle Stengers, "Including Nonhumans in Political Theory," in *Political Matter: Technoscience, Democracy, and Public Life*, ed. Bruce Brahn and Sarah Whatmore (Minneapolis: University of Minnesota Press, 2010), 11–12.

68. Hannah Landecker, *Culturing Life: How Cells Became Technologies* (Cambridge, MA: Harvard University Press, 2007).

69. Hutchins Hapgood, "Cultivate Your Garden," Hapgood Papers, Beinecke, Yale, Box 26, File 704.

70. Hapgood.

71. See David Matless *Landscape and Englishness* (London: Reaktion Books, 1998), 103–70; Frank Trentmann, "Civilization and Its Discontents: English Neo-Romanticism and the Transformation of Anti-Modernism," *Journal of Contemporary History* 29, no. 4 (1994): 583–625.

72. Stopes, *Married Love*, 36, 64, 122.

73. Robert Colls, *Identity of England* (Oxford: Oxford University Press, 2002), 204, 211; Trentmann, "Civilization and Its Discontents," 583–625; T. J. Jackson Lears, *No Place of Grace: Antimodernism and the Transformation of American Culture, 1880–1920* (New York: Pantheon Books, 1981).

74. Stopes, *Married Love*, 18, 36, 64.

75. Richard Drinnon, *Rebel in Paradise* (Chicago: University of Chicago Press, 1961), 147.

76. Emma Goldman and Max Baginski, "Introduction," *Mother Earth* 1, no. 1 (March 1906): 1.

77. Goldman and Baginski, 2.

78. Goldman and Baginski, 2.

79. Goldman and Baginski, 2.

80. See for example, Tom Lutz, *American Nervousness, 1903: An Anecdotal History* (Ithaca, NY: Cornell University Press, 1991), 21, 32, 35, 65–66, 79, 90; Janet Oppenheim, *"Shattered Nerves": Doctors, Patients and Depression in Victorian England* (Oxford: Oxford University Press, 1991).

81. Smith Ely Jelliffe to Mabel Dodge, 7 August 1920, Mabel Dodge Luhan Papers, Beinecke, Yale, Box 20, File 563.

82. Neith Boyce to Hutchins Hapgood, 18 July 1929, Hapgood Papers, Beinecke, Yale, Box 20, File 513.

83. Boyce to Hapgood.

84. Boyce to Hapgood.

85. On points of convergence between social sciences and biology, see Tracy Teslow, *Constructing Race: The Science of Bodies and Cultures in American Anthropology* (New York: Cambridge University Press, 2014); Chris Renwick, *British Sociology's Lost Biological Roots: A History of Futures Past* (Basingstoke, UK: Palgrave Macmillan, 2012).

86. Naomi Mitchison to Mabel Dodge Luhan, 1 March 1935, Mabel Dodge Luhan Papers, Beinecke, Yale, Box 26, File 716.

87. Hapgood, "The Anarchist Farmer," Hapgood Papers, Beinecke, Yale, Box 26, File 681.

88. Stopes, *Married Love*, 21.

89. Stopes, 17, 18.

90. See for example, Trentmann, "Civilization and Its Discontents," 583–625; Lears, *No Place of Grace.*

91. Stopes, *Married Love*, 21.

92. Feminist geographers have discussed how heterosexual norms constitute space. See Lynda Johnston and Robyn Longhurst, eds., *Space, Place, and Sex: Geographies of Sexualities* (Lanham, MD: Rowman & Littlefield, 2010).

93. Johnston and Longhurst, 21, 53, 59.

94. Stopes, *Married Love*, 77.

95. Hutchins Hapgood to Neith Boyce, 1909, Hapgood Papers, Beinecke, Yale, Box 12, File 372.

96. Emma Goldman to Ben Reitman, 2 July 1908, Emma Goldman Papers (Alexandria, VA: Chadwyck-Healy, 1990), Reel 2; Emma Goldman to Ben Reitman, 29 June 1908, Emma Goldman Papers, Reel 2.

97. Elizabeth Hutchinson, *The Indian Craze: Primitivism, Modernism, and Transculturation in American Art, 1890–1915* (Durham, NC: Duke University Press, 2009); Joy Kasson, *Buffalo Bill's Wild West: Celebrity, Memory and Popular History* (New York: Hill and Wang, 2000); Helen Carr, *Inventing the American Primitive* (New York: New York University Press, 1996); Philip Deloria, *Playing Indian* (New Haven, CT: Yale University Press, 1998), 95–117; Marianna Torgovnick, *Gone Primitive: Savage Intellects, Modern Lives* (Chicago: University of Chicago Press, 1990).

98. Neith Boyce to Mabel Dodge, 1915, Mabel Dodge Luhan Papers, Beinecke, Yale, Box 3, File 90.

99. Mabel Dodge Luhan, Diary, 31 August 1946, Mabel Dodge Luhan Papers, Beinecke, Yale, Box 100, File 2293.

100. Mabel Dodge, "On Human Relations," June 1938, Mabel Dodge Luhan Papers, Beinecke, Yale, Box 44, File 1349.

101. Dodge.

102. Dodge.

103. Dodge.

104. Nancy Leys Stepan and Sander Gilman, "Appropriating the Idioms of Science: The Rejection of Scientific Racism," in *The 'Racial' Economy of Science: Toward a Democratic Future*, ed. Sandra Harding (Bloomington: Indiana University Press, 1993), 170–201.

105. Marie Stopes, *Wise Parenthood* (1918; London: G.P. Putnam's Sons, Ltd., 1924), 20.

106. Marie Stopes, *Radiant Motherhood: A Book for Those Who Are Creating the Future* (London: G.P. Putnam's Sons Ltd., 1920), 220.

107. Donna Haraway, *How Like a Leaf: An Interview with Thyrza Nichols Goodeve* (New York: Routledge, 2000).

3. PLANETARY INTIMACIES: PHYSICS, OCCULTISM, AND NONHUMANS IN LOVE

1. Parisi, "Nanoarchitectures"; Luciana Parisi, "Technoecologies of Sensation," in *Deleuze/Guattari and Ecology*, ed. Bernd Herzogenrath (Basingstoke, UK: Palgrave Macmillan, 2009): 182–99; Clough, *Autoaffection*.

2. Karen Barad, "The Inhuman That Therefore I Am," Politics of Care Workshop (York University, 22 April 2012), 4; Jussi Parikka, *Insect Media: An Archaeology of Animals and Technology* (Minneapolis: University of Minnesota Press, 2010); Jake Kosek, "Ecologies of Empire: On the New Uses of the Honeybee," *Cultural Anthropology* 25, no. 4 (November 2010): 650–78; Hird, *The Origins of Sociable Life*; Richard White, *The Organic Machine* (New York: Hill and Wang, 1995).

3. Stengers, "Including Nonhumans in Political Theory," 11–12. Also, see Bruno Latour's discussion of communities of actants, both human and nonhuman, in *Reassembling the Social.*

4. Anne Fausto-Sterling, *Sex/Gender: Biology in a Social World* (New York: Routledge, 2012); Terry, *An American Obsession*; Clarke, *Disciplining Reproduction*; Lynda Birke and Ruth Hubbard, eds., *Reinventing Biology: Respect for Life and the Creation of Knowledge* (Bloomington: Indiana University Press, 1995); Nelly Oudshoorn, *Beyond the Natural Body: An archaeology of Sex Hormones* (London: Routledge, 1994); Haraway, *Simians, Cyborgs, and Women.*

5. Karen Barad, *Meeting the Universe Halfway* (Durham, NC: Duke University Press, 2007), 45-66.

6. For the intersection of ecofeminism and goddess worship, see Val Plumwood, *Environmental Culture: The Ecological Crisis of Reason* (London: Routledge, 2002); Karen Warren, *Ecofeminist Philosophy: On a Western Perspective of What It Is and Why It Matters* (Lanham, MD: Rowman & Littlefield, 2000), and Carol Adams, ed., *Ecofeminism and the Sacred* (New York: Continuum, 1993).

7. Stefan Helmrich, "Kinship in Hypertext: Transubstantiating Fatherhood and Information Flow in Artificial Life," in *Relative Values: Reconfiguring Kinship*, ed. Sarah Franklin and Susan McKinnon (Durham, NC: Duke University Press, 2001), 116–44.

8. Parisi, "Technoecologies of Sensation," 183.

9. Harry Bruinius, *Better for All the World: The Secret History of Forced Sterilization and America's Quest for Racial Purity* (New York: Knopf, 2006); Ivan Crozier, "'All The World's a Stage': Dora Russell, Norman Haire, and the 1929 League for Sexual Reform Congress," *Journal of the History of Sexuality* 12, no. 1 (2003): 16–37; Richardson, *Love and Eugenics in the Nineteenth Century*; Wendy Kline, *Building a Better Race: Gender, Sexuality, and Eugenics from the Turn of the Century to the Baby Boom* (Berkeley: University of California Press, 2001).

10. Grosskurth, *Havelock Ellis*, 27, 33, 39, 93, 226.

11. Havelock Ellis, *My Life* (London: Heinemann, 1940), 130.

12. Chushichi Tsuzuki, *Edward Carpenter, 1844–1929: Prophet of Human Fellowship* (Cambridge: Cambridge University Press, 1980), 2–3, 15–25.

13. Parminder Kaur Bakshi, "Homosexuality and Orientalism: Edward Carpenter's Journey to the East," in *Edward Carpenter and Late Victorian Radicalism*, ed. Tony Brown (London: Frank Cass & Co. Ltd., 1990), 171–72.

14. Gail Bederman, "Chapter 3: 'Teaching Our Sons to Do What We Have Been Teaching the Savages to Avoid': G. Stanley Hall, Racial Reproduction, and the Neurasthenic Paradox," in *Manliness and Civilization* (Chicago: University of Chicago Press, 1995), 77–120. For the teaching of Christian manhood in relation to sexuality, see Axel Bundgaard, *Muscle and Manliness: The Rise of Sport in American Boarding Schools* (Syracuse, NY: Syracuse University Press, 2005), 118.

15. Emma Goldman, "Marriage and Love," 1916, The Emma Goldman Papers (Alexandria, VA: Chadwyck-Healy, 1990): Reel 48.

16. Margaret Sanger, "Happiness," *Woman Rebel* (April 1914); 8.

17. John Corrigan, *Business of the Heart: Religion and Emotion in the Nineteenth Century* (Berkeley: University of California Press, 2002).

18. Havelock Ellis, Diary, 4 January 1880, Havelock Ellis Papers, BL, London, Item 70525.

19. Ellis.

20. Edward Carpenter, *Civilisation; Its Causes and Cure and Other Essays* (London: Allen & Unwin, 1921), 46.

21. Carpenter, 27.

22. Carpenter.

23. Ellen Key, *Love and Marriage*, trans. Arthur G. Chater (New York: G.P Putnam's Sons, 1911), 15.

24. Key, 46.

25. Key, 173.

26. Key, 155.

27. Beryl Satter, *Each Mind a Kingdom: American Women, Sexual Purity, and the New Thought Movement, 1875–1920* (Berkeley: University of California Press, 1999); Catherine Albanese, *A Republic of Mind and Spirit: A Cultural History of Metaphysical Religion* (New Haven, CT: Yale University Press, 2007); Ann Taves, *Fits, Trances, and Visions: Experiencing Religion and Explaining Experience from Wesley to James* (Princeton, NJ: Princeton University Press, 1999).

28. On the Transcendentalists, see Barry Hankins, *Second Great Awakening and the Transcendentalists* (Westport, CT: Greenwood Press, 2004); Catherine Albanese, *Nature Religion in America: From the Algonkian Indians to the New Age* (Chicago: University of Chicago Press, 1990); Sandra Frankiel, *California's Spiritual Frontiers: Religious Alternatives in Anglo-Protestantism, 1850–1910* (Berkeley: University of California Press, 1988).

29. Alex Owen, *The Place of Enchantment: British Occultism and the Culture of the Modern* (Chicago: University of Chicago Press, 2004); Janet Oppenheim, *The Other World: Spiritualism and Psychical Research in England, 1850–1914* (Cambridge: Cambridge University Press, 1985).

30. Malcolm Kottler, "Alfred Russel Wallace, the Origin of Man, and Spiritualism," *Isis* 65, no. 2 (June 1974): 145–92.

31. On physicists and occultism, see Peter J. Bowler, "Physics and Cosmology," in *Reconciling Science and Religion* (Chicago: University of Chicago Press, 2001), 87–121; Erwin Hiebert, "Modern Physics and Christian Faith," in *God and Nature: Historical Essays on the Encounter between Christianity and Science*, ed. David C. Lindberg and Ronald Numbers (Berkeley: University of California Press, 1986), 424–47; Janet Oppenheim, "Physics and Psychic Phenomena," in *The Other World: Spiritualism and Psychical Research in England, 1850–1914* (Cambridge: Cambridge University Press, 1985).

32. Bertrand Russell, "The Study of Mathematics," in *Mysticism and Logic and Other Essays*, 2nd ed. (London: Allen & Unwin, 1959), 66, 68–69.

33. On William Crookes's fascination with spiritualism, see Oppenheim, *The Other World*, 16. On William James and spiritualist phenomena, see Taves, *Fits, Trances, and Visions*, 274, 280; Paul Jerome Croce, *Science and Religion in the Era of William James: Eclipse of Uncertainty, 1820–1880* (Chapel Hill: University of North Carolina Press, 1995), 50, 58, 63.

34. Tsuzuki, *Edward Carpenter, 1844–1929*, 2–3, 15–25.
35. Rowbotham, *Edward Carpenter*, 87, 145.
36. Rowbotham, 145.
37. Rowbotham, 348.
38. Rowbotham, 48–49.
39. Rowbotham, 105–6.
40. Rowbotham, 106.
41. See for example, John C. Burnham, "The New Psychology," in *1915: The Cultural Moment*, ed. Adele Heller and Lois Rudnick (New Brunswick, NJ: Rutgers University Press, 1991), 117–27; Thomson, "Chapter 3, After the New Age," 76–106.
42. Burnham, "The New Psychology," 117–27.
43. See for example, Carla Hustak, "Inventing the Female Self in Greenwich Village, 1900–1930: Mabel Dodge's Encounter with Science and Spirituality," *Subjectivity*, no. 6 (2013): 173–92; Alexander Geppert, "Divine Sex, Happy Marriage, Regenerated Nation: Marie Stopes's Marital Manual *Married Love* and the Making of a Best-Seller, 1918–1955," *Journal of the History of Sexuality* 8, no. 3 (January 1998): 389–33.
44. Lois Palken Rudnick, *Mabel Dodge Luhan: New Woman, New Worlds* (Albuquerque: New Mexico University Press, 1984); Flannery Burke, *From Greenwich Village to Taos: Primitivism and Place at Mabel Dodge Luhan's* (Lawrence: University Press of Kansas, 2008).
45. Mabel Dodge to Alexander Berkman, undated, Mabel Dodge Luhan Papers, Beinecke, Yale, Box 3, File 78.
46. Dodge.
47. Mabel Dodge to Smith Ely Jelliffe, undated, Mabel Dodge Luhan Papers, Beinecke, Yale, Box 20, File 567.
48. On this exchange between Jelliffe and Dodge, see Mabel Dodge to Smith Ely Jelliffe, Mabel Dodge Luhan Papers, Beinecke, Yale, Box 20, File 567.
49. On the influence of Christian Science on Emma Curtis Hopkins, see Gail M. Harley, *Emma Curtis Hopkins: Forgotten Founder of New Thought* (Syracuse, NY: Syracuse University Press, 2002).
50. Mabel Dodge Luhan, *Intimate Memories* vol. 3 (New York: Harcourt Brace & Company, 1933), 468.
51. See for example, Christopher White, *Unsettled Minds: Psychology and the American Search for Spiritual Assurance, 1830–1940* (Berkeley: University of California Press, 2009); Burnham, "The New Psychology," 117–27.
52. On Freud's relationship with Brill, see Kurzweil, *The Freudians*, 49, 52.
53. Luhan, *Intimate Memories*, 511.
54. Mabel Dodge to Neith Boyce, 10 July 1919, Hapgood Papers, Beinecke, Yale, Box 5, File 152.
55. Dodge.
56. Dodge's spiritual outlook took shape at a time of the rise of maternalism in feminist politics and heightened attention to maternal roles in the context of psychoanalysis. Significantly, Dodge situated these relationships in a cosmic register. On maternalism, see Molly Ladd-Taylor, *Mother-Work: Women, Child Welfare, and the State, 1890–1930* (Urbana: University of Illinois Press, 1994).

57. Joscelyn Godwin indicates occultism's "worship of the generative organs." See Joscelyn Godwin, *The Theosophical Enlightenment* (Albany: State University of New York Press, 1994), 1–26.

58. On the magical properties attributed to technologies, see Fred Nadis, *Wonder Shows: Performing Science, Magic, and Religion in America* (New Brunswick, NJ: Rutgers University Press, 2005); Pamela Thurschwell, *Literature, Technology, and Magical Thinking, 1880–1920* (Cambridge: Cambridge University Press, 2001). Histories of birth control technologies place little if any emphasis on the magical and occultist interpretations of bodies in this period. For in-depth analyses of birth control technologies, see Andrea Tone, *Devices and Desires: A History of Contraceptives in America* (New York: Hill & Wang, 2001); Peter Neushal, "Marie C. Stopes and the Popularization of Birth Control Technology," *Technology and Culture* 39, no. 2 (1998): 246–47.

59. Miriam Benn, for instance, highlights how George Drysdale's readers found his works inadequate for addressing the mystical experience of sex. See Miriam Benn, *Predicaments of Love* (London: Pluto Press, 1992), 162.

60. Annie Besant, *Annie Besant: An Autobiography* (London: T. Fisher Unwin, 1893), 165–66, 237–41.

61. Elizabeth Aldrich to Margaret Sanger, 6 February 1922, *The Margaret Sanger Papers* (Bethesda, MD: University Publications of America, 1995): Reel 83.

62. Aldrich.

63. Margaret Sanger, *The Pivot of Civilization* (New York: Brentano's, 1922), 27.

64. Aldrich to Sanger, 6 February 1922.

65. This concept of magnetic fluids traversed both religious and biological discourses in the late eighteenth and early nineteenth century with Jean Baptiste-Lamarck's notion of a magnetic fluid connecting organisms to their environment. See for example, Jean-Baptiste Lamarck, *Zoological Philosophy: An Exposition with Regard to the Natural History of Animals*, trans. Hugh Elliott (London: Macmillan and Co. Limited, 1914), 187, 189, 201, 212.

66. Letter to American President Wilson, September 1915. Marie C. Stopes Collection, Wellcome Library, London, File ML Overseas Correspondence 1915-1957.

67. Margaret Sanger to Marie Stopes, undated. Marie C. Stopes Collection, Wellcome Library, London, File ML Overseas Correspondence 1915-1957.

68. Historian Peter Neushul notes the development of birth control technologies as technologies charged with emotions. See Neushul, "Marie Stopes and the Popularization of Birth Control Technology," 246, 258.

69. Marie Stopes, "Birth Control" (National Birthrate Commission, London, 10 March 1919), Marie Stopes Papers, BL, London, Item 58546.

70. Stopes.

71. See for example, Bruinius, *Better for All the World*; Christine Rosen, *Preaching Eugenics: Religious Leaders and the American eugenics movement* (Oxford: Oxford University Press, 2004); Kline, *Building a Better Race*.

72. Marie Stopes to Duncan Cameron, 8 November 1928, Marie Stopes Papers, Wellcome Library, London, File A298. Cameron also wrote to Stopes to

confirm his lecture to the CBC, "The Race Problem in Scotland." See Duncan Cameron to Marie Stopes, 11 December 1923, Marie Stopes Papers, Wellcome Library, London File A298.

73. On changing meanings of whiteness and Irish and Italian immigration, see for example, Matthew Frye Jacobson, *Whiteness of a Different Color: European Immigrants and the Alchemy of Race* (Cambridge, MA: Harvard University Press, 1998), 41–51. On whiteness and racial representations of fertility, see Irving, *Immigrant Mothers: Narratives of Race and Maternity, 1890–1925* (Urbana: University of Illinois Press, 2000), 36–50; Anna Davin, "Imperialism and Motherhood," in *Tensions of Empire: Colonial Cultures in a Bourgeois World*, ed. Frederick Cooper and Ann Laura Stoler (Berkeley: University of California Press, 1997), 87–151.

74. Margaret Sanger, *Margaret Sanger: An Autobiography* (New York: W.W. Norton, 1938), 28–29.

75. Sanger, 406.

76. See Bruinius, *Better for all the World*; Rosen, *Preaching Eugenics*; Kline, *Building a Better Race*.

77. William Inge to Marie Stopes, 26 January 1918, Marie Stopes Papers, BL, London, Item 58548.

78. "An English Bishop on Birth Control," *BCR* 4, no. 2 (February 1920): 14.

79. On the politics of affect, see Hemmings, "Invoking Affect," 548–67; Brian Massumi, "The Future Birth of the Affective Fact: The Political Ontology of Threat," in Gregg and Seigworth, eds., *The Affect Theory Reader*, 52–70; Ben Anderson, "Modulation the Excess of Affect: Morale in a State of 'Total War,'" in Gregg and Seigworth,eds., *The Affect Theory Reader*, 161–85; Patricia Clough, "The Affective Turn: Political Economy, Biomedia, and Bodies," in Gregg and Seigworth, eds., *The Affect Theory Reader*, 206–25. On love and care in feminist literature, see Fiona Robinson, *The Ethics of Care: A Feminist Approach to Human Security* (Philadelphia: Temple University, 2011); Luce Irigaray, *The Way of Love*, trans. Heidi Bostic and Stephen Pluhacek (London: Continuum, 2002); Hilary Rose, *Love, Power and Knowledge: Towards a Feminist Transformation of the Sciences* (Bloomington: Indiana University Press, 1994); Joan Tronto, *Moral Boundaries: A Political Argument for an Ethic of Care* (New York: Routledge, 1993); Arlie Hochschild, *The Managed Heart: Commercialization of Human Feeling* (Berkeley: University of California Press, 1983).

4. REINVENTING LOVE AS TECHNOLOGIES OF SEX AND MARITAL INTIMACIES

1. Marie Stopes to Jane Hawthorne, 11 June 1920, Marie C. Stopes Collection, Wellcome Library, London, File A272.

2. See for example, Londa Schiebinger, *Nature's Body: Gender's Body in the Making of Modern Science* (Boston: Beacon Press, 1993); Clarke, *Disciplining Reproduction*; Judith Halberstam, *In a Queer Time and Place: Transgender Bodies, Subcultural Lives* (New York: New York University, 2005); Lee Edelman, *No Future: Queer Theory and the Death Drive* (Durham, NC: Duke University Press, 2004); Parisi, *Abstract Sex*; Lynn Margulis, *Symbiogenetic Planet: A New Look at Evolution* (New York: Basic Books, 1998).

3. Many scholars have noted the role of animals in sexual science. See for example, Watkins, *The Estrogen Elixir*; Sengoopta, *The Most Secret Quintessence of Life*; Rader, *Making Mice*, Clarke, *Disciplining Reproduction*, 1998; Harriet Ritvo, *The Platypus and the Mermaid and Other Figments of the Classifying Imagination* (Cambridge, MA: Harvard University Press, 1997).

4. Parisi, "Technoecologies of Sensation," 182–99.

5. Bertrand Russell to Dora Russell, 18 April 1924. Dora Russell fonds, McMaster, Box 7.29.

6. Russell.

7. Bland and Doan, eds. *Sexology in Culture*; Bullough, *Science in the Bedroom.*

8. Havelock Ellis, *Studies in the Psychology of Sex* (Philadelphia: F.A. Davis, 1928), 510.

9. Margaret Sanger, *Happiness in Marriage* (1926; New York: Blue Ribbon Books, 1940), 122.

10. Sanger, 122.

11. Sanger, 130.

12. Sanger, 161.

13. Sanger, 123, 132.

14. Sanger, 132.

15. Sanger, 132.

16. Sanger, 143.

17. Stopes, *Married Love*, 37.

18. Stopes, 83.

19. Stopes, 57.

20. Stopes, 89.

21. Stopes, 53.

22. Hutchins Hapgood to Neith Boyce, Summer 1898, Hapgood Papers, Beinecke, Yale, Box 11, File 348.

23. Hutchins Hapgood to Neith Boyce, June 1898, Hapgood Papers, Beinecke, Yale, Box 11, File 349.

24. Hapgood Box 11, File 349.

25. Hutchins Hapgood to Neith Boyce, 31 October 1905, Hapgood Papers, Beinecke, Yale, Box 12, File 363.

26. Hapgood Box 12, File 363.

27. Dora Russell, *The Right to Be Happy* (London: Harper & Brothers Publishers, 1927), 167.

28. Bertrand Russell, *Marriage and Morals* (New York: Horace Liveright, 1929), 16, 122–23, 127–28.

29. On cultural fears of the decline of white middle-class energies, see John Pettegrew, *Brutes in Suits: Male Sensibility in America, 1890–1920*. Baltimore, MD: Johns Hopkins University Press, 2007; Carolyn Thomas de la Peña, *The Body Electric* (New York: New York University Press, 2003); Marijke Gijswijt-Hoftstra and Roy Porter, eds. *Cultures of Neurasthenia* (New York: Rodopi, 2001); Lutz, *American Nervousness*; Anson Rabinbach, *The Human Motor: Energy, Fatigue and the Origins of Modernity* (New York: Basic Books, 1990).

30. Neith Boyce and Hutchins Hapgood. *Enemies*, 1916, Hapgood Papers, Beinecke, Yale, Box 26, File 673.

31. Alys Weinbaum, *Wayward Reproductions* (Durham, NC: Duke University Press, 2004), 145–86.

32. Judith Butler, *Gender Trouble* (New York: Routledge, 1990).

33. Neith Boyce to Mabel Dodge, 1915, Mabel Dodge Luhan Papers, Beinecke, Yale, Box 3, File 90.

34. Neith Boyce to Hutchins Hapgood, 16 May 1916, Hapgood Papers, Beinecke, Yale, Box 19, File 506.

35. Hutchins Hapgood, "The Passion of the Conservative," Hapgood Papers, Beinecke, Yale, Box 27, File 770.

36. Hapgood.

37. Hutchins Hapgood, "The Criminal Monkey," Hapgood Papers, Beinecke, Yale, Box 48, File 1537.

38. See, for example, Cynthia Eagle Russett, *Sexual Science: The Victorian Construction of Womanhood* (Cambridge, MA: Harvard University Press, 1991).

39. Henri Bergson, *Creative Evolution*, translated by Arthur Mitchell (New York: Holt, 1913), 126, 225.

40. Hutchins Hapgood, "The Criminal Monkey," Hapgood Papers, Beinecke, Yale, Box 48, File 1537.

41. See for example, Dan Stone, *Breeding Superman: Nietzsche, Race and Eugenics in Edwardian and Interwar Britain* (Liverpool: Liverpool University Press, 2002); Jennifer Ratner-Rosenhagen, *American Nietzsche* (Chicago: University of Chicago Press, 2012).

42. Neith Boyce to Hutchins Hapgood, 1901, Hapgood Papers, Beinecke, Yale, Box 19, File 496.

43. Hutchins Hapgood, "The Drama of the Italians," Hapgood Papers, Beinecke, Yale, Box 28, File 847.

44. Hutchins Hapgood, "The Fall of the Bowery," Hapgood Papers, Beinecke, Yale, Box 26, File 714.

45. Seth Koven, *Slumming: Sexual and Social Politics in Victorian London* (Princeton, NJ: Princeton University Press, 2004); Chad Heap, *Slumming: Sexual and Racial Encounters in American Nightlife, 1885–1940* (Chicago: University of Chicago Press, 2009).

46. Bertrand Russell to Dora Russell, 11 October 1927. Dora Russell fonds, McMaster University, Box 7.29.

47. Historians of sex reformers have discussed the intersection of reforming gender relations and reforming sex. See for example, Christina Simmons, "Women's Power in Sex Radical Challenges to Marriage in the Early-Twentieth-Century United States," *Feminist Studies* 29, no. 1 (Spring 2003): 168–98; George Robb, "The Way of All Flesh: Degeneration, Eugenics, and the Gospel of Free Love," *Journal of the History of Sexuality* 6, no. 4 (April 1996): 589–603; Lesley Hall, "Uniting Science and Sensibility," 118–36.

48. On utopian socialism, see for example Barbara Taylor, *Eve and the New Jerusalem: Socialism and Feminism in the Nineteenth Century* (London: Virago, 1983). On women in the New Left, see Ellen Kay Trimberger, "Women in the

Old and New Left: The Evolution of a Politics of Personal Life," *Feminist Studies* 5, no. 3 (Autumn 1979): 431–50.

49. Margaret Jackson, *The Real Facts of Life: Feminism and the Politics of Sexuality c.1985–1940* (London: Taylor & Francis, 1994); Sheila Jeffreys, "Sex Reform and Anti-feminism in the 1920s," in *The Sexual Dynamics of History*, ed. London Feminist History Group (London: Pluto Press, 1983); John Spurlock, "The Problem of Modern Married Love for Middle-Class Women," in *An Emotional History of the United States*, ed. Peter Stearns and Jan Lewis (New York: New York University Press, 1998), 319–32. Also, Dale Bauer discusses women writers' reaction to "the inequality of modern love" and how "sex power remained a problem for most middle-class and working women." See Dale Bauer, *Sex Expression and American Women Writers, 1860–1940* (Chapel Hill: University of North Carolina Press, 2009), 106–7.

50. Historians have indicated that the early twentieth century marked a transformation in higher emotional expectations of relationships and the significance of sexual intimacy in marriage. See for example, Elaine Tyler May, *Great Expectations: Marriage and Divorce in Post-Victorian America* (Chicago: University of Chicago Press, 1980). Stephanie Coontz, *The Way We Never Were: American Families and the Nostalgia Trap* (New York: Basic Books, 1992). John D'Emilio and Estelle Freedman, *Intimate Matters: The History of Sexuality in America* (New York: Harper & Row, 1988). On this same intensification of marital love and greater sexual expectations in Britain, see Lesley Hall, *Hidden Anxieties: Male Sexuality, 1900–1950* (Cambridge, MA: Blackwell, 1990); Marcus Collins, *Modern Love: An Intimate History of Men and Women in Twentieth-Century Britain* (London: Atlantic Books, 2003); and Kate Fisher, *Birth Control, Sex and Marriage in Britain, 1918–1960* (Oxford: Oxford University Press, 2006).

51. Sex reformers recognized connections between New York City's Greenwich Village and London's Bloomsbury. See the correspondence between British sex reformer Naomi Mitchison and American sex reformer Mabel Dodge. Naomi Mitchison to Mabel Dodge Luhan, 21 November 1935, Mabel Dodge Luhan Papers, Beinecke, Yale, Box 26, File 716. Also, Dora Russell's romantic relationship with Greenwich Village journalist Griffin Barry highlights the intimate connections between these two bohemian communities. See for example, their daughter Harriet Barry's biography. Harriet Ward, *A Man of Small Importance: My Father Griffin Barry* (Debenham, UK: Dormouse Books, 2003).

52. Hutchins Hapgood, *A Victorian in Modern World* (New York: Harcourt, Brace and Company, 1939), 207.

53. Hapgood, 202.

54. Hapgood, 320.

55. Dora Russell, *The Tamarisk Tree: My Quest for Love and Liberty* (London: Elek/Pemberton, 1975), 69.

56. Neith Boyce to Hutchins Hapgood, 2 January 1899, Hapgood Family Papers, Beinecke, Yale, Box 18, File 491.

57. Ellen Kay Trimberger, ed., *Intimate Warriors: Portraits of a Modern Marriage 1899–1944—Selected Works by Neith Boyce and Hutchins Hapgood* (New York: The Feminist Press, 1991), 33.

58. Hutchins Hapgood to Neith Boyce, December 1915, Hapgood Papers, Beinecke, Yale, Box 12, File 377.

59. Neith Boyce to Hutchins Hapgood, 16 May 1916, Hapgood Papers, Beinecke, Yale, Box 19, File 506.

60. Bertrand Russell to Dora Russell, 4 December 1927, Bertrand Russell Archives, McMaster University.

61. Bertrand to Dora Russell, 20 October 1927, Bertrand Russell Archives, McMaster University.

62. Dora Russell to Bertrand Russell, 9 March 1933, Dora Russell Papers, IISH, Amsterdam, Box 78–92, File 82.

63. Hutchins Hapgood to Neith Boyce, 1904, Hapgood Papers, Beinecke, Yale, Box 12, File 360.

64. Neith Boyce to Hutchins Hapgood, 1907, Hapgood Papers, Beinecke, Yale, Box 19, File 502.

65. Bertrand Russell to Dora Russell, 26 October 1927, Bertrand Russell Archives, McMaster.

66. Russell.

67. Bertrand Russell to Dora Russell, 22 November 1929, Dora Russell fonds, McMaster, Box 7.29.

68. Bertrand Russell to Dora Russell, 6 September 1929, Dora Russell fonds, McMaster, Box 7.29; Bertrand Russell to Dora Russell, 9 September 1929, Dora Russell fonds, McMaster, Box 7.29.

69. Margaret Marsh, "Suburban Men and Masculine Domesticity, 1870–1915," *American Quarterly* 40 (June 1988): 165–86. On the shaping of new emotional ideals of fatherhood, see Robert Griswold, *Fatherhood in America: A History* (New York: Basic Books, 1993); Tim Fisher, "Fatherhood and the British Fathercraft Movement, 1919–1939," *Gender & History* 17, no. 2 (August 2005): 441–62.

70. Hutchins Hapgood to Neith Boyce, 11 September 1908, Hapgood Papers, Beinecke, Yale, Box 12, File 369.

71. Hutchins Hapgood to Neith Boyce, 25 March 1917, Hapgood Papers, Beinecke, Yale, Box 13, File 378.

72. Stephen Brooke, *Sexual Politics: Sexuality, Family Planning, and the British Left from the 1880s to the Present Day* (Oxford: Oxford University Press, 2011).

73. Russell, *The Right to Be Happy*, 5, 259.

74. On the class and racial politics of sex manuals, see Julian Carter, *The Heart of Whiteness: Normal Sexuality and Race in America, 1880–1940* (Durham, NC: Duke University Press, 2007), 75–117; Christina Simmons, "'Modern Marriage' for African Americans, 1920–1940," *Canadian Review of American Studies* 30 (2000): 273–300; Simmons, "Women's Power in Sex Radical Challenges to Marriage in the Early-Twentieth-Century United States," 168–98.

75. See for example, Johanna Schoen, *Choice and Coercion: Birth Control, Sterilization, and Abortion in Public Health and Welfare* (Chapel Hill: University of North Carolina Press, 2005); Angela Franks, *Margaret Sanger's Eugenic Legacy* (Jefferson, NC: McFarland, 2005); Laura Briggs, *Reproducing Empire:*

Race, Sex, Science, and U.S. Imperialism in Puerto Rico (Berkeley: University of California Press, 2002).

76. Richardson, *Love and Eugenics in the Late Nineteenth Century*; Kline, *Building a Better Race*; Richard Soloway, *Demography and Degeneration* (Chapel Hill: University of North Carolina Press, 1990).

77. Dora Russell, Untitled, 1923–1924, Dora Russell Papers, IISH, Amsterdam, Netherlands, Box 402-406, File 402.

78. Norman Haire to Marie Stopes, 23 September 1921, Stopes Papers, BL, London, Item 58567.

79. Norman Haire to Marie Stopes, 26 May 1921, Stopes Papers, BL, London, Item 58567.

80. Marie Stopes to Helena Wright, 5 October 1927, Stopes Papers, BL, London, Item 58567.

81. Janet Hawthorne to Marie Stopes, 30 May 1920, Stopes Papers, BL, London, Item 58566.

82. BCCRB Reports, 1928–1930, Sophia Smith Collection, Northampton, Massachusetts, Box 38, File 1.

83. BCCRB Reports, 1932, Sophia Smith Collection, Northampton, Massachusetts, Box 38, File 5.

5. ROMANCING EVOLUTIONARY BIOLOGY: DARWINISM IN THE METROPOLIS

1. Neith Boyce to Hutchins Hapgood, 16 June 1898, Hapgood Papers, Beinecke, Yale, Box 18, File 488.

2. Boyce.

3. Hutchins Hapgood to Neith Boyce, 16 June 1898, Hapgood Papers, Beinecke, Yale, Box 11, File 350.

4. See for example, Donna Haraway, "Teddy Bear Patriarchy: Taxidermy in the Garden of Eden, New York City, 1908–1936," *Social Text*, no. 11 (Winter 1984–1985), 26–64; Russett, *Sexual Science*, 63–64, 205; Sandilands and Erickson, "Introduction: A Genealogy of Queer Ecologies," 1–42; Parisi, *Abstract Sex*, 16, 46–47, 49; Louise Michele Newman, *White Women's Rights: The Racial Origins of Feminism in the United States* (New York: Oxford University Press, 1999), 22–55.

5. See for example, Daniel Bender, *American Abyss: Savagery and Civilization in the Age of Industry* (Ithaca, NY: Cornell University Press, 2009); Bederman, *Manliness and Civilization*; Haraway, "Teddy Bear Patriarchy," 26–58; Nancy Leys Stepan, "Race and Gender: The Role of Analogy in Science," *Isis* 7, no. 2 (June 1986): 261–77; Sander Gilman, "Sexology, Psychoanalysis, and Degeneration," in *Degeneration: The Dark Side of Progress*, ed. J. Edward Chamberlain and Sander Gilman (New York: Columbia University Press, 1985), 72–96.

6. See for example, Emily Martin, "The Egg and the Sperm: How Science Has Constructed a Romance Based on Stereotypical Male and Female Roles," *Signs* 16, no. 3 (Spring 1991): 485–501; Lynda Birke, *Women, Feminism, and Biology: The Feminist Challenge*. New York: Methuen, 1986), 25, 78; Corinne Hayden, "Biodiversity Sampler for the Millennium," in *Reproducing Reproduction:*

Kinship, Power, and Technological Innovation, ed. Sarah Franklin and Helena Ragoné (Philadelphia: University of Pennsylvania Press, 1998), 196–98.

7. See for example, Elizabeth Grosz's feminist interpretations of Darwin. Elizabeth Grosz, "Darwinism and Feminism" and "Darwin and the Ontology of Life" in *Time Travels: Feminism, Nature, Power* (2005), 13–34, 35–42.

8. Sandilands and Erickson, "Introduction: A Genealogy of Queer Ecologies," in *Queer Ecologies*, 7.

9. Recent historical scholarship has addressed the aesthetic and affective aspects of Darwin's work. See for example, Barbara Larson and Fae Brauer, eds., *The Art of Evolution: Darwin, Darwinisms, and Visual Culture* (Hanover, NH: Dartmouth College Press, 2009); Jonathan Smith, *Darwin and Victorian Visual Culture* (Cambridge: Cambridge University Press, 2006).

10. Adrian Desmond and James Moore, *Darwin* (London: Michael Joseph Ltd., 1991), 264–65, 278, 520, 627–28.

11. Desmond and Moore, 232.

12. Desmond and Moore, 132–33, 251.

13. Desmond and Moore, 580.

14. Desmond and Moore, 556.

15. Desmond and Moore, 557.

16. Desmond and Moore, 290, 375, 447, 551, 580.

17. Charles Darwin, *The Descent of Man* (London: John Murray, 1871), 38, 48–50.

18. Darwin, 336.

19. Darwin, 38, 52, 336.

20. The popularity of eugenics at this time shaped intellectuals' particular interest in Darwinian mate selection and evolution. Bert Bender has argued that Darwinian sexual selection rather than natural selection became a prevalent theme in American literature. See Bender, *The Descent of Love*. On prominent intellectuals framing of love and eugenics in the 1890s, see Richardson, *Love and Eugenics*.

21. Charles Darwin, *The Expression of Emotion in Man and Animals*, 3rd ed. (London: HarperCollins Publishers, 1999), 99–100, 117–19, 126–27, 213.

22. Darwin, 169.

23. Darwin, *The Descent of Man,* 168.

24. Laura Doan, "'The Outcast of One Age Is the Hero of Another': Radclyffe Hall, Edward Carpenter and the Intermediate Sex," in *Palatable Poison*, ed. Laura Doan and Jay Prosser (New York: Columbia University Press, 2001), 162–78.

25. Edward Carpenter, *Love's Coming of Age* (1896; repr., London: George Allen & Unwin Ltd., 1913), 8, 21.

26. Havelock Ellis, *The Objects of Marriage* (New York: Medical Review of Reviews, 1917), 6, 13.

27. J. W. Slaughter "Selection in Marriage," *ER* 1 (April 1909–January 1910): 152, 156, 162.

28. C. W. Saleeby, "The Psychology of Parenthood," *Eugenics Review* (April 1909–January 1910,): 41.

29. On Darwinism and the conflation of temporalities in cultural life, see Seitler, *Atavistic Tendencies*.

30. Havelock Ellis to Edward Carpenter, 16 May 1920, Havelock Ellis Papers, British Library, London, Item 70536.

31. Havelock Ellis, "Birth Control and Eugenics," *ER* 9(1)(April 1917): 35, 37.

32. Margaret Sanger, *Margaret Sanger: An Autobiography* (New York: W.W. Norton & Company Publishers, 1938), 89–91.

33. Sanger, *The Pivot of Civilization*, 139.

34. On Sanger's eugenics, see for example, Linda Gordon, *Woman's Body, Woman's Right* (New York: Grossman, 1976), 260–80; Franks, *Margaret Sanger's Eugenic Legacy*.

35. Goldman, "Marriage and Love."

36. Emma Goldman, "Marriage and Love," 1916, The Emma Goldman Papers (Alexandria, VA: Chadwyck-Healy, 1990): Reel 48.

37. Bonnie Haaland notes Goldman's support of eugenics. See Haaland, *Emma Goldman*, 41.

38. Goldman, "Marriage and Love."

39. On this model of the sexuality of the Victorian woman, see Nancy Cott, "Passionlessness," *Signs* 4, no. 2 (Autumn 1978): 219–36.

40. Havelock Ellis, *The Love Rights of Women* (New York: Birth Control Review, 1921), 12.

41. On the development of sciences of sex in this period, see for example, Russett, *Sexual Science*; Bullough, *Science in the Bedroom*; Bland and Doan, *Sexology in Culture*.

42. In the American context, see for example, Simmons, "Women's Power in Sex; Nancy Cott, *The Grounding of Modern Feminism* (New Haven, CT: Yale University Press, 1987). In the British context, see for example, Brooke, *Sexual Politics*; Collins, *Modern Love*.

43. On Gilman's objections to the New Feminist exaltation of sexual pleasure, see Ellen Chesler, *Woman of Valor: Margaret Sanger and the Birth Control Movement in America* (New York: Simon & Schuster, 1992), 60–61. Also, see Cott, *The Grounding of Modern Feminism*, 49; Charlotte Perkins Gilman, *Women and Economics* (Boston: Small, Maynard & Company, 1898).

44. See for example, Jackson, *The Real Facts of Life*; Jeffreys, "Sex Reform and Anti-feminism in the 1920s."

45. Joanne Passet, *Sex Radicals and the Quest for Women's Equality* (Urbana: University of Illinois Press, 2003), 14, 49, 163–65, 168–70; D'Emilio and Freedman, *Intimate Matters*, 161; Cott, *The Grounding of Modern Feminism*.

46. Carpenter, *Love's Coming-of-Age*, 27, 35, 40.

47. Carpenter, 43, 55, 78.

48. Richardson, *Love and Eugenics*; Kline, *Building a Better Race*. Also, see Carter, *The Heart of Whiteness* and Robb, "The Way of All Flesh."

49. Nancy Ordover, *American Eugenics: Race, Queer Anatomy, and the Science of Nationalism* (Minneapolis: University of Minnesota Press, 2003).

50. Terry, *An American Obsession*, 120.

51. Edward Carpenter, "Homogenic Love: An Essay," (Manchester, UK: Labour Press Society, 1895), 18, 45, 47–48. http://search.library.utoronto.ca/details?7290027.

52. Edelman, *No Future.*

53. Roughgarden, *Evolution's Rainbow.*

54. Terence Kissack, *Free Comrades* (Oakland, CA: AK Press, 2008).

55. Emma Goldman to Havelock Ellis, 27 December 1924, Emma Goldman Papers, Reel 14.

56. Phyllis Grosskurth, *Havelock Ellis: A Biography* (London: Allen Lane, 1980), 380, 384.

57. Phyllis Grosskurth discusses the details of Olive Schreiner and Havelock Ellis's relationship. See Grosskurth, 69, 77–99, 139–40.

58. Grosskurth, 144, 154.

59. Grosskurth, 140–42.

60. Rowbotham, *Edward Carpenter*, 337.

61. Rowbotham, 294, 315.

62. See for example, George Chauncey, *Gay New York: Gender, Urban Culture and the Making of the Gay Male World, 1890–1940* (New York: Basic Books, 1994).

63. Ruth Livesey, *Socialism, Sex, and the Culture of Aestheticism in Britain, 1880–1914* (Oxford: Oxford University Press, 2007), 1–8, 105,117. Also, see Jeffrey Weeks, *Against Nature* (London: Rivers Oram Press, 1991), 170–83.

64. Marian Morton, *Emma Goldman and the American Left* (New York: Twayne Publishers, 1992), 67.

65. Biographer Richard Drinnon focuses on the friendship between Goldman and Berkman. See Drinnon, *Rebel in Paradise.*

66. Goldman, "Marriage and Love."

67. Emma Goldman discusses many of the details of her reactions to Freud, Kropotkin, and Edward Carpenter in Emma Goldman, *Living My Life* (New York: AMS Press, 1970).

68. On primitivism in Britain and the United States, see Shane Vogel, *The Scene of Harlem Cabaret: Race, Sexuality, Performance* (Chicago: University of Chicago Press, 2009); Hutchinson, *The Indian Craze*; Koven, *Slumming*; Torgovnick, *Gone Primitive*; Dolores LaChapelle, *D. H. Lawrence: Future Primitive* (Denton, TX: University of North Texas Press, 1996).

69. Candace Falk, *Love, Anarchy, and Emma Goldman* (New York: Holt, Rinehart & Winston, 1984).

70. Emma Goldman to Ben Reitman, 29 June 1908. The Emma Goldman Papers (Alexandria, VA: Chadwyck-Healy, 1990): Reel 2.

71. Emma Goldman to Ben Reitman, 1908–1917, The Emma Goldman Papers (Alexandria, VA: Chadwyck-Healy, 1990): Reel 2.

72. Westermarck, *The Future of Marriage in Western Civilisation*, 1.

73. Westermarck, 29.

74. Historians have discussed early twentieth-century marriage experiments as a specific development among avant-garde middle-class intellectuals in Britain and the United States. See for example, Katie Roiphe, *Uncommon Arrangements: Seven Portraits of Married Life in London Literary Circles, 1910–1939*

(New York: The Dial Press, 2007); Christine Stansell, *American Moderns: Bohemian New York and the Creation of a New Century* (New York: Metropolitan Books, 2000).

75. Sociologist Steven Seidman's history of the changing relationship between love and sex from the Victorian period through the twentieth century notes this shift to sex as love. See Steven Seidman, *Romantic Longings: Love in America, 1830–1980* (New York: Routledge, 1991).

76. Westermarck, *The Future of Marriage in Western Civilisation*, 28, 31, 32, 46, 71, 74, 157.

77. Westermarck, 199.

78. Westermarck, 155.

79. Westermarck, 155.

80. Westermarck, 156.

CONCLUSION. GENEALOGIES OF LOVE: DARWINIAN ROMANCES IN REPRODUCTIVE SCIENCES

1. See Sarah Franklin's association of biotechnologies with "millennial medicine." Sarah Franklin, "Ethical Biocapital," in *Remaking Life and Death*, ed. Sarah Franklin and Margaret Lock (Santa Fe, NM: School of American Research Press, 2003), 121.

2. H. G. Wells, *The Time Machine*, ed. Patrick Parrinder (London: Penguin Books, 2005).

3. Wells, 18–20.

4. See Patricia Clough`s discussion of the joint implications for feminism and science studies in the affective turn. Clough, "The Affective Turn," 1–22.

5. Wells, *The Time Machine*, 26, 29, 30, 49.

6. Edward Chamberlain and Sander Gilman, eds., *Degeneration: The Dark Side of Progress*. New York: Columbia University Press, 1985.

7. Latour, *Reassembling the Social*, 25.

8. Wells, *The Time Machine*, 51, 61, 67.

9. Clough, "The Affective Turn," 1–22.

10. See for example, Massumi, "The Future Births of the Affective Fact," 52–70; Anderson, "Modulating the Excess of Affect," 161–85.

11. See for example, Bruinius, *Better for All the World*; Stern, *Eugenic Nation*; Franks, *Margaret Sanger's Eugenic Legacy*; Ordover, *American Eugenics*; Kline, *Building a Better Race*; Linda Gordon, *The Moral Property of Women: A History of Birth Control Politics in America* (Urbana: University of Illinois Press, 2002), chap. 5, 72–85.

12. Karin Weis, "Introduction," *The New Psychology of Love*, eds. Robert Sternberg and Karin Weis (New Haven, CT: Yale University Press, 2006), 3.

13. Paul Ekman, ed., *Darwin and Facial Expression* (New York: Academic Press, 1973); Silvan Tomkins, *Affect, Imagery Consciousness: Volume 1 The Positive Affects* (New York: Springer Publishing Company, 2008), 13, 23, 185; Damasio, *Looking for Spinoza: Joy, Sorrow, and the Feeling Brain*. Orlando, FL: Harcourt, 2003, 48; Damasio, *The Feeling of What Happens: Body and Emotion in the Making of Consciousness*. New York: Harcourt Brace, 1999, 39, 53, 285.

14. Irigaray, *The Way of Love.*

15. Thrift, *Non-representational Theory*, 56–57, 68, 91–92.

16. For examples of affect theorists' turn to Darwinian evolution, see Clough, "The Affective Turn," 216; Thrift, *Non-representational Theory*, 181; Massumi, *Parables for the Virtual*, 12, 114, 123.

Bibliography

ARCHIVAL SOURCES

Hapgood Papers, Beinecke Library, Yale University, New Haven, CT
Havelock Ellis Papers, British Library, London, United Kingdom
The Emma Goldman Papers (microfilm edition). Alexandria, VA: Chadwyck-Healy.
Mabel Dodge Luhan Collection, Beinecke Library, Yale University, New Haven, CT
Mabel Dodge Luhan Papers, Beinecke Library, Yale University, New Haven, CT
Bertrand Russell Papers, Russell Archives, McMaster University, Hamilton, ON, Canada
Dora Russell Papers, International Institute for Social Research, Amsterdam, Netherlands
Margaret Sanger Papers, Sophia Smith Collection, Smith College, Northampton, MA
Marie Stopes Papers, British Library, London, United Kingdom

PUBLISHED PRIMARY SOURCES

Baginski, Max, and Emma Goldman. "Introduction." *Mother Earth* no. 1 (March 1906): 1.
Bailey, Liberty Hyde. *Plant Breeding: Being Six Lectures upon the Amelioration of Domestic Plants.* New York: The Macmillan Company, 1906.

Baker, John R. *Sex in Man and Animals*. London: George Routledge & Sons Ltd., 1926.

Bergson, Henri. *Creative Evolution*. Translated by Arthur Mitchell. New York: Holt, 1913.

Besant, Annie. *Annie Besant: An Autobiography*. London: T. Fisher Unwin, 1893.

Burbank, Luther. "Some of the Fundamental Principles of Plant Breeding." In *Proceedings: International Conference on Plant Breeding and Hybridization 1902–1907*, 35–39. New York: The Horticultural Society, 1904.

———. *The Training of the Human Plant*. New York: Century, 1907.

Burbank, Luther, John Whitson, Robert John, and Henry Smith Williams. *Luther Burbank: His Methods and Discoveries and Their Practical Application* Vols. 1–9. New York: Luther Burbank Society, 1914.

Breuer, Josef and Sigmund Freud. *Studies in Hysteria*. Translated by James Strachey. New York: Basic Books Inc., 1957.

Carpenter, Edward. *Civilisation; Its Causes and Cure and Other Essays*. London: Allen & Unwin, 1921.

———. *Love's Coming of Age*. 1896. Reprint, London: George Allen & Unwin Ltd., 1913.

———. "Homogenic Love: An Essay." Manchester, UK: Labour Press Society, 1895. http://search.library.utoronto.ca/details?7290027.

Cole, L. J. "Animal Aristocracy and Human Democracy." *Birth Control Review (BCR)*, January 1924.

Darwin, Charles. *The Descent of Man*. London: John Murray, 1871.

———. *The Different Forms of Flowers*. London: John Murray, 1877.

———. *The Effects of Cross and Self Fertilisation in the Vegetable Kingdom*. New York: D. Appleton and Company, 1877.

———. *The Expression of Emotion in Man and Animals*. 3rd ed. London: Harper Collins Publishers, 1999.

———. *On the Origin of Species*. 1859. Cambridge, MA: Harvard University Press, 1964.

Diedrich, Gideon. "Biological Reasons for Family Limitation." *BCR*, February 1920.

Duggar, B.M. ed. *Proceedings of the International Congress of Plant Sciences, Ithaca, New York, August 16–23, 1926*. Menasha, WI: Banta, 1929.

Ellis, Havelock. *The Love Rights of Women*. New York: Birth Control Review, 1921.

———. *Man and Woman: A Study of Human Secondary Sexual Characters*. London: Walter Scott, Ltd., 1894.

———. *My Life*. London: Heinemann, 1940.

———. *The Objects of Marriage*. New York: Medical Review of Reviews, 1917.

———. *Studies in the Psychology of Sex*. Philadelphia: F.A. Davis, 1928.

———. "The World's Racial Problem." *BCR*, October 1920.

Engberg, Robert, and Donald Wesling, eds. *John Muir: To Yosemite and Beyond—Writings from the Years 1863 to 1875*. Madison: University of Wisconsin Press, 1980.

Freud, Sigmund. *Civilization and its Discontents*. Translated by David McLintock, with introduction by Leo Bersani. London: Penguin Books, 2004.

Freud, Sigmund. *Psychopathology of Everyday Life*. Harmondsworth, UK: Penguin Books Limited, 1939.

Gilman, Charlotte Perkins. *Women and Economics*. Boston: Small, Maynard & Company, 1898.

Goldman, Emma. *Living My Life*. New York: AMS Press, 1970.

Hall, Granville Stanley. *Adolescence: Volume II*. New York: D. Appleton, 1907.

Harwood, W. S. *New Creations in Plant Life: An Authoritative Account of the Life and Work of Luther Burbank*. New York: The Macmillan Company, 1905.

Hooker, Donald. "The Effect of X-Ray upon Reproduction in the Rat," *BCR*, September 1922.

Hapgood, Hutchins. *A Victorian in the Modern World*. New York: Harcourt, Brace and Company, 1939.

Horticultural Society of New York: *Proceedings: International Conference on Plant Breeding and Hybridization*. New York: Horticultural Society, 1902–1907.

James, William. *Principles of Psychology*. Vol. 2. Cambridge, MA: Harvard University Press, 1981.

James, William. "What Is an Emotion?" In *The Emotions*. Baltimore, MD: Williams & Wilkins Co., 1922.

Jones, Ernest. *On the Nightmare*. London: Hogarth Press and the Institute of Psychoanalysis, 1931.

Key, Ellen. *Love and* Marriage. Translated by Arthur G. Chater. New York: G.P. Putnam's Sons, 1911.

Lamarck, Jean-Baptiste. *Zoological Philosophy: An Exposition with Regard to the Natural History of Animals*. Translated by Hugh Elliott. London: Macmillan and Co. Limited, 1914.

Luhan, Mabel Dodge. *Intimate Memories*. Vol. 3. New York: Harcourt Brace & Company, 1933.

Marshall, F. H. A. *Physiology of Reproduction*. Vol. 2. 3rd ed. London: Longmans Green & Co., 1952.

McDougall, William. *An Introduction to Social Psychology*. Boston: John W. Luce & Co., 1910.

———. "Psychology in the Service of Eugenics." *Eugenics Review* 5 (April 1913): 295–308.

Meisel, Perry, and Walter Kendrick, eds. *Bloomsbury/Freud: The Letters of James and Alix Strachey, 1924–1925*. London: Chatto & Windus Ltd., 1986.

Morris, Daniel. "Improvement of the Sugar Cane by Selection and Cross-Fertilization." In *Proceedings: International Conference on Plant Breeding and Hybridization 1902*, 80–81. New York: The Horticultural Society, 1904.

Olmsted, Frederick Law. *Public Parks and the Enlargement of Towns*. Cambridge, MA: Riverside Press, 1870.

Russell, Bertrand. *The Autobiography of Bertrand Russell: 1872–1914*. London: George Allen and Unwin Ltd., 1967.

———. *Marriage and Morals*. New York: Horace Liveright, 1929.

Russell, Bertrand. "The Study of Mathematics." In *Mysticism and Logic and Other Essays*, 55–73. 2nd ed. London: Allen & Unwin, 1959.

Russell, Dora. *Hypatia.* London: Kegan, Pual, Trench, Trubner & Co., Ltd., 1925.
———. *The Right to Be Happy.* London: Harper & Brothers Publishers, 1927.
———. *The Tamarisk Tree: My Quest for Liberty and Love.* London: Elek/ Pemberton, 1975.
Saleeby, C. W. "The Psychology of Parenthood." *Eugenics Review*, April 1909–January 1910.
Sanger, Margaret. *Happiness in Marriage.* New York: Blue Ribbon Books, 1926.
———. *Margaret Sanger: An Autobiography.* New York: W.W. Norton, 1938.
———. *The Pivot of Civilization.* New York: Brentano's, 1922.
Slaughter, J. W. "Selection in Marriage." *Eugenics Review*, April 1909–January 1910.
Stopes, Marie. *Ancient Plants.* London: Blackie and Son, 1910.
———. *Botany; or the Modern Study of Plants.* London: T.C. & E.C. Jack, 1912.
———. *The Human Body and Its Functions.* London: The Gill Publishing Co., Ltd., 1926.
———. *Married Love; or, Love in Marriage.* New York: Eugenics Publishing Co., 1927.
———. *Radiant Motherhood: A Book for Those Who Are Creating the Future.* London: G.P. Putnam's Sons Ltd., 1920.
———. *Wise Parenthood.* 1918. Reprint, London: G.P. Putnam's Sons, Ltd., 1924.
Sutton, S. B., ed. *Civilizing American Cities: A Selection of Frederick Law Olmsted's Writings on City Landscapes.* Cambridge, MA: The MIT Press, 1971.
Wells, H. G. *Experiment in Autobiography.* New York: The MacMillan Company, 1934.
———. *The Island of Dr. Moreau: A Critical Text of the 1896 London First Edition.* Edited by Leon Stover. Jefferson, NC: McFarland & Company, 1996.
———. *The Time Machine.* Edited by Patrick Parrinder. London; Penguin Books, 2005.
Westermarck, Edward. *The Future of Marriage in Western Civilisation.* London: Macmillan and Co., Limited, 1936.
Whitson, John, Robert John, and Henry Smith Williams, eds. *Luther Burbank: His Methods and Discoveries and Their Practical Application.* 12 volumes. New York: Luther Burbank Press, 1914.

SECONDARY SOURCES

Adams, Carol. "Caring about Suffering: A Feminist Exploration." In *The Feminist Care Tradition in Animal Ethics*, edited by Carol Adams and Josephine Donovan, 198–226. New York: Columbia University Press, 2007.
———, ed. *Ecofeminism and the Sacred.* New York: Continuum, 1993.
———. "War on Compassion." In *The Feminist Care Tradition in Animal Ethics*, edited by Carol Adams and Josephine Donovan, 21–38. New York: Columbia University Press, 2007.
Ahmed, Sara. *The Cultural Politics of Emotion.* New York: Routledge, 2004.

Albanese, Catherine. *Nature Religion in America: From the Algonkian Indians to the New Age*. Chicago: University of Chicago Press, 1990.

———. *A Republic of Mind and Spirit: A Cultural History of American Metaphysical Religion*. New Haven, CT: Yale University Press, 2007.

Anderson, Ben. "Modulating the Excess of Affect: Morale in a State of 'Total War.'" In Gregg and Seigworth, *The Affect Theory Reader*, 161–85.

Bakshi, Parminder Kaur. "Homosexuality and Orientalism: Edward Carpenter's Journey to the East." In *Edward Carpenter and Late Victorian Radicalism*, edited by Tony Brown. London: Frank Cass & Co. Ltd., 1990.

Barad, Karen. "The Inhuman That Therefore I Am." Faculty Working Paper, Politics of Care Workshop, York University, 2012.

———. *Meeting the Universe Halfway*. Durham, NC: Duke University Press, 2007.

Bauer, Dale. *Sex Expression and American Women Writers, 1860–1940*. Chapel Hill: University of North Carolina Press, 2009.

Beard, George. *American Nervousness*. New York: G.P. Putnam's Sons, 1881.

Bederman, Gail. *Manliness and Civilization: A Cultural History of Gender and Race in the United States, 1880–1917*. Chicago: University of Chicago Press, 1995.

Bender, Bert. *The Descent of Love: Darwin and the Theory of Sexual Selection in American Fiction, 1871–1926*. Philadelphia: University of Pennsylvania Press, 1996.

Bender, Daniel. *American Abyss: Savagery and Civilization in the Age of Industry*. Ithaca, NY: Cornell University Press, 2009.

Benn, Miriam. *Predicaments of Love*. London: Pluto Press, 1992.

Benson, Etienne. "Animal Writes: Historiography, Disciplinarity, and the Animal Trace," 3–16. In *Making Animal Meaning*. Edited by Linda Kalof and Georgina Montgomery. East Lansing: Michigan State University Press, 2011.

Berger, Gwen. *Taboo Subjects: Race, Sex, and Psychoanalysis*. Minneapolis: University of Minnesota Press, 2005.

Berlant, Lauren. *The Female Complaint: The Unfinished Business of Sentimentality in American Culture*. Durham, NC: Duke University Press, 2008.

Birke, Lynda. *Feminism, Animals, and Science*. Philadelphia: University of Pennsylvania Press, 1998.

———. *Women, Feminism, and Biology: The Feminist Challenge*. New York: Methuen, 1986.

Birke, Lynda, and Ruth Hubbard, eds. *Reinventing Biology: Respect for Life and the Creation of Knowledge*. Bloomington: Indiana University Press, 1995.

Bland, Lucy, and Laura Doan, eds. *Sexology in Culture: Labelling Bodies and Desires*. Chicago: University of Chicago Press, 1998.

Boulter, Michael. *Darwin's Garden: Down House and the Origin of Species*. London: Constable & Robinson Ltd., 2008.

Bourke, Joanna. "Fear and Anxiety: Writing about Emotion in Modern History." *History Workshop Journal* 55, no. 1 (April 2003): 111–33.

Bowler, Peter. *Life's Splendid Drama*. Chicago: University of Chicago Press, 1996.

———. *Reconciling Science and Religion: The Debate in Early Twentieth-Century Britain*. Chicago: University of Chicago Press, 2001.

Braidotti, Rosi. *Metamorphoses: Towards a Materialist Theory of Becoming*. Cambridge: Polity Press, 2002.

Brickman, Celia. *Aboriginal Populations in the Mind: Race and Primitivity in Psychoanalysis*. New York: Columbia University Press, 2003.

Briggs, Laura. *Reproducing Empire: Race, Sex, Science, and U.S. Imperialism in Puerto Rico*. Berkeley: University of California Press, 2002.

Brooke, Stephen. *Sexual Politics: Sexuality, Family Planning, and the British Left from the 1880s to the Present Day*. Oxford: Oxford University Press, 2011.

Bruinius, Harry. *Better for All the World: The Secret History of Forced Sterilization and America's Quest for Racial Purity*. New York: Knopf, 2006.

Buettinger, Craig. "Antivivisection and the Charge of ZooPhil-Psychosis in the Early Twentieth Century." *The Historian* 55, no. 2 (Winter 1993): 277–88.

Buhle, Mari Jo. *Feminism and Its Discontents*. Cambridge, MA: Harvard University Press, 1998.

Bullough, Vern. *Science in the Bedroom: A History of Sex Research*. New York: Basic Books, 1994.

Bundgaard, Axel. *Muscle and Manliness: The Rise of Sport in American Boarding Schools*. Syracuse, New York: Syracuse University Press, 2005.

Burke, Flannery. *From Greenwich Village to Taos: Primitivism and Place at Mabel Dodge Luhan's*. Lawrence: University Press of Kansas, 2008.

Burkhardt, Frederick. "Darwin and the Copley Medal." *Proceedings of the American Philosophical Society* 145, no. 4 (December 2001): 510–18.

Burnham, John. "The New Psychology." In *1915: The Cultural Moment: New Politics, the New Woman, the New Psychology, the New Art, and the New Theatre in America*, edited by Adele Heller and Lois Rudnick, 117–27. New Brunswick, NJ: Rutgers University Press, 1991.

Burton, Antoinette. *Burdens of History: British Feminists, Indian Women, and Imperial Culture, 1865–1915*. Chapel Hill: University of North Carolina Press, 1994.

Butler, Judith. *Gender Trouble*. New York: Routledge, 1990.

Carr, Helen. *Inventing the American Primitive*. Cork: Cork University Press, 1996.

Carstensen, Vernon. "The Genesis of an Agricultural Experiment Station." *Agricultural History* 34, no. 1 (January 1960): 13–20.

Carter, Julian. *The Heart of Whiteness: Normal Sexuality and Race in America, 1880–1940*. Durham, NC: Duke University Press, 2007.

Castricano, Jodey, ed. *Animal Subjects: An Ethical Reader in a Posthuman World*. Waterloo, ON: Wilfrid Laurier University Press, 2008.

Cellulo, Kristin. *Making Marriage Work*. Chapel Hill: University of North Carolina Press, 2009.

Chaloner, W .G. "The Palaeobotanical Work of Marie Stopes." In *History of Palaeobotany: Selected Essays*, 127–35. London: The Geological Society, 2005.

Chamberlain, Edward, and Sander Gilman, eds. *Degeneration: The Dark Side of Progress*. New York: Columbia University Press, 1985.

Chapman, Mary, and Glenn Hendler, eds. *Sentimental Men: Masculinity and the Politics of Affect in American Culture*. Berkeley: University of California Press, 1999.

Chauncey, George. *Gay New York: Gender, Urban Culture, and the Making of the Gay Male World, 1890–1940*. New York: Basic Books, 1994.

Chen, Mel. *Animacies: Biopolitics, Racial Mattering, and Queer Affect*. Durham, NC: Duke University Press, 2012.

Chesler, Ellen. *Woman of Valor: Margaret Sanger and the Birth Control Movement in America*. New York: Simon & Schuster, 1992.

Cittadino, Eugene. *Nature as the laboratory: Darwinian Plant Ecology in the German Empire, 1880–1900*. Cambridge: Cambridge University Press, 1990.

Clarke, Adele. *Disciplining Reproduction: Modernity, American Life Sciences, and "the Problems of Sex."* Berkeley: University of California Press, 1998.

Clough, Patricia Ticineto. "The Affective Turn: Political Economy, Biomedia, and Bodies." In Gregg and Seigworth, eds., *The Affect Theory Reader*, 206–25.

———. *Autoaffection: Unconscious Thought in the Age of Teletechnology*. Minneapolis: University of Minnesota Press, 2000.

Clough, Patricia Ticineto, and Jean Halley, *The Affective Turn: Theorizing the Social*. Durham, NC: Duke University Press, 2007.

Collins, Marcus. *Modern Love: An Intimate History of Men and Women in Twentieth-Century Britain*. London: Atlantic Books, 2003.

Colls, Robert. *Identity of England*. Oxford: Oxford University Press, 2002.

Coontz, Stephanie. *The Way We Never Were: American Families and the Nostalgia Trap*. New York: Basic Books, 1992.

Corrigan, John. *Business of the Heart: Religion and Emotion in the Nineteenth Century*. Berkeley: University of California Press, 2002.

Cott, Nancy. *The Grounding of Modern Feminism*. New Haven, CT: Yale University Press, 1987.

———. "Passionlessness: An Interpretation of Victorian Sexual Ideology, 1790–1850." *Signs: Journal of Women or Culture and Society* 4, no. 2 (Autumn 1978): 219-236.

Croce, Paul Jerome. *Science and Religion in the Era of William James: Eclipse of Uncertainty, 1820–1880*. Chapel Hill: University of North Carolina Press, 1995.

Crozier, Ivan. "'All the World's a Stage': Dora Russell, Norman Haire, and the 1929 League for Sexual Reform Congress." *Journal of the History of Sexuality* 12, no. 1(2003): 16–37.

Damasio, Antonio. *The Feeling of What Happens: Body and Emotion in the Making of Consciousness*. New York: Harcourt Brace, 1999.

———. *Looking for Spinoza: Joy, Sorrow, and the Feeling Brain*. Orlando, FL: Harcourt, 2003.

Daston, Lorraine and Gregg Mitman. *Thinking with Animals: New Perspectives on Anthropomorphism*. New York: Columbia University Press, 2005.

Davin, Anna. "Imperialism and Motherhood," 87–151. In *Tensions of Empire: Colonial Cultures in a Bourgeois World*. Edited by Frederick Cooper and Ann Laura Stoler. Berkeley: University of California Press, 1997.

Davis, Rebecca. "'Not Marriage at All, But Simple Harlotry': The Companionate Marriage Controversy." *Journal of American History* 94, no. 4 (2008): 1137–63.

DeBoer-Langworthy, Carol, ed. *The Modern World of Neith Boyce*. Albuquerque: University of New Mexico Press, 2003.

Deleuze, Gilles, and Felix Guattari, *A Thousand Plateaus: Capitalism and Schizophrenia*. Trans. Brian Massumi. Minneapolis: University of Minnesota Press, 1987.

Deloria, Philip. *Playing Indian*. New Haven, CT: Yale University Press, 1998.

D'Emilio, John, and Estelle Freedman. *Intimate Matters: The History of Sexuality in America*. New York: Harper & Row, 1988.

Desmond, Adrian, and James Moore. *Darwin*. London: Michael Joseph Ltd., 1991.

Doan, Laura. "'The Outcast of One Age Is the Hero of Another': Radclyffe Hall, Edward Carpenter and the Intermediate Sex." In *Palatable Poison*, edited by Laura Doan and Jay Prosser,162–78. New York: Columbia University Press, 2001.

Dobson, Andrew, ed. *The Green Reader: Essays Toward a Sustainable Society*. San Francisco, CA: Mercury House, Incorporated, 1991.

Doyle, Richard. *Darwin's Pharmacy: Sex, Plants, and the Evolution of the Noösphere*. Seattle: University of Washington Press, 2011.

Dreyer, Peter. *A Gardener Touched with Genius*. Revised Edition. Berkeley: University of California Press, 1985.

Drinnon, Richard. *Rebel in Paradise*. Chicago: University of Chicago Press, 1961.

Dunlap, Thomas. *Nature and the English Diaspora: Environment and History in the United States, Canada, Australia, and New Zealand*. Cambridge: Cambridge University Press, 1999.

Edelman, Lee. *No Future: Queer Theory and the Death Drive*. Durham: Duke University Press, 2004.

Ekman, Paul, ed. *Darwin and Facial Expression*. New York: Academic Press, 1973.

Falcon-Lang, Howard. "Marie Stopes and the Discovery of Pteridosperms and the Origin of Carboniferous Coal Balls." *Earth Sciences History* 27, no. 1 (2008): 78–99.

Falk, Candace. *Love, Anarchy, and Emma Goldman*. New York: Holt, Rinehart & Winston, 1984.

Fausto-Sterling, Anne. *Sex/Gender: Biology in a Social World*. New York: Routledge, 2012.

Felski, Rita. *Doing Time: Feminist Theory and Postmodern Culture*. New York: New York University Press, 2000.

Fields, Jill. "'Fighting the Corsetless Evil': Shaping Corsets and Culture, 1900–1930." *Journal of Social History* 33, no. 2 (Winter 1999): 355–84.

Fisher, Kate. *Birth Control, Sex and Marriage in Britain, 1918–1960*. Oxford: Oxford University Press, 2006.

Fisher, Tim. "Fatherhood and the British Fathercraft Movement, 1919–1939." *Gender & History* 17, no. 2 (August 2005): 441–62.

Foucault, Michel. *History of Sexuality, Vol. 1: An Introduction*. New York: Random House, 1978.

———. *Madness and Civilization: A History of Insanity in the Age of Reason*. Translated by Richard Howard. New York: Pantheon Books, 1965.

———. "Nietzsche, Genealogy, History." In *Language, Counter-Memory, Practice: Selected Essays and Interviews*, edited by Donald F. Bouchard and Sherry Simon, 139–64. Ithaca, NY: Cornell University Press, 1977.

Fox, Stephen. *The American Conservation Movement: John Muir and His Legacy*. Madison: University of Wisconsin Press, 1985.

Frank, Stephen M. *Life with Father: Parenthood and Masculinity in the Nineteenth-Century American North*. Baltimore: Johns Hopkins University Press, 1998.

Frankiel, Sandra. *California's Spiritual Frontiers: Religious Alternatives in Anglo-Protestantism, 1850–1910*. Berkeley: University of California Press, 1988.

Franklin, Sarah. *Dolly Mixtures: The Remaking of Genealogy*. Durham, NC: Duke University Press, 2007.

Franklin, Sarah, and Margaret Lock, eds. *Remaking Life and Death*. Santa Fe, NM: School of American Research Press, 2003.

Franks, Angela. *Margaret Sanger's Eugenic Legacy*. Jefferson, NC: McFarland, 2005.

Gandhi, Leela. *Affective Communities: Anti-Colonial Thought, Fin-de-siècle Radicalism, and the Politics of Friendship*. Durham, NC: Duke University Press, 2006.

Garland, David. "What Is a 'History of the Present'? On Foucault's Genealogies and Their Preconditions." *Punishment & Society* 16, no. 4 (2014): 365–84.

George, Sam. *Botany, Sexuality, and Women's Writing, 1760–1830: From Modest Shoot to Forward Plant*. Manchester: Manchester University Press, 2007.

Geppert, Alexander. "Divine Sex, Happy Marriage, Regenerated Nation: Marie Stopes's Marital Manual *Married Love* and the Making of a Best-Seller, 1918–1955." *Journal of the History of* Sexuality 8, no. 3 (January 1998): 389–433.

Ghattacharyya, Gargi. *Dangerous Brown Men: Exploiting Sex, Violence and Feminism in the War on Terror*. London: Zed Books, 2008.

Gifford, Sanford. "The American Reception of Psychoanalysis, 1908–1922." In *1915: The Cultural Moment*, edited by Adele Helle and Lois Rudnick, 128–45. New Brunswick, NJ: Rutgers University Press, 1991.

Gijswijt-Hoftstra, Marijke, and Roy Porter, eds. *Cultures of Neurasthenia*. Cambridge: Rodopi, 2001.

Gilfoyle, Tim. *City of Eros: New York City, Prostitution, and the Commercialization of Sex, 1790–1920*. New York: Norton, 1992.

Gilman, Sander. "Sexology, Psychoanalysis, and Degeneration," 72–96. In *Degeneration: The Dark Side of Progress*. Edited by J. Edward Chamberlain and Sander Gilman. New York: Columbia University Press, 1985.

Godwin, Joscelyn. *The Theosophical Enlightenment*. Albany: State University of New York Press, 1994.

Gordon, Linda. *The Moral Property of Women: A History of Birth Control Politics in America*. Urbana: University of Illinois Press, 2002.

Gordon, Linda. *Woman's Body, Woman's Right*. New York: Grossman, 1976.

Gregg, Melissa. "White Collar Intimacy." In *Digital Cultures and the Politics of Emotion: Feelings, Affect and Technological Change*, edited by Athina Karatzogianni and Adi Kuntsman, 147–64. London: Palgrave Macmillan, 2012.

Gregg, Melissa, and Gregory J. Seigworth, eds. *The Affect Theory Reader*. Durham, NC: Duke University Press, 2010.

Griswold, Robert. *Fatherhood in America: A History*. New York: Basic Books, 1993.

Gross, Charles. "Alfred Wallace and the Evolution of the Human Mind." *The Neuroscientist* 16(5): 496–507.

Grosskurth, Phyllis. *Havelock Ellis: A Biography*. London: Allen Lane, 1980.

Grosz, Elizabeth. *Becoming Undone: Darwinian Reflections on Life, Politics, and Art*. Durham, NC: Duke University Press, 2011.

———. *Time Travels: Feminism, Nature, Power.* Durham, NC: Duke University Press, 2005.

———. *Volatile Bodies: Toward a Corporeal Feminism*. Bloomington: Indiana University Press, 1994.

Haaland, Bonnie. *Emma Goldman: Sexuality and the Impurity of the State*. New York: Black Rose Books, 1993.

Hacking, Ian. *Historical Ontology*. Cambridge, MA: Harvard University Press, 2002.

Hagen, Joel B. *An Entangled Bank: The Origins of Ecosystem Ecology*. New Brunswick, NJ: Rutgers University Press, 1992.

Halberstam, Judith. *In a Queer Time and Place: Transgender Bodies, Subcultural Lives*. New York: New York University Press, 2005

Hale, Nathan. *The Rise and Crisis of Psychoanalysis in the United States*. Oxford: Oxford University Press, 1995.

Hall, Catherine. *Civilizing Subjects: Colony and Metropole in the English Imagination*. Chicago: University of Chicago Press, 2002.

Hall, Lesley. *Hidden Anxieties: Male Sexuality 1900–1950*. Cambridge, MA: Blackwell, 1990.

———. "Uniting Science and Sensibility: Marie Stopes and the Narratives of Marriage in the 1920s," 118–36. In *Rediscovering Forgotten Radicals: British Women Writers, 1889–1939*. Edited by Angela Ingram and Daphne Patal. Chapel Hill: University of North Carolina Press, 1993.

Hall, Ruth. *Marie Stopes: A Biography*. London: André Deutsch Limited, 1977.

Hankins, Barry. *Second Great Awakening and the Transcendentalists*. Westport, CT: Greenwood Press, 2004.

Haraway, Donna. *How Like a Leaf: An Interview with Thyrza Nichols Goodeve*. New York: Routledge, 2000.

———. *Modest_Witness@Second_Millennium. FemaleMan_Meets_OncoMouse: Feminism and Technoscience*. New York: Routledge, 1997.

———. "The Promises of Monsters: A Regenerative Politics for Inappropriate/d Others." In *Cultural Studies*, edited by Lawrence Grossberg, Cary Nelson, and Paula Treichler, 295–337. New York: Routledge, 1992.

———. *Simians, Cyborgs, and Women: The Reinvention of Nature*. London: Free Association Books, 1991.

———. "Teddy Bear Patriarchy: Taxidermy in the Garden of Eden, New York City, 1908–1936." *Social Text*, no. 11 (Winter 1984–1985): 20–64.

———. *When Species Meet.* Minneapolis: University of Minnesota Press, 2008.

Harding, Sandra. *Objectivity and Diversity: Another Logic of Scientific Research.* Chicago: University of Chicago Press, 2015.

———, ed. *The Postcolonial Science and Technology Reader.* Durham, NC: Duke University Press, 2011.

Harley, Gail M. *Emma Curtis Hopkins: Forgotten Founder of New Thought.* Syracuse, NY: Syracuse University Press, 2002.

Hayden, Corinne. "Biodiversity Sampler for the Millennium." In *Reproducing Reproduction: Kinship, Power, and Technological Innovation*, edited by Sarah Franklin and Helena Ragoné, 173–206. Philadelphia: University of Pennsylvania Press, 1998.

Heap, Chad. *'Slumming:' Sexual and Racial Encounters in American Nightlife, 1885–1940.* Chicago: University of Chicago Press, 2009.

Helmrich, Stefan. "Kinship in Hypertext: Transubstantiating Fatherhood and Information Glow in Artificial Life." In *Relative Values: Reconfiguring Kinship*, edited by Sarah Franklin and Susan McKinnon, 116–44. Durham, NC: Duke University Press, 2001.

Hemmings, Clare. "Invoking Affect." *Cultural Studies* 19, no. 5 (2005): 548–67.

Hiebert, Erwin. "Modern Physics and Christian Faith." In *God and Nature: Historical Essays on the Encounter between Christianity and Science*, edited by David C. Lindberg and Ronald Numbers, 424–47. Berkeley: University of California Press, 1986.

Hird, Myra. *The Origins of Sociable Life: Evolution after Science Studies.* New York: Palgrave Macmillan, 2009.

Hirshbein, Laura Davidow. "The Glandular Solution: Sex, Masculinity, and Aging in the 1920s." *Journal of the History of Sexuality* 9, no. 3 (1999): 277–304.

Hochadel, Oliver. "Darwin in the Monkey Cage: The Zoological Garden as a Medium of Evolutionary Theory," 81–107. In *Beastly Natures: Animals, Humans and the Study of History.* Edited by Dorothee Brantz. Charlottesville: University of Virginia Press, 2010.

Hochschild, Arlie. *The Managed Heart: Commercialization of Human Feeling.* Berkeley: University of California Press, 1983.

Hofstadter, Richard. *Social Darwinism in American Thought* (Boston: Beacon Press, 1992).

Houlbrook, Matt. *Queer London.* Chicago: University of Chicago Press, 2005.

Hustak, Carla. "Inventing the Female Self in Greenwich Village, 1900–1930: Mabel Dodge's Encounter with Science and Spirituality." *Subjectivity*, no. 6 (2013): 173–92.

Hustak, Carla, and Natasha Myers. "Involutionary Momentum: Affective Ecologies and the Sciences of Plant/Insect Encounters." *differences* 23, no. 3, (2012): 74–118.

Hutchinson, Elizabeth. *The Indian Craze: Primitivism, Modernism, and Transculturation in American Art, 1890–1915.* Durham, NC: Duke University Press, 2009.

Inhorn, Marcia, Tine Tjornhoj-Thomsen, Helene Goldberg, Maruska Lacour Mosegaard, eds. *Reconceiving the Second Sex*. New York: Berghahn Books, 2009.

Irigaray, Luce. *The Way of Love*. Trans. Heidi Bostic and Stephen Pluhacek. London: Continuum, 2002.

Irving, Katrina. *Immigrant Mothers: Narratives of Race and Maternity, 1890–1925*. Urbana and Chicago: University of Illinois Press, 2000.

Jackson, Margaret. *The Real Facts of Life: Feminism and the Politics of Sexuality, c 1850–1940*. London: Taylor & Francis, 1994.

Jacobson, Matthew Frye. *Whiteness of a Different Colour*. Cambridge, MA: Harvard University Press, 1998.

Jeffreys, Sheila. "Sex Reform and Anti-feminism in the 1920s." In *The Sexual Dynamics of History: Men's Power, Women's Resistance*, edited by the London Feminist History Group. London: Pluto Press, 1983.

Johnson, Benjamin. "Wilderness Parks and Their Discontents." In *American Wilderness: A New History*, edited by Michael Lewis, 113–30. Oxford: Oxford University Press, 2007.

Johnston, Lynda, and Robyn Longhurst, eds. *Space, Place, and Sex: Geographies of Sexualities*. Lanham, MD: Rowman & Littlefield, 2010.

Kalof, Linda, and Georgina Montgomery, eds. *Making Animal Meaning*. East Lansing: Michigan State University Press, 2011.

Kasson, Joy. *Buffalo Bill's Wild West: Celebrity, Memory and Popular History*. New York: Hill and Wang, 2000.

Keeney, Elizabeth. *The Botanizers: Amateur Scientists in Nineteenth-Century America*. Chapel Hill, NC: University of North Carolina Press, 1992.

Kern, Stephen. *The Culture of Love: From Victorians to Moderns*. Cambridge, MA: Harvard University Press, 1992.

Kimmelman, Barbara. "The American Breeders' Association: Genetics and Eugenics in an Agricultural Context, 1903–13." *Social Studies of Science* 13, no. 2 (1983): 163–204.

Kingsbury, Noel. *Hybrid*. Chicago: University of Chicago Press, 2009.

Kingsland, Sharon. *The Evolution of American Ecology, 1890–2000*. Baltimore: Johns Hopkins University Press, 2005.

———. *Modelling Nature: Theoretical and Experimental Approaches to Population Ecology, 1920–1950*. Chicago: University of Chicago, 1995.

Kissack, Terence. *Free Comrades*. Oakland, CA: A.K. Press, 2008.

Kline, Wendy. *Building a Better Race*. Berkeley: University of California Press, 2001.

Kloppenburg, Jack. *First the Seed*. 2nd edition. Madison: University of Wisconsin Press, 2004.

Kollar, Rene. *Searching for Raymond: Anglicanism, Spiritualism and Bereavement between the Two World Wars*. Lanham, MD: Lexington Books, 2000.

Kosek, Jake. "Ecologies of Empire: On the New Uses of the Honeybee." *Cultural Anthropology* 25, no. 4 (November 2010): 650–78.

Kottler, Malcolm. "Alfred Russel Wallace, the Origin of Man, and Spiritualism." *Isis* 65, no. 2 (June 1974): 145–92.

Koven, Seth. *Slumming: Sexual and Social Politics in Victorian London*. Princeton, NJ: Princeton University Press, 2004.

Kuhn, Thomas. *Structures of Scientific Revolutions*. Chicago: University of Chicago Press, 1970.

Kurzweil, Edith. *The Freudians: A Comparative Perspective*. New Haven, CT: Yale University Press, 1989.

LaChapelle, Dolores. *D.H. Lawrence: Future Primitive*. Denton, TX: University of North Texas Press, 1996.

Ladd-Taylor, Molly. *Mother-Work: Women, Child Welfare, and the State, 1890–1930*. Urbana: University of Illinois Press, 1994.

Landecker, Hannah. *Culturing Life: How Cells Became Technologies*. Cambridge, MA: Harvard University Press, 2007.

Lansbury, Coral. *The Old Brown Dog: Women, Workers, and Vivisection in Edwardian England*. Madison: University of Wisconsin Press, 1985.

Larson, Barbara, and Fae Brauer, eds. *The Art of Evolution: Darwin, Darwinisms, and Visual Culture*. Hanover, NH: Dartmouth College Press, 2009.

Latour, Bruno. *Reassembling the Social: An Introduction to Actor-Network Theory*. New York: Oxford University Press, 2005.

Lears, T. J. Jackson. *No Place of Grace: Antimodernism and the Transformation of American Culture, 1880–1920*. New York: Pantheon Books,1981.

Lederer, Susan. *Subjected to Science: Human Experimentation in America before the Second World War*. Baltimore, MD: Johns Hopkins University Press, 1995.

Lewis, Jan, and Peter Stearns. "Introduction," 1–14. In *An Emotional History of the United States*. Edited by Peter Stearns and Jan Lewis. New York: New York University Press, 1998.

Lightman, Bernard. *Victorian Popularizers of Science: Designing Nature for New Audiences*. Chicago: University of Chicago Press, 2007.

Livesey, Ruth. *Socialism, Sex, and the Culture of Aestheticism in Britain, 1880–1914*. Oxford: Oxford University Press, 2007.

Logan, Cheryl. "The Altered Rationale for the Choice of a Standard Animal in Experimental Psychology: Henry A. Donaldson, Adolf Meyer, and 'the Albino Rat.'" *History of Psychology* 2, nos. 1–3 (February 1999): 3–24.

Longino, Helen. *Science as Social Knowledge: Values and Objectivity in Scientific Inquiry*. Princeton, NJ: Princeton University Press, 1990.

Lorimer, Douglas. "Nature, Racism, and Late Victorian Science." *Canadian Journal of History* 25, no. 3 (December 1990): 369–85.

———. "Theoretical Racism in Late-Victorian Anthropology, 1870–1900." *Victorian Studies* 31, no. 3 (Spring 1988): 405–30.

Lutz, Tom. *American Nervousness, 1903: An Anecdotal History*. Ithaca, NY: Cornell University Press, 1991.

Marcus, Alan. *Agricultural Science and the Quest for Legitimacy: Farmers, Agricultural Colleges, and Experiment Stations, 1870–1890*. Ames: Iowa State University Press, 1985.

Margulis, Lynn. *Symbiogenetic Planet: A New Look at Evolution*. New York: Basic Books, 1998.

Marsh, Margaret. "Suburban Men and Masculine Domesticity, 1870–1915." *American Quarterly* 40 (June 1988): 165–86.

Martin, Emily. "The Egg and the Sperm: How Science Has Constructed a Romance Based on Stereotypical Male and Female Roles." *Signs* 16, no. 3 (Spring 1991): 485–501.

Martin, Ronald E. *The Language of Difference: American Writers and Anthropologists Reconfigure the Primitive, 1878–1940*. Newark: University of Delaware Press, 2005.

Mason, Jennifer. *Civilized Creatures: Urban Animals, Sentimental Culture, and American Literature, 1850–1900*. Baltimore: Johns Hopkins University Press, 2005.

Massumi, Brian. "The Future Birth of the Affective Fact: The Political Ontology of Threat." In Gregg and Seigworth, eds., *The Affect Theory Reader*, 52–70.

———. *Parables for the Virtual: Movement, Affect, Sensation*. Durham, NC: Duke University Press, 2002.

Matless, David. *Landscape and Englishness*. London: Reaktion Books, 1998.

May, Elaine Tyler. *Great Expectations: Marriage and Divorce in Post-Victorian America*. Chicago: University of Chicago Press, 1980.

Mayberry, Maralee, Banu Subramaniam, and Lisa H. Weasel, eds. *Feminist Science Studies*. New York: Routledge, 2001.

McCook, Stuart. "'The World Was My Garden': Tropical Botany and Cosmopolitanism in American Science, 1898–1935," 499–507. In *Colonial Crucible: Empire in the Making of the American State*. Edited by Alfred McCoy and Francisco Scarano. Madison: University of Wisconsin Press, 2009.

Melosi, Martin. *Garbage in the Cities*. Revised Edition. Pittsburgh, PA: University of Pittsburgh Press, 2005.

Merchant, Carolyn. *American Environmental History: An Introduction*. New York: Columbia University Press, 2007.

———. *Reinventing Eden: The Fate of Nature in Western Culture*. New York: Routledge, 2003.

Midgley, Clare. *Women against Slavery: The British Campaigns, 1780–1870*. London: Routledge, 1992.

Milton, Kay. *Loving Nature: Towards an Ecology of Emotion*. New York: Routledge, 2002.

Mitman, Gregg. *Breathing Space: How Allergies Shape Our Lives and Landscapes*. New Haven, CT: Yale University Press, 2007.

Mitman, Gregg, Michelle Murphy, and Christopher Sellers, eds. *Landscapes of Exposure: Knowledge and Illness in Modern Environments*. Chicago: University of Chicago Press, 2004.

Monk, Ray. *Bertrand Russell: The Spirit of Solitude, 1872–1921*. New York: The Free Press, 1996.

Morton, Marion. *Emma Goldman and the American Left*. New York: Twayne Publishers, 1992.

Muncy, Robin. *Creating a Female Dominion in American Reform, 1890–1935*. New York: Oxford University Press, 1991.

Nadis, Fred. *Wonder Shows: Performing Science, Magic, and Religion in America*. New Brunswick, NJ: Rutgers University Press, 2005.

Nash, Linda. "The Fruits of Ill-Health: Pesticides and Workers' Bodies in Post–World War II California." In *Landscapes of Exposure: Knowledge and Illness in Modern Environments*, edited by Gregg Mitman, Michelle Murphy, and Chirstopher Sellers, 203–19. Chicago: University of Chicago Press, 2004.

Neuhaus, Jessamyn. "The Importance of Being Orgasmic: Gender and Marital Sex Manuals in the United States, 1920–1963." *Journal of the History of Sexuality* 9, no.4 (October 2000): 447–73.

Neushul, Peter. "Marie C. Stopes and the Popularization of Birth Control Technology." *Technology and Culture* 39, no. 2 (1998): 245–72.

Newman, Louise. *White Women's Rights: The Racial Origins of Feminism in the United States*. New York: Oxford University Press, 1999.

Nicholson, Virginia. *Among the Bohemians: Experiments in Living 1900–1939*. London: Viking, 2000.

Nigianni, Chrysanthi. "The Taste of Living." In *The Animal Catalyst: Towards Ahuman Theory*, edited by Patricia MacCormack, 111–30. New York: Bloomsbury Academic, 2014.

Numbers, Ronald L. *Darwin Comes to America* (Cambridge, MA: Harvard University Press, 1998).

Olmstead, Alan, and Paul Rhode. *Creating Abundance: Biological Innovation and American Agricultural Development*. Cambridge: Cambridge University Press, 2008.

Oppenheim, Janet. *The Other World: Spiritualism and Psychical Research in England, 1850–1914*. Cambridge: Cambridge University Press, 1985.

———. "*'Shattered Nerves': Doctors, Patients and Depression in Victorian England*. Oxford: Oxford University Press, 1991.

Ordover, Nancy. *American Eugenics: Race, Queer Anatomy, and the Science of Nationalism*. Minneapolis: University of Minnesota Press, 2003.

Oudshoorn, Nelly. *Beyond the Natural Body: An Archaeology of Sex Hormones*. London: Routledge, 1994.

———. *The Male Pill*. Durham, NC: Duke University Press, 2003.

Overfield, Richard. "The Agricultural Experiment Station and Americanization: The Hawaiian Experience, 1900–1910." *Agricultural History* 60, no. 2 (Spring 1986): 256–66.

Owen, Alex. *The Place of Enchantment: British Occultism and the Culture of the Modern*. Chicago: University of Chicago Press, 2004.

Palladino, Paolo. "Wizards and Devotees: On the Mendelian Theory of Inheritance and the Professionalization of Agricultural Science in Great Britain and the United States, 1880–1930." *History of Science* 32, no. 98 (December 1994): 409–44.

Pandora, Katherine. "Knowledge Held in Common: Tales of Luther Burbank and Science in the American Vernacular." *Isis* 92, no. 3 (September 2001): 484–517.

Parikka, Jussi. *Insect Media: An Archaeology of Animals and Technology*. Minneapolis: University of Minnesota Press, 2010.

Parisi, Luciana. *Abstract Sex: Philosophy, Biotechnology, and the Mutations of Desire*. London: Continuum, 2004.

———. "Nanoarchitectures: The Synthetic Design of Extensions and Thoughts." In *Digital Cultures and the Politics of Emotion: Feelings, Affect and Technological Change*, edited by Athina Karatzogianni and Adi Kuntsman, 33–51. London: Palgrave MacMillan, 2012.

———. "Technoecologies of Sensation." In *Deleuze/Guattari and Ecology*, edited by Bernd Herzogenrath, 182–99. Basingstoke, UK: Palgrave Macmillan, 2009.

Parrenas, Rhacel Salazar. "The Care Crisis in the Philippines: Children and Transnational Families in the New Global Economy." In *Global Woman: Nannies, Maids, and Sex Workers in the New Economy*, edited by Barbara Ehrenreich and Arlie Hochschild, 39–54. New York: Henry Holt and Company, 2003.

Passet, Joanne. *Sex Radicals and the Quest for Women's Equality*. Urbana: University of Illinois Press, 2003.

Peña, Carolyn Thomas de la. *The Body Electric*. New York: New York University Press, 2003.

Pettegrew, John. *Brutes in Suits: Male Sensibility in America, 1890–1920*. Baltimore, MD: Johns Hopkins University Press, 2007.

Pettit, Michael. "The Problem of Raccoon Intelligence in Behaviourist America." *The British Journal* for *the History of Science* 43, no. 3 (September 2010): 391–421.

Pfister, Joel. "Glamorizing the Psychological: The Politics of the Performances of Modern Psychological Identities." In *Inventing the Psychological*, edited by Joel Pfister and Nancy Schnog, 167–200. New Haven, CT: Yale University Press, 1997, 167–200.

Plumwood, Val. *Environmental Culture: The Ecological Crisis of Reason*. London: Routledge, 2002.

Pollan, Michael. *Botany of Desire: A Plant's Eye View of the World*. New York: Random House, 2001.

Porter, Roy, and Lesley Hall. *The Facts of Life: The Creation of Sexual Knowledge in Britain, 1650–1950*. New Haven, CT: Yale University Press, 1995.

Porter, Theodore. *Trust in Numbers: The Pursuit of Objectivity in Science and Public Life*. Princeton, NJ: Princeton University Press, 1995.

Rabinbach, Anson. *The Human Motor: Energy, Fatigue and the Origins of Modernity*. New York: Basic Books, 1990.

Rader, Karen. *Making Mice: Standardizing Animals for American Biomedical Research, 1900–1955*. Princeton, NJ: Princeton University Press, 2004.

Ratner-Rosenhagen, Jennifer. *American Nietzsche*. Chicago: University of Chicago Press, 2012.

Reed, Christopher. *Bloomsbury Rooms: Modernism, Subculture, and Domesticity*. New Haven, CT: Yale University Press, 2004.

Reddy, William. *The Navigation of Feeling: A Frameworks for the History of Emotions*. Cambridge: Cambridge University Press, 2001.

Renwick, Chris. *British Sociology's Lost Biological Roots: A History of Futures Past*. Basingstoke, UK: Palgrave Macmillan, 2012.

Richardson, Angelique. *Love and Eugenics in the Late Nineteenth Century: Rational Reproduction and the New Woman*. Oxford: Oxford University Press, 2003.

Richardson, Robert. *William James: In the Maelstrom of American Modernism*. Boston: Houghton Mifflin Company, 2006.

Ritvo, Harriet. *The Platypus and the Mermaid and Other Figments of the Classifying Imagination*. Cambridge, MA: Harvard University Press, 1997.

Robb, George. "The Way of All Flesh: Degeneration, Eugenics, and the Gospel of Free Love." *Journal of the History of Sexuality* 6, no. 4 (April 1996): 589–603.

Robinson, Fiona. *The Ethics of Care: A Feminist Approach to Human Security*. Philadelphia: Temple University, 2011.

Roiphe, Katie. *Uncommon Arrangements: Seven Portraits of Married Life in London Literary Circles, 1910–1939*. New York: The Dial Press, 2007.

Roper, Michael. "Slipping Out of View: Subjectivity and Emotion in Gender History." *History Workshop Journal* 59, no. 1 (April 2005): 57–72

Rose, Anne C. "Animal Tales: Observations of the Emotions in American Experimental Psychology, 1890–1940." *Journal of the History of Behavioral Sciences* 48, no. 4 (Fall 2012): 301–17.

Rose, Hilary. *Love, Power and Knowledge: Towards a Feminist Transformation of the Sciences*. Bloomington: Indiana University Press, 1994.

Rose, June. *Marie Stopes and the Sexual Revolution*. Stroud, Gloucestershire: Tempus Publishing Limited, 1992, 2007.

Rosen, Christine. *Preaching Eugenics: Religious Leaders and the American Eugenics Movement*. Oxford: Oxford University Press, 2004.

Rosen, Robyn. *Reproductive Health, Reproductive Rights: Reformers and the Politics of Maternal Welfare, 1917–1940*. Columbus: The Ohio State University Press, 2003.

Rosenberg, Charles E. "Science, Technology and Economic Growth: The Case of the Agricultural Experiment Station Scientist, 1875–1914." *Agricultural History* 45, no. 1 (January 1971): 1-20.

Rosenwein, Barbara. *Emotional Communities in the Early Middle Ages*. Ithaca, NY: Cornell University Press, 2007.

Rossiianov, Kirill. "Beyond Species: Il'ya Ivanov and His Experiments on Cross-Breeding Humans with Anthropoid Apes." *Science in Context* 15, no. 2 (2002): 277–316.

Roughgarden, Joan. *Evolution's Rainbow*. Berkeley: University of California Press, 2009.

Rowbotham, Sheila. *Edward Carpenter: A Life of Liberty and Love*. London: Verso, 2008.

Rudnick, Lois Palken. *Mabel Dodge Luhan: New Woman, New Worlds*. Albuquerque: New Mexico University Press, 1984.

Russett, Cynthia. *Darwin in America: The Intellectual Response, 1865-1912*. San Francisco: W.H. Freeman and Company, 1976.

———. *Sexual Science: The Victorian Construction of Womanhood*. Cambridge, MA: Harvard University Press, 1989.

Sandilands, Catriona, and Bruce Erickson, eds. *Queer Ecologies: Sex, Nature, Politics, Desire*. Bloomington: Indiana University Press, 2010.

Satter, Beryl. *Each Mind a Kingdom: American Women, Sexual Purity and the New Thought Movement, 1875–1920*. Berkeley: University of California Press, 1999.

Sawyer, Richard. *To Make a Spotless Orange: Biological Control in California*. Ames: Iowa State University Press, 1996.

Schiebinger, Londa. *Nature's Body: Gender in the Making of Modern Science*. Boston: Beacon Press, 1993.

Schoen, Johanna. *Choice and Coercion: Birth Control, Sterilization, and Abortion in Public Health and Welfare*. Chapel Hill: University of North Carolina Press, 2005.

Sears, Hal. *The Sex Radicals: Free Love in High Victorian America*. Lawrence: The Regents Press of Kansas, 1977.

Seidman, Steven. *Romantic Longings: Love in America, 1830–1980*. New York: Routledge, 1991.

Seigworth, Gregory J., and Melissa Gregg, "An Inventory of Shimmers." In *The Affect Theory Reader*, 1–25. Durham, NC: Duke University Press, 2010.

Seitler, Dana. *Atavistic Tendencies: The Culture of Science in American Modernity*. Minneapolis: University of Minnesota Press, 2008.

Sengoopta, Chandak. *The Most Secret Quintessence of Life: Sex, Glands, and Hormones, 1850–1950*. Chicago: University of Chicago Press, 2006.

Shanley, Mary Lyndon. *Making Babies, Making Families: What Matters Most in an Age of Reproductive Technologies, Surrogacy, Adoption, Same-Sex and Unwed Parents*. Boston: Beacon Press, 2001.

Sheail, John. *Nature Conservation in Britain*. London: The Stationery Office, 1998.

Shteir, Ann. *Cultivating Women, Cultivating Science: Flora's Daughters and Botany in England, 1760–1860*. Baltimore, MD: Johns Hopkins University Press, 1996.

Simmons, Christina. "'Modern Marriage' for African Americans, 1920–1940." *Canadian Review of American Studies* 30 (2000): 273–300.

———. "Modern Sexuality and the Myth of Victorian Repression," in *Passion and Power*, eds. Kathy Peiss and Christina Simmons. Philadelphia: Temple University Press, 1989.

———. "Women's Power in Sex Radical Challenges to Marriage in the Early-Twentieth-Century United States." *Feminist Studies* 29, no. 1 (Spring 2003): 168–98.

Sirisena, Mihirini. "Virtually Yours: Reflecting on the Place of Mobile Phones in Romantic Relationships." *Digital Cultures and the Politics of Emotion: Feelings, Affect and Technological Change*, 181–93. Edited by Athina Karatzogianni and Adi Kuntsman. London: Palgrave Macmillan, 2012.

Sklar, Kathryn Kish. *Florence Kelley and the Nation's Work*. New Haven, CT: Yale University Press, 1995.

Slavet, Eliza. *Racial Fever: Freud and the Jewish Question*. New York: Fordham University Press, 2009.

Smith, Jane. *The Garden of Invention: Luther Burbank and the Business of Breeding Plants*. New York: Penguin Press, 2009.

Smith, Jonathan. *Darwin and Victorian Visual Culture*. Cambridge: Cambridge University Press, 2006.

Soloway, Richard. *Demography and Degeneration*. Chapel Hill: University of North Carolina Press, 1990.

———. "The Galton Lecture 1996: Marie Stopes, Eugenics and the English Birth Control Movement," 46–76. In *Marie Stopes, Eugenics, and the English Birth. Control Movement: Proceedings Organized by the Galton Institute London 1996*. Edited by Robert A. Peel. London: The Galton Institute, 1997.

Sorenson, John, ed. *Critical Animal Studies: Thinking the Unthinkable*. Toronto, ON: Canadian Scholars' Press Inc., 2014.

Spivak, Gayatri. "Can the Subaltern Speak?" In *Marxism and the Interpretation of Culture*, ed. Cary Nelson and Lawrence Grossberg, 271–313. Urbana: University of Illinois Press, 1988.

Spurlock, John. *Free Love: Marriage and Middle-Class Radicalism in America, 1825–1860*. New York: New York University Press, 1988.

———. "The Problem of Modern Married Love for Middle-Class Women." In *An Emotional History of the United States*, edited by Peter Stearns and Jan Lewis, 319–32. New York: New York University Press.

Stansell, Christina. *American Moderns: Bohemian New York and the Creation of a New Century*. New York: Metropolitan Books, 2000.

Stearns, Peter, and Carol Z. Stearns. "Emotionology: Clarifying the History of Emotions and Emotional Standards." *American Historical Review* 90 (October 1985): 813–36.

Stengers, Isabelle. "Including Nonhumans in Political Theory." In *Political Matter: Technoscience, Democracy, and Public Life*, edited by Bruce Braun and Sarah Whatmore, 3–34. Minneapolis: University of Minnesota Press, 2010.

Stepan, Nancy Leys. "Race and Gender: The Role of Analogy in Science." *Isis* 7, no. 2 (June 1986): 261–77.

Stepan, Nancy Leys, and Sander Gilman. "Appropriating the Idioms of Science: The Rejection of Scientific Racism." In *The 'Racial' Economy of Science: Toward a Democratic Future*, edited by Sandra Harding, 170–201. Bloomington: Indiana University Press, 1993.

Stern, Alexandra Minna. *Eugenic Nation: Faults and Frontiers of Better Breeding in Modern America*. Berkeley: University of California Press, 2005.

Sternberg, Robert, and Karin Weis, ed. *The New Psychology of Love*. New Haven, CT: Yale University Press, 2006.

Stoler, Ann Laura. *Carnal Knowledge and Imperial Power: Race and the Intimate in Colonial Rule*. Berkeley: University of California Press, 2002.

Stone, Dan. *Breeding Superman: Nietzsche, Race, and Eugenics in Edwardian and Interwar Britain*. Liverpool: Liverpool University Press, 2002.

Storey, William. "Plants, Power, and Development: Founding the Imperial Department of Agriculture for the West Indies, 1880–1914." In *States of Knowledge: The Co-Production of Science and Social Order*, edited by Sheila Jasanoff, 109–30. New York: Routledge, 2004.

Subramaniam, Banu. "And the Mirror Cracked! Reflections of Natures and Cultures." In *Feminist Science Studies: A New Generation*, edited by Maralee

Mayberry, Banu Subramaniam, and Lisa H. Weasel, 55–62. New York: Routledge, 2001.

Subramaniam, Banu. *Ghost Stories for Darwin: The Science of Variation and the Politics of Diversity*. Urbana: University of Illinois Press, 2014.

Taves, Ann. *Fits, Trances and Visions: Experiencing Religion and Explaining Experience from Wesley to James*. Princeton, NJ: Princeton University Press, 1999.

Taylor, Barbara. *Eve and the New Jerusalem: Socialism and Feminism in the Nineteenth Century*. London: Virago, 1983.

Terada, Rei. *Feeling in Theory: Emotion after the "Death of the Subject."* Cambridge, MA: Harvard University Press, 2001.

Terry, Jennifer. *An American Obsession*. Chicago: University of Chicago Press, 1999.

Teslow, Tracy. *Constructing Race: The Science of Bodies and Cultures in American Anthropology*. New York: Cambridge University Press, 2014.

Thompson, Charis. *Making Parents: The Ontological Choreography of Reproductive Technologies*. Cambridge, MA: The MIT Press, 2005.

Thomson, Mathew. *Psychological Subjects: Identity, Culture and Health in Twentieth-Century Britain*. Oxford: Oxford University Press, 2006.

Thorsheim, Peter. "Green Space and Class in Imperial London." In *The Nature of Cities*, edited by Andew Isenberg. Rochester, NY: University of Rochester Press, 2006.

Thrift, Nigel. *Knowing Capitalism*. London: Sage Publications, 2005.

———. *Non-representational Theory: Space, Politics, Affect*. London: Routledge, 2008.

Thurschwell, Pamela. *Literature, Technology, and Magical Thinking, 1880–1920*. Cambridge: Cambridge University Press, 2001.

Thurtle, Philip. *The Emergence of Genetic Rationality*. Seattle: University of Washington, Press, 2007.

Todd, Pamela. *Bloomsbury at Home*. London: Pavilion Books Limited, 1999.

Tomkins, Sylvan. *Affect, Imagery, Consciousness: Volume 1 The Positive Affects*. New York: Springer Publishing Company, 2008.

Tone, Andrea. *Devices and Desires: A History of Contraceptives in America*. New York: Hill & Wang, 2001.

Torgovnick, Marianna. *Gone Primitive: Savage Intellects, Modern Lives*. Chicago: University of Chicago Press, 1990.

Tosh, John. *A Man's Place: Masculinity and the Middle Class Home*. New Haven, CT: Yale University Press, 1999.

Townsend, Kim. *Manhood at Harvard*. New York: W.W. Norton, 1996.

Trentmann, Frank. "Civilization and Its Discontents: English Neo-Romanticism and the Transformation of Anti-Modernism." *Journal of Contemporary History* 29, no. 4 (1994): 583–625.

Trimberger, Ellen Kay, ed. *Intimate Warriors: Portraits of a Modern Marriage, 1899–1944—Selected Works by Neith Boyce and Hutchins Hapgood*. New York: The Feminist Press, 1991.

———. "Women in the Old and New Left: The Evolution of a Politics of Personal Life." *Feminist Studies* 5, no. 3 (Autumn 1979): 431–50.

Tronto, Joan. *Moral Boundaries: A Political Argument for an Ethic of Care*. New York: Routledge, 1993.

Tsuzuki, Chushichi. *Edward Carpenter, 1844–1929: Prophet of Human Fellowship*. Cambridge: Cambridge University Press, 1980.

Vìëtslav, Orel. "History of Plant Hybridization According to Mendel's Contemporary Rudolf Geschwind." *History & Philosophy of the Life Sciences* 8, no. 2 (1986): 251–63.

Vogel, Shane. *The Scene of Harlem Cabaret: Race, Sexuality, Performance*. Chicago and London: University of Chicago Press, 2009.

Waldby, Catherine, and Robert Mitchell. *Tissue Economies: Blood, Organs, and Cell Lines in Late Capitalism*. Durham, NC: Duke University Press, 2006.

Ward, Harriet. *A Man of Small Importance: My Father Griffin Barry*. Debenham, UK: Dormouse Books, 2003.

Warren, Karen. *Ecofeminist Philosophy: On a Western Perspective of What It Is and Why It Matters*. Lanham, MD: Rowman & Littlefield, 2000.

Waters, Chris. *British Socialists and Politics of Popular Culture, 1884–1914*. Manchester: Manchester University Press, 1990.

Watkins, Elizabeth. *The Estrogen Elixir: A History of Hormone Replacement Therapy in America*. Baltimore: Johns Hopkins University Press, 2007.

Weeks, Jeffrey. *Against Nature*. London: Rivers Oram Press, 1991.

Weinbaum, Alys Eve. *Wayward Reproductions*. Durham, NC: Duke University Press, 2004.

Weis, Karin. "Introduction," In *The New Psychology of Love*. Edited by Robert Sternberg and Karin Weis, 1–14. New Haven, CT: Yale University Press, 2006.

Wexler, Laura. *Tender Violence: Domestic Visions in an Age of U.S. Imperialism*. Chapel Hill: University of North Carolina Press, 2000.

Whatmore, Sarah, and Bruce Brahn, eds. *Political Matter: Technoscience, Democracy and Public Life*. Minneapolis: University of Minnesota Press, 2010.

Wheeler, Roxann. *The Complexion of Race*. Philadelphia: University of Pennsylvania Press, 2000.

White, Christopher. *Unsettled Minds: Psychology and the American Quest for Spiritual Assurance, 1830–1940*. Berkeley: University of California Press, 2009.

White, Paul. "The Experimental Animal in Victorian Britain." In *Thinking with Animals*, edited by Lorraine Daston and Gregg Mitman, 59–82. New York: Columbia University Press, 2005.

White, Richard. *The Organic Machine*. New York: Hill and Wang, 1995.

Wilson, William H. *The City Beautiful Movement*. Baltimore: Johns Hopkins University Press, 1989.

Wolfe, Cary. *Before the Law: Humans and Other Animals in a Biopolitical Frame*. Chicago: University of Chicago Press, 2013.

Worster, Donald. *The Wealth of Nature: Environmental History and the Ecological Imagination*. Oxford: Oxford University Press, 1993.

Index

Founded in 1893,
UNIVERSITY OF CALIFORNIA PRESS
publishes bold, progressive books and journals on topics in the arts, humanities, social sciences, and natural sciences—with a focus on social justice issues—that inspire thought and action among readers worldwide.

The UC PRESS FOUNDATION
raises funds to uphold the press's vital role as an independent, nonprofit publisher, and receives philanthropic support from a wide range of individuals and institutions—and from committed readers like you. To learn more, visit ucpress.edu/supportus.